Social Media, Technology, and New Generations

Social Media, Technology, and New Generations

Digital Millennial Generation and Generation Z

Edited by
Ahmet Atay and Mary Z. Ashlock

LEXINGTON BOOKS
Lanham • Boulder • New York • London

Published by Lexington Books
An imprint of The Rowman & Littlefield Publishing Group, Inc.
4501 Forbes Boulevard, Suite 200, Lanham, Maryland 20706
www.rowman.com

86-90 Paul Street, London EC2A 4NE, United Kingdom

Copyright © 2022 by The Rowman & Littlefield Publishing Group, Inc.

All rights reserved. No part of this book may be reproduced in any form or by any electronic or mechanical means, including information storage and retrieval systems, without written permission from the publisher, except by a reviewer who may quote passages in a review.

British Library Cataloguing in Publication Information Available

Library of Congress Cataloging-in-Publication Data

Names: Atay, Ahmet, editor. | Ashlock, Mary Z., editor.
Title: Social media, technology, and new generations : digital millennial generation and Generation Z / edited by Ahmet Atay, Mary Z. Ashlock.
Description: Lanham : Lexington Books, [2022] | Includes bibliographical references and index. | Summary: "This book examines millennials and Generation Z in the context of media and visual culture, considering three interrelated areas: how millennials and Gen Z use new media technologies in different contexts; what they do with media; and the relationship between media and the two generations that make up their target audience"—Provided by publisher.
Identifiers: LCCN 2022009030 (print) | LCCN 2022009031 (ebook) | ISBN 9781498550703 (cloth) | ISBN 9781498550727 (paperback) | ISBN 9781498550710 (ebook)
Subjects: LCSH: Mass media—Technological innovations—United States. | Social media—United States. | Generation Z—Attitudes. | Generation Y—Attitudes. | Mass media and technology—United States. | Technology—Social aspects—United States.
Classification: LCC P96.T422 U638 2022 (print) | LCC P96.T422 (ebook) | DDC 302.20973—dc23/eng/20220309
LC record available at https://lccn.loc.gov/2022009030
LC ebook record available at https://lccn.loc.gov/2022009031

Contents

Introduction: New Media Technologies, Social Media, Millennials, and Generation Z   1
Ahmet Atay and Mary Z. Ashlock

SECTION 1: SOCIAL MEDIA IN EVERYDAY LIFE   11

1. Strike a Po(z)e!: Generation Z's Engagement with Fashion Brands on Social Media   13
   Sophie Nightingale and Cristina Miguel

2. Millennials/Gen Z, Dating Applications and Tinder: Living on Social Network Sites and Searching for Love and Community   29
   Ahmet Atay

3. Everything Is an App (Including Us): The Media Ecology of Generation Z   43
   Brian Gilchrist

4. Millennials and the Gen Z in the Era of Social Media   61
   Anca Serbanescu

SECTION 2: MILLENNIALS AND GENERATION Z IN DIFFERENT CONTEXTS   79

5. Observations in the Classroom: Bridging the Gaps among Media, Technology, and College Students   81
   Mary Z. Ashlock, Yi Jasmine Wang, Lindsay J. Della, Siobhan E. Smith-Jones, and Ralph S. Merkel

6	Welcoming Gen Z to the Workforce: Leveraging Digital Literacy for Recruitment and Retention *Stephanie Smith and Michael Strawser*	93
7	The Representations of *Generation Millennials* and *Z* in the Mass Media: A Text Mining Analysis *Kenneth C. C. Yang and Yowei Kang*	107

SECTION 3: GLOBAL EXAMPLES   129

8	The Role of Technological Change in Facilitating Young People's Experiences with Computer-Mediated Communication (CMC) in the United Kingdom *Lauren Dempsey*	131
9	Media and Technology: Generational Differences and Attitude of Nigerian Media Users in Nigeria *Oluwafunmilayo 'Bode Alakija and Anthony Amedu*	149
10	Digital Children of the Digital Era: A Case Study of Generation Z on Instagram *H. Hale Künüçen and Leyla Akbaş*	167

Index	177
About the Contributors	179

Introduction

New Media Technologies, Social Media, Millennials, and Generation Z

Ahmet Atay and Mary Z. Ashlock

This project is an outcome of our continual interest and ongoing academic curiosity with the Millennial culture. We are not Millennials; however, we work with Millennials in our academic settings, and we had (and still have) students who are members of this generation. Hence, we are surrounded by them, and we interact with them on a regular basis. We also realize that Millennials played a paramount role in the last two US presidential elections. As a generation, they might still not have economic power; however, they will continue to have a political impact and have certain cultural powers, including the power of consumption. While they continue to shape our current political and social life, they will also dictate the future of our politics, media, and popular culture.

In 2016, we built a larger research project on Millennials, and we began tackling different aspects of the Millennial generation and their culture. When we completed our first two books on Millennials, *Millennial Culture and Communication Pedagogies: Narratives from the Classroom and Higher Education* (2018) and *Examining Millennials Reshaping Organization Cultures: From Theory to Practice* (2019), our sole focus was on the Millennial generation. However, during that time, Generation Z was coined. Soon after it entered into our everyday lexicon, it emerged as an area of inquiry. We realized that our students were changing, and we were changing with them. Hence our academic interest expanded to include Generation Z as well because they were in our classroom, they were part of our families, and they began influencing our popular culture. Since the older members of Generation Z were eligible to vote, they also began impacting our political and social lives. Hence, this book focuses on the Millennial generation and Generation Z; it features aspects of both generations in the context of media and examines how members of these generations use new media technologies and social media in different contexts.

Different scholars in generation studies mark the beginning of the Millennial generation differently. For the purpose of this book, we describe the Millennial generation (or Generation Y) as a generation whose members were born between the early 1980s and the early 2000s (Coomes & DeBard, 2004; Howe & Strauss, 2000; Whitehouse & Flippin, 2017). Similarly, the starting year of Generation Z is also debated. While some scholars argue that the starting year is 2000, others, such as Dimock (2017), argue that anybody who is born after 1997 would be described as a member of Generation Z. They are also the most diverse of the two generations, at least in the US context.

Most Millennials came of age and entered the workforce during a global recession. Besides global economics, their culture and experiences were also shaped by the 9/11 terrorist attacks. These two significant cultural and political moments greatly influenced their generation and shaped their cultural practices (Dimock, 2017).

The growing body of research on the Millennial generation and the media prove that this is a timely and important topic for the scholars of media and communication studies to examine. When we started this project, not much research focused on media aspects of Millennial culture (Botterill et al., 2015; Kundanis, 2003; Moore, 2012; Novak, 2016; Poindexter, 2012). Alison Novak's (2016) book *Media, Millennials, and Politics: The Coming of Age of the Next Political Generation* pioneered a new phase of scholarship in this area. Novak's research emphasized the importance of focusing on the relationship between Millennials and their media consumption. She also articulated the new political and consumer power of Millennials. Following the footsteps of Novak's research, Loren Saxton Coleman and Christopher P. Campbell's (2019) edited collection "Media, Myth, and Millennials: Critical Perspectives on Race and Culture" carried the conversation one step further by examining race and cultural diversity in the context of the Millennial generation. Finally, Anthony Cristiano and Ahmet Atay's edited book *Millennials and Media Ecology: Culture, Pedagogy, and Politics* examined how Millennials are using media to participate in different aspects of cultural life.

Although there is a growing body of literature on the Millennial generation, not many scholars studied Generation Z, its culture, and its members in-depth. While some research is being done in *Education and Leadership Studies* (Seemiller & Grace, 2016, 2018; Zarra, 2017), scholars in communication studies are yet to closely examine this particular generation.

THE GOAL OF THE BOOK

In this book, we expanded the discussion on the Millennial generation and media to include Generation Z and their engagement with new media technologies. We took a bit of a different path in this project. First, we focused on how Millennials and members of Generation Z use new media technologies and platforms in different contexts. Second, we were highly interested in examining how Millennials and Gen Z use media and what they do with it. Third, we were also interested in understanding the relationship between these two generations and the media, and how media outlets attempt to use Millennials and Gen Z as their targeted audience group. We believe that by looking at these issues closely, we will generate a richer discussion about the cultures of Millennials and Generation Z and their complex relationship with media texts and platforms, media creators, and teachers who use media to teach.

Millennials, compared to the members of the previous generations, lead the adoption of new media technologies. They also believe that new media technologies have a positive impact on our society. According to Vogels (2019):

> While generations differ in their use of various technologies, a 2018 Center survey found that younger internet users also were more likely than older Americans who use the internet to say the internet has had a positive impact on *society:* 73% of online Millennials said the internet has been mostly a good thing for society, compared with 63% of users in the Silent Generation.

These numbers are even higher for members of Generation Z.

Today, a vast majority of Americans, regardless of their age, use social media. Online research suggests that around seven-in-ten Americans use social media to connect, access news content, share information about their daily lives, and for entertainment purposes (Pew Research). Millennials came of age during the Internet explosion, and they also grew with computers and media technologies. Gen Zers, however, were born into digital culture and grew up with the Internet, smartphones and tablets, social media applications, online gaming, and other online platforms. What is unique about Generation Z is that these technologies have always been part of their lives. As Dimock (2017) reminds, "The iPhone launched in 2007 when the oldest Gen Zers were 10." Hence, in so many ways, these technologies influenced their education, socialization, and development. Parker and Igielnik (2020) remind us that

> we know it's different from previous generations in some important ways, but similar in many ways to the Millennial generation that came before it. Members

of Gen Z are more racially and ethnically diverse than any previous generation, and they are on track to be the most well-educated generation yet. They are also digital natives who have little or no memory of the world as it existed before smartphones.

Hence, in this book, we explore these different forces and realities that continue to shape the lives of Millennials and Generation Z.

The main goal of this book is to examine Millennials and the members of Generation Z in the context of media and visual culture. In order to do so, we have to consider three interrelated areas: the ways Millennials and Generation Z use social media and other online platforms, how media outlets, mainly online platforms, treat Millennials and Generation Z as consumers and laborers, and finally what do Millennials and the members of Generation Z do within online domains. The examination of the Millennial generation and Generation Z and their cultures would be incomplete without understanding these areas.

This book has several interrelated goals:

1. Examining representations of the Millennial generation and Generation Z in social media and visual culture.
2. Examining media and visual culture texts and social media content produced by members of the Generation Z and Millennial generation.
3. Theorizing media in the context of Millennial culture and Generation Z.
4. Bridging the gap between media and youth/generations studies by looking at the mediated representation of the Millennial culture as well as the culture of Generation Z.
5. Taking a cultural studies perspective to explore the mediated and visual aspects of the Millennial culture and the culture of Generation Z by primarily focusing on their online presence.
6. Understanding how Millennials and Generation Z use media forms, social media, and online platforms to socialize and how as educators we use them to educate the members of these two generations.

OUTLINE OF THE BOOK

We divided this book into three sections: social media in everyday life, Millennials and Generation Z in different contexts, and global examples. In each section, authors engage with different aspects of the culture of the Millennial generation and Gen Z as they intersect with new media technologies and social media.

The first section of the book particularly focuses on how Millennials use social media, and what do they do on these platforms. Authors in this section collectively argue that Millennials and Gen Zers are extremely connected and wired, and they live in a highly digitalized culture. While they examine these connectivities, they also discuss both positive and negative impacts of these technologies or applications on individuals and in our larger culture.

"Strike a Po(z)e!: Generation Z's Engagement with Fashion Brands on Social Media" is addressed by Cristina Miguel and Sophie Nightingale. This chapter explores the motivations to use Instagram and Snapchat by Generation Z, identifying the primary reasons young users interact, create content, and connect with brands on these platforms. The authors investigate fashion online branding strategies and users' engagement with fashion brands on these types of social media in the United Kingdom. Results show that Generation Z perceives Instagram as a brand discovery platform and a tool for self-promotion, keeping their accounts public to reach larger audiences. Conversely, they use Snapchat to post less staged content to entertain their friends and communicate at a more intimate level since most participants had their Snapchat accounts set to private. Interaction with brands was through the use of geofilters in line with the informal and entertaining nature of the communication they engage in the platform.

Ahmet Atay examines in his chapter, "Millennials, Dating Applications and Tinder: Living on Social Network Sites and Searching for Love and Community," the reflection of US Millennial culture and his participation in it. As a younger member of Generation X, he embodies the characteristics of both Millennials and Gen Xers as neither fully an insider nor a complete outsider of the Millennial generation and its culture. The author situates himself as in this liminal space and occupies a particular positionality as a transnational and queer body. Important concepts are addressed such as how our culture has become increasingly more digitalized with social network sites and quick media applications. These continue to occupy a significant role in our daily lives with others including online dating applications, such as Tinder. Atay concludes it is not by accident that the majority of Millennials and Gen Zers are members as technologies represent many aspects of their culture, including fast dating and hookup culture.

In *Everything is an App (Including US): The Media Ecology of Generation Z*, Brian Gilcrist provides an interpretive analysis of stereotypes associated with Generation Z. He offers an overview using media ecology as the guiding theory throughout the chapter. Brian submits a brief analysis on some of the common stereotypes associated with Generation Z. Finally, he identifies the effects of new media on Generation Z as the origins of these stereotypes. He contends that new media has influenced members of Generation Z to elevate interaction with smartphones over face-to-face communication. Generation Z has affirmed individualism, rejected community, and developed smartphone addiction, a threat to their mental health. This chapter considers how new media has influenced Generation Z's behavior and offers suggestions for how they could use their smartphones as tools rather than allow smartphones to use them as tools.

In the last chapter of this section, Anca Serbanescu addresses the questions: "How do Millennials and Gen Z enjoy online content?" "How can we communicate effectively with the new generation?" and "How do Millennials and the Gen Z negotiate their public and private lives in the Era of Social Media." Main differences are discussed as to how Millennials and Gen Z choose their information given that modern life has been particularly shaped by the rise of new communication technologies. Anonymous social media platforms like Secret and Snapchat are more appealing to Gen Z than Facebook and similar platforms that leave permanent records. They use social networks for fun and not for sharing one's private life, while Millennials prefer to update their statuses and remain in contact with friends. Given these premises, the role of communicators is to observe, listen, store, and manage information, analyze data, and produce a strategic communication output in line with the user's needs.

The authors in the second section of the book examine Millennials in different contexts and their engagement with new media platforms and social media within these contexts. The authors studied how changing new media technologies are impacting Millennials and Gen Z and their presence in the workplace, in the classroom, or in the media.

Mary Z. Ashlock, Yi Jasmine Wang, Lindsay J. Della, Siobhan E. Smith-Jones, and Ralph S. Merkel narrate their shared experiences in *Observations in the Classroom: Bridging the Gap between Media, Technology and College Students*. The authors apply the concept that college professors perceive Gen Z and Millennial students through different lenses in various ways. Cultural backgrounds, education, societal forces, and biases affect how we approach our students and the subjects we choose to teach. This chapter outlines teaching experiences among colleagues with Gen Z and Millennial students. Although these accounts vary, especially due to the generational differences between professors and students, there are key learning points. Each of the authors shares their observations and experiences from a wide range of courses.

In their chapter, "Welcoming Gen Z to the workforce: Leveraging digital literacy for recruitment and retention," Stephanie Smith and Michael G. Strawser examine both the strengths and areas of weakness among Generation Z and what this means to the American workforce. The authors use the theoretical framework of digital literacy, recruitment, retention, and communication strategies as a foundation to help explain and present the existing media representations of Millennials and Generation Z. Organizations must shift into thinking of their workplace as a brand that needs to be developed and nurtured to secure top talent among Generation Z. Strategies to do so are provided in this chapter. Foundations of digital literacy posit how organizations can create a mutually beneficial communication environment for Millennials and Generation Z.

Kenneth C. C. Yang and Yowei Kang use framing theory in selecting, organizing, and editing information in their chapter "The Representations of Generation M and Z in the Mass Media: A Texting Mining Analysis." Important questions are posed such as the following: How are Generations M and Z represented in the media around the world? To be specific, what are the recurrent images of Generations M and Z? Are there any cross-country variations of these images to describe these two market segments? The authors use text mining to analyze media data collected from the mainstream English-language media to explore relationships among these recurrent concepts.

The last section of the book focuses on three global case studies about Millennials and Generation Z. In these chapters, the authors study how Millennials and Gen Z use social media and other new media technologies and platforms in the UK, Nigeria, and Turkey. Hence, the authors lead us to see connections between Millennials and Gen Zers in the United States and in other countries.

Lauren Dempsey considers "The Role of Technological Change in Facilitating Young People's Experiences with Computer-Mediated Communication (CMC) in the United Kingdom." This chapter describes the existing dichotomies between Millennials and Generation Z, exploring the differences (and similarities) between these two generations longitudinally to build an understanding of their use of technology in relationship management. The focus is on the younger generations' engagement with computer-mediated communication (CMC) including any hardware that facilitates CMC (such as smartphones, laptops, and tablets) and CMC platforms (such as social media, email, and video calling). Technological innovation coincides with a shift in young peoples' behaviors and media portrayals.

Oluwafunmilayo'Bode Alakija and Anthony Amedu's exploratory chapter "Media and Technology: Generational Differences and Attitude of Nigerian Media Users in Nigeria" situates Nigerians within the debates that have conceptualized various categories of the United States of generations according to the age and technology in which each grew up. The authors investigate generational differences and attitudes to media and digital technologies among three different generations of Nigerian media users based on the transformative power of the media on society. Alakija and Amedu's chapter shows how media has been influential in the social, cultural, political, and economic fabrics of the nation and continues to serve educative and transformative purposes even though the different generation configurations and attitudes to the media have not been subjected to scholarly inquiry. Despite varying competencies, the three generations acknowledged the social and transformative power of the media and use both mediums, traditional and social media, as such.

In their chapter, "Digital Children of the Digital Era: A Case Study of Generation Z on Instagram," H. Hale Künüçen and Leyla Akbaş identify the impact of Instagram reference groups of role models on members of Generation Z in Turkey. The authors take a keen interest in samples of Instagram accounts from Turkish members who Generation Z follows. This qualitative case study examines the effects of these role models in the lives of members of Generation Z. It also identifies the communication features of members of Generation Z on Instagram.

Therefore, collectively the authors in this book present rich discussions on different aspects of the culture of the Millennial Generation and Generation Z. Moreover, they provide rich discussions about how Millennials and Gen Zers use media, what they do on media and with media, and how are they being seen as consumers and content producers of social media applications and other online platforms.

REFERENCES

Ashlock, M. Z., & Atay, A. (Eds). (2019). *Millennial culture and communication pedagogies: Narratives from the classroom and higher education.* Lanham, MD: Lexington Books.

Atay, A., & Ashlock, M. Z. (Eds). (2018). *Examining millennials reshaping organization cultures: From theory to practice.* Lanham, MD: Lexington Books.

Botterill, J., Bredin, M., & Dun, T. (2015). Millennials' media use: It is a matter of time. *Canadian Journal of Communication*, 40 (3), 537–541.

Campbell, C., & Coleman, L. S. (Eds). (2019). *Media, myth, and millennials: Critical perspectives on race and culture.* Lanham, MD: Lexington Books.

Coomes, M. D., & DeBard, B. (2004). A generational approach to understanding students. *New Direction for Student Services*, 106, Summer, 5–16.

Cristiano, A., & Atay, A. (Eds). (2020). *Millennials and media ecology: Culture, pedagogy, and politics.* London, UK: Routledge.

Dimock, M. (2019, January 17). Defining generations: Where millennials and generation z begins. *Pew Research Center.* https://www.pewresearch.org/fact-tank/2019/01/17/where-millennials-end-and-generation-z-begins/.

Howe, N., & Strauss, W. (2000). *Millennials rising: The next great generation.* New York, NY: Vintage Books.

Kundanis, R. M. (2003). *Children, teens, families, and mass media: The millennial generation.* New York, NY: Routledge.

Moore, M. (2012). Interactive media usage among millennial consumers. *Journal of Consumer Marketing*, 29 (6), 436–444. https://doi.org/10.1108/07363761211259241.

Novak, A. N. (2016). *Media, millennials, and politics: The coming of age of the next political generation.* Lanham, MD: Lexington Books.

Parker, K., & Igielnik, R. (2020, May). On the cusp of adulthood and facing an uncertain future: What we know about gen z so far. *Pew Research Center.* https://www.pewresearch.org/social-trends/2020/05/14/on-the-cusp-of-adulthood-and-facing-an-uncertain-future-what-we-know-about-gen-z-so-far-2/.

Poindexter, P. M. (2012). *Millennials, news, and social media: Is news engagement a thing of the past?* New York, NY: Peter Lang.

Seemiller, C., & Grace, M. (2016). *Generation Z goes to college.* San Francisco, CA: Jossey-Bass.

Seemiller, C., & Grace, M. (2019). *Generation Z: A century in the making.* London, UK: Routledge.

Social media fact sheet. *Pew Research Center.* https://www.pewresearch.org/internet/fact-sheet/social-media/.

Vogels, E. A. (2020, February 6). 10 Facts about American and online dating. *Pew Research Center.* https://www.pewresearch.org/fact-tank/2020/02/06/10-facts-about-americans-and-online-dating/.

Whitehouse, P. J., & Flippin, C. S. (2017). From diversity to intergenerativity: Addressing the mystery and opportunities of Generation X. *Journal of the American Society on Aging,* 41 (3), 6–11.

Zarra, E. T., III. (2017). *The entitled generation: Helping teachers teach and reach the minds and hearts of generation z.* Lanham, MD: Lexington Books.

Section 1

SOCIAL MEDIA IN EVERYDAY LIFE

Chapter 1

Strike a Po(z)e!

Generation Z's Engagement with Fashion Brands on Social Media

Sophie Nightingale and Cristina Miguel

Consumers are increasingly actively engaging with fashion brands through likes and shares on social media. Thus, it is becoming more important than ever to establish online relationships with customers to facilitate a more personable brand (Tsai & Men, 2013). Munnukka et al. (2015) explain that attitudinal loyalty can be used as a measurement of brand engagement on social media, involving consumers actively corresponding with brands through likes and shares, but without purchase. At the same time, users meticulously self-brand, where an online persona is created using narratives and images influenced by culture (Hearn, 2008), to encourage likes and follows. In the case of Instagram, some users may become *instafamous* (Marwick, 2015) as Instagram allows regular people to attract copious amounts of attention through photos and craft their personal brand.

Using the fashion industry, in particular, ASOS and Topshop brands, in this chapter, we analyze Generation Z's brand engagement through social media. We composed a qualitative study of content analysis and two focus groups, including a sample of 14 British social media users (aged 18–24 years old). First, this chapter explores the motivations to use Instagram and Snapchat by Generation Z and identifies the primary reasons young users interact and connect with brands on these platforms. Second, we investigate fashion online branding strategies and consumer engagement with fashion brands on these types of social media. The study focuses on Instagram and Snapchat because they are among the most popular and engaging social media platforms for young users in the UK (Ofcom, 2018), the so-called Generation Z, a term used to group people who were born in the middle nineties (Van den Bergh & Behrer, 2016). Instagram is a photo/video sharing app with 1 billion users, where 80% of their users follow a business on the platform (Instagram, 2019). Around 74% of total Instagram users belong to Generation Z (GlobalWebIndex, 2019). According to We Are Social (2019), 42% of the Internet users (aged 13+) in the UK can be reached through Instagram. Snapchat is also a photo/video sharing app that has over 186 million daily users and claims to be the perfect platform to reach young people (Snapchat, 2019). In the UK, 30% of total Internet users aged 13+ can be reached with advertisements on Snapchat (We Are Social, 2019).

MOTIVATIONS TO USE INSTAGRAM AND SNAPCHAT

Previous studies about Instagram and Snapchat have looked at motivations to use the platforms (Alhabash & Ma, 2017; Pittman & Reich, 2016), self-presentation on Instagram, for example, of athletes (e.g., Geurin-Eagleman & Burch, 2016; Watkins & Lee, 2016) or pregnancy (e.g., Tiidenberg & Baym, 2017), branding on Instagram (e.g., Carah & Shaul, 2016; Çukul, 2015; Waninger, 2015) or Snapchat (Sashittal et al., 2016), and personal relationships on Snapchat (e.g., Utz et al., 2015; Vaterlaus et al., 2016; Young, 2014).

Multiple scholars (e.g., Alhabash, 2017; Phua et al., 2017; Sheldon & Bryant, 2016; Stafford & Schkade, 2004; Whiting & Williams, 2013) explore the uses and gratifications theory to understand what motivates people to use social media. Studies by Sheldon and Bryant (2016) and Whiting and Williams (2013) highlighted surveillance and knowledge of others as key social media motivators. In this context, surveillance is referring to the close observation and monitoring undertaken of a person's activity on their social media channels. Botterill et al. (2015) argue that young users are hooked on social media because it is a convenient tool for socializing as well as due to the demand for keeping up to date owing to the availability and constant monitoring of social media. Research shows that Instagram is used for self-documentation (Alhabash, 2017) and self-presentation (Waninger, 2015) and that content is often organized and manipulated (Kofeod & Larson, 2016). Conversely, young users turn to Snapchat for privacy and to avoid the public display on Facebook (Alhabash, 2017; Stanley, 2015; Utz et al., 2015). Utz et al. (2015) explain that Snapchat is a more personal app that individuals use to reach only their closest group of friends. The intimacy of Snapchat is vital for its use, making it a popular platform among adolescents to tell stories and share private photos (Kofeod & Larson, 2016; Vaterlaus et al., 2016; Young, 2014). Carah and Shaul (2016) describe Instagram as an "image machine" (p. 83) used to persuade, initiate, and create social and personal ideologies. Therefore, content is uploaded on Instagram and Snapchat differently due to the type of recipients.

Both Instagram and Snapchat have a variety of filters and editing techniques for users that allow them to control what they post of themselves and how they look, encouraging them to manage the self they wish to portray online (Karahanna et al., 2015). Geurin-Eagleman and Burch (2016) draw on Goffman's (1959) theory of self-presentation to detail the motives of using social media to present the desired self. Goffman (1959) describes self-presentation as an act that individuals put on to project an idealized image of themselves. Presenting the desired self is related to the concept of self-branding (Hearn, 2008). Schiffman et al. (2010) previously spoke of how social media provides a platform for users to experiment with personalities and the self, which Hollenbeck and Kaikati (2012) support in their study explaining how Facebook encourages users to reveal only certain elements of themselves they wish others to see. This argument aligns with Karahanna et al. (2015) concept of psychological ownership motivation, in that individual's need to express self-identity can be fulfilled using social media platforms.

Fashion has been a motivator for Internet use for a long time. with fashion blogs starting to appear in 2002 (Rocamora, 2012). The growth of this leads the way for fast-paced, easily accessible fashion on social media. Phua et al. (2017), in their study about the use of social media to follow brands, found that Instagram is commonly used to follow fashion. Instagram states on its website that users who like to upload fashion images were among the earliest people using the platform and that they consume five times as many photos as other users (Instagram, 2016). Dolbec and Fischer (2015) studied the use of online platforms to share fashion imagery and found that users post content they deem fashionable, using hashtags and style advice whether they have millions of followers or very few. They found that users want to appear fashionable while following and taking photos of others (street style fashion blogging) for inspiration. Likewise, Waninger (2015), in his study about online branding within the Islamic fashion industry, concluded that Muslim women are increasingly using Instagram for fashion networking, but that authenticity is key in self-presentation on Instagram for both people and brands.

While it is proven that consumers self-brand online to portray their ideal self and for fashion inspiration, Munichor and Steinhart (2016) warn of arrogant brands deterring individuals with high self-threat or low self-esteem. In particular, consumers with high levels of self-threat will avoid arrogant brands to maintain a positive self-perception. Arrogant brands believe they are too good to listen to customers or competitors. Munichor and Steinhart (2016) continue to explain that consumers will actively seek brands or products that may enhance the self, therefore, protecting their self-image and self-esteem. Brand avoidance can also occur from jealousy. For example, when consumers feel negative about themselves, they may remove that threat (DeStano & Salovey, 1996), in this instance, unfollow a brand or person. Understanding

Generation Z's motivations to use social media and their contribution to brand publics will allow marketers to effectively engage with them online.

STRATEGIES TO ENGAGE CONSUMERS THROUGH SOCIAL MEDIA

Brands can encourage followers to interact with them in a number of ways on Instagram and Snapchat, for instance, by launching a competition using hashtags (Chaney, 2016), creating Snapchat filters (Cicero, 2015), offering style advice from in-house stylists, or collaborating with influencers (Uzunoglu & Kip, 2014). Çukul (2015) found that Instagram is useful in creating two-way communication with the brand and consumer; however, Sashittal et al. (2016) encourage brands to use Snapchat to reach customers on a friend level. In order to understand how members of Generation Z engage with brands on social media, the concept of consumer-brand engagement must be analyzed to identify significant steps of the engagement process. Consumer-brand engagement is the "psychological state that occurs in interactive, co-creative experiences with a focal brand" (Leckie et al., 2016, p. 558), which can generate online brand communities (highly engaged) or brand publics. Brand publics are described as "an organized media space kept together by a continuity of practices of mediation" (Arvidsson & Caliandro, 2015, p. 1). Arvidsson and Caliandro (2016) explain that brand publics are fuelled by user-generated content posted intentionally by users who have not been directly influenced to interact with the brand. They describe this concept as a passive way of interacting with brands where content surrounding a brand amalgamates using a common sharing method, such as a hashtag (ibid.). Carah and Shaul (2016) studied the effectiveness of brand hashtagging, finding that just one use can stimulate multiple cultural intermediaries to use the hashtag across social media, in particular on Instagram.

Nevertheless, frequently, the stimulus to post has derived from an influencer or friend. Influencers such as YouTubers, Instagramers, and bloggers broadcast to an audience seeking advice and inspiration. Several researchers (e.g., Abidin, 2015; Dolbec & Fischer, 2015; Parrott et al., 2015; Uzunoglu & Kip, 2014; Weijo et al., 2014) have taken an interest in influencers and the power they have over purchasing habits. Influencers are digital users that have a large following from posting personal content that others engage with, curating affiliations with brands as well as becoming their own brand (Marwick & Boyd, 2011). The name derives from the persuasive effect and inspirational positioning they have within social networks. Co-creation with influencers will allow brands to increase consumer reach as the co-creation centrality of specific interest is localized (Weijo et al., 2014). James (2016) supports this by stating that social media influencers are becoming more desirable for brands to head with marketing campaigns than celebrities, due to the higher levels of engagement influencers generate. Influencers can be used to anthropomorphize a brand (creating human-like characteristics) (Hudson et al., 2016), connecting the consumer with someone they view as a friend. Hudson et al. (2016) studied the influence of social media interactions on consumer-brand relationships and recommended that anthropomorphizing a brand works hand in hand with social media marketing and has the potential to increase the value of consumer-brand relationships. Guese and Haelg (2009) explain that brand intimacy can occur when a brand anthropomorphizes, which can increase trust and consumer-brand engagement.

RESEARCH METHODS

The fashion brands used as case studies were ASOS and Topshop due to both being English-based high-street fashion brands suitable for both genders, which have a large following on Instagram. At the moment of writing, ASOS holds 8.1 million followers (ASOS, 2019) while Topshop has 9.7 million followers (Topshop, 2019). The study included 14 participants aged 19–24 who participated in two focus groups after the initial data was collected and analyzed from ASOS and Topshop's Instagram and Snapchat accounts to understand how these brands use the platforms for branding. Participants were recruited using convenience sampling by contacting people from the personal circle of one of the researchers who belonged to Gen Z, which prevented a lengthy recruitment stage (Ritchie & Lewis, 2006). An even number of men and women with varying interests and social media habits were contacted via Facebook through one of the researchers' personal networks to see if they were willing to participate. Homogeneity among participants was sought to decrease the likelihood of participants feeling uncomfortable and less willing to communicate within the group. Participants were allocated a pseudonym to maintain anonymity while still informing the reader of environmental factors that may influence their social media habits, gender, age, and occupation.

The study was composed of two data collection techniques content analysis and focus groups. Content analysis was undertaken during a month to explore how ASOS and Topshop used the platforms to reach their target audience. Field notes were taken while analyzing ASOS and Topshop's Instagram and Snapchat accounts to see how consumers and brands interact with them. Focus groups were used to encourage an informal discussion about the topics raised, noting the opinions and behaviors of participants. Focus groups were conducted in person to understand opinions and behaviors. Participant packs were created using screenshots of ASOS and Topshop on Instagram and

Snapchat, giving examples of the style of content the brands post to use as stimulus materials to provoke discussion. Names were not recorded to ensure confidentiality. The information sheet provided to participants before they took part in the focus groups included a "Guidelines" section notifying participants that they should discuss their ideas contributing equally; however, they did have the right to leave the room if they felt uncomfortable.

Thematic analysis was used to interpret the data, as it is a method that allows flexibility in producing an opulent set of data (Braun & Clarke, 2006). In thematic analysis, themes "capture something important about the data in relation to the research question" (Braun & Clarke, 2006, p. 10). The sequential steps of thematic analysis include preparing the data, data familiarization, coding, reviewing of themes, data reduction, and taxonomy of themes (e.g., Braun & Clarke, 2006). The focus groups' transcripts were coded assigning specific themes with codes. Next, a thematic map was created pulling quotes from the transcript codes of significant themes. The data reduction process followed in which unnecessary data or themes that were not succinct were removed from the data set to avoid confusion or saturation of findings (Alhojailan, 2012). To organize the data left, a table was drawn to align quotes, themes, and research objectives.

MOTIVATIONS TO USE INSTAGRAM AND SNAPCHAT IN FASHION BRAND PUBLICS

Instagram is used to edit, upload, like, and comment, as well as follow brands, influencers, and friends. The study identified that female participants uploaded pictures more frequently than males, and more fashion-related photos. The male participants were most likely to post a photo about a trip or friends. In relation to Snapchat, all participants agreed to use Snapchat filters because it is funny, they make people look pretty, and it offers something different than other social media apps. Stories encourage users to post content revealing insights into their life and apply filters to alter the way they are perceived by viewers. A review of the main motivations to use Instagram and Snapchat is presented hereafter.

Self-branding

All participants use Instagram and Snapchat at least once a day, but they do not necessarily upload content every day. Oliver (22, Events Manager) specified that he would post to Instagram twice a week, but it depends on how exciting his life is, suggesting he uses Instagram to self-brand, only showing the best bits that he wants people to see. On Instagram, participants use color-changing filters to show off where they are or what they are doing, as well as tag fashion brands to show off what they have bought. Participants want their followers to know that they are out somewhere exciting and not just at home. According to most participants, images on Instagram are designed to make followers envious and engage with the photo. Harriet (24, Sports Student) summarizes Instagram as "a base to promote yourself," ultimately describing it as a platform for self-branding.

All participants have their Instagram accounts set to public, while their Snapchat was used for private interaction, where they can choose which friends view them in which way. Hannah (24, Teacher) compared Instagram and Snapchat interaction arguing that "people can see everything you've ever uploaded," noting that the exposure of her Instagram profile requires her to think more about who will see her images, altering what she might post freely on Snapchat. For Snapchat, Hannah clarified: "It's people that you're friends with. People aren't going to be accessing your videos unless you're friendly enough with them," implying Snapchat is used to send images to specific people. Likewise, Harriet claimed Snapchat is "more about people" because of the social privacy, editing features, and comic nature. This control of private images and insights into users' lives makes the content more intimate. Privacy of the images and videos sent between friends was a key factor for participants in the sharing of information. The use of (geo)filters on pictures was a common practice on Snapchat. Although a few participants, like Lucy (23, Marketing and Events), use Snapchat filters to make herself "look pretty," most participants use them to make their friends laugh. Humorous content and quick location snapshots are sent on Snapchat to communicate with friends.

Fashion Inspiration

Instagram claims it provides around the clock, real-time fashion (Instagram, 2016). Female participants expressed their use of social media for fashion and style inspiration, explaining they gather this information through hashtags, tagging friends, influencers, and celebrities, and using links in captions to find an item. The gathering of this content contributes to brand publics (Arvidsson & Caliandro, 2016). For the female participants, keeping up with what friends and influencers are doing is important, and Snapchat and Instagram allow them to do this. Inspiration is gathered from searching on Instagram, which can help participants discover new brands. In particular, Harriet described the way she searches for hashtags and her interest in getting inspiration from others, "I like seeing what people put together," and how she actively searches, "I do find myself flicking through hashtags" implying she invests a lot of time in using Instagram. Some of the most popular tags on Instagram are #fashion and #style proving the motivation to create a visual conversation of images that can be searched for and added to (Instagram, 2016). Preferences of appearance of the images were stated by Lucy, for example: "I like the pretty dress that's pink," proving congruence between image aesthetic and brand image. This was seen less among male participants, suggesting they are less concerned with the aesthetic of an image.

This idea of using Instagram to discover new brands was raised again when asked about motivations to follow brands. Participants indicated they follow brands they find on the platform that are not easily accessed elsewhere. Oliver stated he is "more likely to follow something that hasn't got a physical shop" as well as "brands that are new and up and coming to see what kind of stuff they're bringing out," further describing Instagram as a platform of brand discovery. This process indicates participants access brand publics to source information. They explained engaging with brands online due to the fear of missing out and pressure to keep up with trends. From here they may purchase, follow, or like images of brands on Instagram. Hannah's preference for having brands on Instagram is due to the 24-hour limit on Snapchat "I look at stuff and you don't know how much it is," saying that Instagram is useful for searching for images of clothes that will always be there that she can return to in the future. The digital photo album style of the platform creates a separate way for users to shop without accessing the site directly. Yet participants like to engage with brands on Snapchat, getting insights into what goes on behind the scenes. Charlie (21, Events Management Student) pointed out that although he may be interested in seeing brands on Snapchat, the number of images shared is important "I wanna see it but not a 400-second long Snapchat story," implying that attention spans must be noted when sharing multiple images. It is known that younger generations have shorter attention spans due to them growing up with quick, up-to-date online messaging at their fingertips (Törőcsik et al., 2014; Van den Bergh & Behrer, 2016).

INTERACTION WITH FASHION BRANDS ON INSTAGRAM AND SNAPCHAT

On Instagram, users can actively follow the brand, use their hashtags and tags, but brands can also pay for a sponsored post, as well as use hashtags and influencers to promote products. Links can be added to direct users to a web page, and images can be shared across multiple social media sites. This makes Instagram ideal for branding and engaging with users via visual content as the platform is based upon image interactions. For Snapchat, there are two ways a brand can reach the consumer: by being added as a friend and by advertising directly on the platform through snap ads, sponsored (geo)filters, or sponsored lenses (Snapchat, 2017). The addition of Snapchat's (geo)filters (Snapchat, 2017) allows brands to pay for their own filter for users to apply to images and videos. Snapchat says that (geo)filters "allow brands to take part in the hundreds of millions of snaps sent between friends each day" (Snapchat, 2017). Sponsored lenses are a similar concept but are animated filters that distort the user's image that Snapchat says offers "a completely new take on brand activation, offering not just an impression, but 'play time'" (Snapchat, 2016). These filters and lenses work similarly to product placement in which paid-for content is broadcasted in the media by a product or brand identifier (Liu et al., 2015). The aim of this is to influence audience behavior, encouraging participation in brand publics. The use of tags, sponsored filters, and sponsored lenses allow consumers to self-brand while interacting with brand publics.

Topshop and ASOS use Instagram and Snapchat for branding, however, neither use sponsored ads on the platforms, only influencer partnerships and employee features. On Instagram, Topshop and Topman post primarily editorial-style shoots taken on a professional camera, rather than a phone. The pictures include famous models and celebrities they have partnered with, like, Cara Delevingne, shots from the catwalk, and images from Topshop and Topman personal stylist's accounts. The majority of the captions tell the audience to "Check our link in the bio to shop the style," as well as hashtags such as #TopshopStyle. However, some participants feel the perceived perfection Topshop seeks to portray on Instagram is intimidating "Topshop I unfollowed because all they did was put pretty pictures up all the time" (Harriet, 21, Sports Student). As Munichor and Steinhart (2016) found, consumers will avoid brands they find arrogant to maintain a positive self-perception. Conversely, participants described ASOS as relatable and therefore preferred on Instagram because of the emoji use, colloquial captions, and transparency of the brand. ASOS encourages the tag #AsSeenOnMe to collate images of people wearing its clothes, as well as spread the word about the brand. An account is dedicated to sharing these photos. ASOS has a laid-back approach to Instagram, using colloquial language as if talking to a friend. Emojis are often featured, as well as its own employees. This broadens ASOS' reach of promotions as employees are already linked to the brand spreading the name on every post.

Topshop posts more frequently than Topman, which usually only posts of catwalks or collaborations. When Topshop posts a story, it will be for an occasion such as a photo shoot, a catwalk, or a new release. Snaps will be posted throughout the day: a mix of photos and videos, but always starting with an image saying "Welcome back to TOPSHOP SNAPS." Following this will be a descriptor of where and why they are Snapchatting. For example, "We're at the Oxford Circus store for the launch of Lady Garden." Behind the scenes, snaps from the backstage of the catwalk are often uploaded. ASOS posts similar to this, publicizing new products, behind-the-scenes clips, and interviews with stylists and ASOS employees. Emojis and the pen tool are often used to decorate the content ASOS posts to its story. Product clothes are included to encourage the audience to search for the product. In addition, Instagram accounts are also promoted through Snapchat.

All participants follow fashion brands on social media. Instagram and Snapchat provide a number of ways for consumers to engage with brands. For Instagram, this includes editing and uploading self-branded, visual content, interacting with content to express interest in an image the same way they would to a friend. Users also tag and hashtag brands in their own images. These photos are often fashion-related and other users sometimes comment, expressing their love for the outfit. This style of self-branding contributes to brand publics. While Instagram is used to post images relevant to the brand, using hashtags, name tags, and location tags to add information, Snapchat is used to interact more personally, watching behind-the-scenes videos or using sponsored filters in one's picture. Behind-the-scenes style content published on social media contributes to the development of brand intimacy (Guese & Haelg, 2009). Sponsored filters usually last for 24 hours and participants liked them. The congruency of the sponsored filters within the original Snapchat filters makes them seem less like sponsored content, which could increase their use. Nevertheless, neither Topshop nor ASOS uses sponsored filters.

Influencers (e.g., Fleur De Force and Jess Woodley) and celebrities (e.g., Kate Moss) are often used to communicate a brand's image, further promoting the brand. By tagging the location and brand, the post will appear if someone searches for it. This method of advertisement is used by Topshop and ASOS. The brands use influencers to tag the brand and write a caption promoting it. Using the hash symbol creates a tag collating content with the same tag, making it more visible (Page, 2012). This is commonly used on Instagram allowing users to easily search for specific things. Influencers are increasingly being used by brands to expand exposure and engagement, often by promoting paid-for advertisements or sponsorship (Abidin, 2015). When influencers post authentic content that is not exposed as an ad, it contributes to brand publics (Arvidsson & Caliandro, 2016). Participants follow and interact with influencers on Instagram and claimed to be more influenced by influencers than brands' posts, for example: "You see people like Jess Woodley—she's so cool I wanna wear what she's wearing" (Jane, 19, HR Student). Likewise, Carrie (24, Sport PhD Student) explained she wants to wear the brand of someone she follows that she finds inspiring.

Participants are more inclined to like than comment from the motivation of an aesthetically pleasing image or an object they wish to own. This can be seen with Jane "I'd like one of the ASOS ones, the girl looks quite cool," explaining the reason for liking the image is because she feels either a connection or admiration of the person featured. Lucy agreed she would like one of the images that showed a "pretty little dress" indicating the motivation to be a digital way to say she likes the item. It was clear they regularly like photos, with Matt (21, Engineering Student) exclaiming that he will "Just throw them around" emphasizing the understanding that although likes are sought after, they are also common enough to be used with little thought. Munnukka et al. (2015) describe these interactions as attitudinal loyalty to a brand, as consumers are engaging with the brand, but not purchasing.

According to participants, comments require a greater investment of time and thought. The key motivation for commenting on an Instagram branded photo was to communicate with friends. Oliver stated "Yeah tagging someone like a friend," indicating that the comment section is used for further interaction with friends to direct them to the image, rather than interaction with a brand. Carrie asked "Who are you talking to?" and that "A brand is just selling things, like what are you going to talk about?" These thoughts suggest brands are not human-like enough on social media for consumers to interact with them the same way they do with friends, calling for further brand personification to increase engagement on Instagram.

CONCLUSION

The purpose of this chapter was to explore how Generation Z engages with fashion brands on Instagram and Snapchat. Using Topshop and ASOS as fashion brand examples, we explored what motivates participants to use the platforms and the ways they engage with these brands. Editing features and documentation motivation make Instagram a platform for self-branding, allowing users to strategically craft their uploads. The time limit of Snapchat content creates a more rounded image of users, revealing intimate playful content. A clear gender difference in motivations to use Instagram and Snapchat was found in our study. Most female participants stated that fashion inspiration and peer surveillance were reasons for using the platforms, while most male participants pointed out that they use them to document and communicate with others. Both commented on using the platforms for self-promotion, as well as to connect with brands for fashion advice and to browse their products. All participants followed brands on Instagram, and most followed brands on Snapchat. Even though they found regular uploading of images and videos annoying, they were still consuming those communication and therefore creating a channel between the brand and the consumer. Thus, Generation Z engages with fashion brands on Instagram and Snapchat while crafting their own personal brand.

Fashion inspiration verified a catalyst for multiple engagement behaviors. Most prominently, participants spoke of searching Instagram for style inspiration accessing brand publics. From this, they follow influencers, search for new and established brands, and fashion-related hashtags in order to keep up with trends. Influencers are followed on both Snapchat and Instagram; however, Instagram is the preferred platform to search and keep up with fashion. Moreover, on Instagram, some participants tagged themselves with the brands' names or used branded hashtags such as ASOS' #AsSeenOnMe when uploading pictures wearing the brand's clothing. These interactions contribute to brand publics creating content about a brand without directly engaging with it. Participants liked to be able to scroll and click through content they were not interested in and were more inclined to like a picture than comment on it as commenting was perceived as a tool to communicate with friends not brands. Therefore, brands must alter the content posted on social media to appear less corporate and to maintain brand intimacy.

REFERENCES

Abidin, C. (2015). Communicative intimacies: Influencers and perceived interconnectedness. *Ada: A Journal of Gender, New Media, and Technology*, 8.

Alhabash, S., & Ma, M. (2017). A tale of four platforms: Motivations and uses of Facebook, Twitter, Instagram, and Snapchat among college students? *Social Media+ Society*, 3(1), 1–13.

Alhojailan, M. I. (2012). Thematic analysis: A crucial review of its process and evaluation. *West East Journal of Social Sciences*, 1(1), 39–47.

Arvidsson, A., & Caliandro, A. (2015). Brand public. *Journal of Consumer Research*, 42, 1.

ASOS. (2019). *ASOS (@asos) • Instagramphotos and videos*. Instagram.com. https://www.instagram.com/asos/?hl=en.

Arvidsson, A., & Caliandro, A. (2016). Brand public. *Journal of Consumer Research*, 42, 727–747.

Botterill, J., Bredin, M., & Dun, T. (2015). Millennials' media use: It is a matter of time. *Canadian Journal of Communication*, 40(3), 537–551.

Braun, V., & Clarke, V. (2006). Using thematic analysis in psychology. *Qualitative Research in Psychology*, 3(2), 77–101.

Carah, N., & Shaul, M. (2016). Brands and Instagram: Point, tap, swipe, glance. *Mobile Media & Communication*, 4(1), 69–84.

Chaney, P. (2016). *7 Ways to improve your Instagram presence*. Social Media Today. http://www.socialmediatoday.com/social-networks/7-ways-improve-your-instagram-presence.

Cicero, N. (2015). *Are branded geofilters the future of advertising on Snapchat?* Marketing Land. http://marketingland.com/branded-geofilters-future-advertising-snapchat-134606.

Constine, J. (2016). *Instagram launches "Stories," a Snapchatty feature for imperfect sharing*. TechCrunch. https://techcrunch.com/2016/08/02/instagram-stories/.

Çukul, D. (2015). Fashion marketing in social media: Using Instagram for fashion branding. *Proceedings from Business & Management Conference*. Vienna: International Institute of Social and Economic Sciences.

Dolbec, P., & Fischer, E. (2015). Refashioning a field? Connected consumers and institutional dynamics in markets. *Journal of Consumer Research, 41*(6), 1447–1468.

Geurin-Eagleman, A. N., & Burch, L. M. (2016). Communicating via photographs: A gendered analysis of Olympic athletes' visual self-presentation on Instagram. *Sport Management Review, 19*(2), 133–145.

GlobalWebIndex. (2019). *Social media across generations*. https://www.globalwebindex.com/reports/social-media-across-generations.

Goffman, E. (1959). *The presentation of self in everyday life*. New York: Doubleday.

Guese, K., & Haelg, K. (2009). The effects of intimacy on consumer-brand relationships. *Advances in Consumer Research, 36*, 1001–1002.

Hearn, A. (2008). Meat, mask, burden: Probing the contours of the branded self. *Journal of Consumer Culture, 8*(2), 197–217.

Hollenbeck, C., & Kaikati, A. (2012). Consumers' use of brands to reflect their actual and ideal selves on Facebook. *International Journal of Research in Marketing, 29*, 395–405.

Hudson, S., Huang, L., Roth, M., & Madden, T. (2016). The influence of social media interactions on consumer-brand relationships: A three-country study of brand perceptions and marketing behaviours. *International Journal of Research in Marketing, 33*, 27–41.

Instagram. (2016). *Feed fashion*. http://feedfashion-instagram.com/media/pdf/feed-fashion-en.pdf.

Instagram. (2019). *Instagram business*. https://business.instagram.com/?locale=en_GB.

James, S. (2016). *Social influencers now more popular for brand campaigns than traditional celebs*. Campaignlive. http://www.campaignlive.co.uk/article/social-influencers-popular-brand-campaigns-traditional-celebs/1398680.

Karahanna, E., Xu, S., & Zhang, N. (2015). Psychological ownership motivation and use of social media. *Journal of Marketing Theory and Practice, 23*(2), 185–207.

Kofoed, J., & Larson, M. C. (2016). A snap of intimacy: Photo sharing practices among young people on social media. *First Monday, 21*(11). http://firstmonday.org/ojs/index.php/fm/article/view/6905/5648.

Lang, N. (2015). *Why teens are leaving Facebook: It's "meaningless."* The Washington Post. https://www.washingtonpost.com/news/the-intersect/wp/2015/02/21/why-teens-are-leaving-facebook-its-meaningless.

Leckie, C., Nyadzayo, M., & Johnson, L. (2016). Antecedents of consumer brand engagement and brand loyalty. *Journal of Marketing Management, 32*(5–6), 558–578.

Liu, S. H., Chou, C. H., & Liao, H. L. (2015). An exploratory study of product placement in social media. *Internet Research, 25*(2), 300–316.

Marwick, A. (2015). Instafame: Luxury selfies in the attention economy. *Public Culture, 27,* 137–160.

Marwick, A., & Boyd, D. (2011). To see and be seen: Celebrity practice on Twitter. *Convergence: The International Journal of Research into New Media Technologies, 17*(2), 139–158.

Munichor, N., & Steinhart, Y. (2016). Saying no to the glow: When consumers avoid arrogant brands. *Journal of Consumer Psychology, 26*(2), 179–192.

Munnukka, J., Karjaluoto, H., & Tikkanen, A. (2015). Are Facebook brand community members truly loyal to the brand? *Computers in Human Behavior, 51,* 429–439.

Ofcom. (2018). *Adults' media use and attitudes report.* https://www.ofcom.org.uk/__data/assets/pdf_file/0011/113222/Adults-Media-Use-and-Attitudes-Report-2018.pdf.

Page, R. (2012). The linguistics of self-branding and micro-celebrity in Twitter: The role of hashtags. *Discourse & Communication, 6*(2), 181–201.

Parrott, G., Danbury, A., & Kanthavanich, P. (2015). Online behaviour of luxury fashion brand advocates. *Journal of Fashion Marketing and Management, 19*(4), 360–383.

Phua, J., Jin, S., & Kim, J. (2017). Gratifications of using Facebook, Twitter, Instagram, or Snapchat to follow brands: The moderating effect of social comparison, trust, tie strength, and network homophily on brand identification, brand engagement, brand commitment, and membership intention. *Telematics and Informatics, 34,* 412–424.

Pittman, M., & Reich, B. (2016). Social media and loneliness: Why an Instagram picture may be worth more than a thousand Twitter words. *Computers in Human Behavior, 62,* 155–167.

Ritchie, J., & Lewis, J. (2006). *Qualitative research practice.* London: Sage.

Rocamora, A. (2012). Hypertextuality and remediation in the fashion media: The case of fashion blogs. *Journalism Practice, 6*(1), 92–106.

Roderick, L. (2017). *How fashion brands are taking Instagram from gimmick to strategic.* Marketing Week. https://www.marketingweek.com/2016/02/17/how-fashion-brands-are-taking-instagram-from-gimmick-to-strategic.

Ryan, D. (2016). *Understanding digital marketing: Marketing strategies for engaging the digital generation.* London: Kogan Page Publishers.

Sashittal, H. C., DeMar, M., & Jassawalla, A. R. (2016). Building acquaintance brands via Snapchat for the college student market. *Business Horizons, 59*(2), 193–204.

Schiffman, L., Kanuk, L., & Wisenblit, J. (2010). *Consumer behavior* (10th ed.). London: Pearson.

Sheldon, P., & Bryant, K. (2016). Instagram: Motives for its use and relationship to narcissism and contextual age. *Computers in Human Behaviour, 58,* 89–97.

Snapchat. (2019). *Overview.* Snapchat for Business. https://forbusiness.snapchat.com/home.

Stanley, B. (2015). *Uses and gratifications of temporary social media: A comparison of Snapchat and Facebook.* Fullerton: California State University.

Tiidenberg, K., & Baym, N. K. (2017). Learn it, buy it, work it: Intensive pregnancy on Instagram. *Social Media+ Society, 3*(1), 1–13.

Topshop. (2019). *Topshop (@topshop) • Instagram photos and videos.* Instagram.com. https://www.instagram.com/topshop/?hl=en.

Törőcsik, M., Szűcs, K., & Kehl, D. (2014). How generations think: Research on generation z. *ActauniversitatisSapientiae, communicatio, 1*(1), 23–45.

Utz, S., Muscanell, N., & Khalid, C. (2015). Snapchat elicits more jealousy than Facebook: A comparison of Snapchat and Facebook use. *Cyberpsychology, Behaviour and Social Networking, 18*(3), 141–145.

Uzunoglu, E., & Kip, S. (2014). Brand communication through digital influencers: Leveraging blogger engagement. *International Journal of Information Management, 34*(5), 592–602.

Van den Bergh, J., & Behrer, M. (2016). *How cool brands stay hot: Branding to generations Y and Z.* London: Kogan Page Publishers.

Vaterlaus, J., Barnett, K., Roche, C., & Young, J. (2016). "Snapchat is more personal": An exploratory study on Snapchat behaviors and young adult interpersonal relationships. *Computers in Human Behavior, 62*, 594–601.

Waninger, K. (2015). *The veiled identity: Hijabistas, Instagram and branding in the online Islamic fashion industry.* Master's Thesis, Georgia State University, Atlanta, GA.

Watkins, B., & Lee, J. W. (2016). Communicating brand identity on social media: A case study of the use of Instagram and Twitter for collegiate athletic Branding. *International Journal of Sport Communication, 9*(4), 476–498.

We are Social. (2019). *Digital in 2019: Global internet use accelerates.* https://wearesocial.com/blog/2018/01/global-digital-report-2018.

Weijo, H., Heitanen, J., & Mattila, P. (2014). New insights into online consumption communities and netnography. *Journal of Business Research, 67*(10), 2072–2078.

Whiting, A., & Williams, D. (2013). Why people use social media: A uses and gratifications approach. *Qualitative Market Research: An International Journal, 16*(4), 362–369.

Young, D. (2014). Now you see it, now you don't . . . or do you?: Snapchat's deceptive promotion of vanishing messages violates Federal Trade Commission regulations. *The John Marshall Journal of Information Technology & Privacy Law, 30*(4), 827–884.

Chapter 2

Millennials/Gen Z, Dating Applications and Tinder

Living on Social Network Sites and Searching for Love and Community

Ahmet Atay

I am neither a Millennial nor a digital native in the traditional sense. However, as an older member of Generation X, I embody the characteristics of both Millennials and Gen Xers. I was not born into the new media technologies we know of today, but I am deeply situated in the digital culture that surrounds us in many ways. I need to make it clear that I am not writing this chapter as a Millennial, nor am I reflecting on the Millennial culture. Instead, I am writing this chapter as someone who is a hybrid, sitting on both sides of the fence. I am neither fully an insider nor a complete outsider of the Millennial generation and its culture. As I sit in this liminal space and occupy a particular positionality as a transnational and queer body, I reflect on the US Millennial culture and my participation in it. Digitally speaking, I consider myself a Millennial because my engagements with US culture have been impacted and shaped by new media technologies since my arrival as an international student in the United States more than two decades ago. Since then, I have constructed an American identity through these technologies. Hence, I embody and perform certain Millennial ideals.

I began this chapter by situating myself such that my positionality is clear, and my arguments will make more sense as I share my digitalized story. As an immigrant, I live in a very digitalized society, and I am constantly surrounded by visual culture materials. Media texts, social media platforms, new media technologies, popular culture artifacts, and consumer culture products influence my interaction with others in so many ways. They also shape how I perform my identity and how I communicate with my family members, friends, and colleagues, especially during the COVID-19 pandemic. I fully depend on new media technologies for communication as well as media texts and social media for companionship. The same technologies also allow me to perform my job as a media educator and teach various (new) media literacies to my students. Moreover, these technologies also enable me to feel connected to the rest of the world, as I feel very isolated in a small town in the middle of Ohio. During the last several months, media texts, social media platforms, and visual culture products have served as a lifeline. They have also allowed me to feel connected to my home culture and combat isolation by consuming media from around the world.

I am sure I am not the only one who uses social media and new media technologies to connect with others to feel less isolated, less bored, and more connected. Hence, in so many ways, I represent certain characteristics of Millennials, especially when it comes to media consumption and the need for connectivity. In the absence of face-to-face communication during the global pandemic, these technologies have enabled us to survive and fulfill some basic human needs, such as accessing food (through digital means) and interacting with other people.

While this chapter is not about surviving a global pandemic through new media technologies, to a degree, it is about social media platforms and how they could function as venues to facilitate connections and cope with isolation. In this chapter, I focus on Tinder as a dating site and discuss how its platform facilitates communication and connection between individuals (predominantly Millennials). I argue that the COVID-19 pandemic has heightened the importance of and engagement with social media applications, particularly dating and hookup sites, as the pandemic has limited our interpersonal interactions, our opportunities to meet people, and, more importantly, our in-person communication with others. Moreover, I argue that Tinder continues to occupy a significant role in Millennials' lives and in our digital culture. In this narrative-based chapter, I narrate my own story as a hybrid Millennial to examine the role that Tinder played in my life in 2020 and in the first half of 2021.

SOCIAL MEDIA AND DIGITAL CULTURE

Before talking about online dating sites, it is important to provide a contextual discussion about the digital culture we are situated in. The scholars of digital media studies (Atay 2015, 2018, 2019; boyd, 2014; Chayko, 2021; Jenkins, 2015; Sujon, 2021) have long articulated the role of new media technologies in our lives. Jenkins (2015) reminds us that we live in a convergent culture. Because of the invasive presence of our smartphones and tablets and the fact that we live in a highly wired society, we often use these devices to conduct different dimensions of our everyday lives. By using these technologies and various quick media applications, we conduct business, teach our classes, do online shopping, check the weather, keep track of our daily steps, take photos, scan receipts for coupons and rebates, record videos, access databases, read the news, enjoy novels or blogs, watch films and videos, talk to people, send and receive text messages, and look for love interests or sexual partners. All of these activities are available to us through our phones and other portable devices. We receive and process a vast amount of information and communication from different people throughout the day. We read and construct emails, look at the news even though it is fragmented, send and receive continuous text messages, communicate through instant messengers, and post tweets, Instagram photos, and information in numerous quick media applications. We live our lives in fragments and continuously engage with messages, texts, and information. In essence, we live in a "click culture." With one click, we buy things, delete information, connect to people, take and share photos, and engage in so many other daily activities.

Regardless of the generation we belong to, we are surrounded by new media technologies and are highly embedded in the digital culture. In his Pew Center online essay, Tom Rosenstiel (2020) writes, "First of all, Millennials are the leading edge. They're doing things with technology, and older generations are following." Similarly, in his Pew Center online essay, Michael Dimock (2019) reminds us that the role of technology and the way the members of a particular generation engage with technology determine the shape and characteristics of their generation. He writes, "Baby Boomers grew up as television expanded dramatically, changing their lifestyles and connection to the world in fundamental ways. Generation X grew up as the computer revolution was taking hold, and Millennials came of age during the internet explosion." To further explain how members of different generations engage with new technologies, let us examine some data. For example, Rosenstiel suggests that 94% of Millennials have cell phones, and fewer than 40% of them have landlines, suggesting that Millennials choose to use only their cellphones to talk with people on the phone. While Millennials grew up with new media technologies and use them widely to conduct their everyday lives, the data suggests that the members of Generation Z rather than Millennials dominate Internet searches and social media presence. As Dimock articulates, Generation Z was born into these technologies. He writes:

> The iPhone launched in 2007, when the oldest Gen Zers were 10. By the time they were in their teens, the primary means by which young Americans connected with the web was through mobile devices, Wi-Fi and high-bandwidth cellular service. Social media, constant connectivity and on-demand entertainment

and communication are innovations Millennials adapted to as they came of age. For those born after 1996, these are largely assumed.

Hence, it is important to realize that even though the experiences of these two generations are highly shaped and guided by new media technologies and social media applications, there are still differences in how they consume media, which platforms they use to connect, and what they do on these platforms.

Social media platforms and quick media applications are being used for several reasons, ranging from connecting with people to calculating one's daily exercise and calorie intake to shopping. Finding love, relationships, long-term partners, and hookups emerged as a widely used function of quick media applications.

HISTORY OF DATING AND MATCHMAKING

The idea of dating sites is built on the notion of matchmaking, which has been a crucial part of romantic and family relationships throughout the centuries. Informal matchmaking morphed into personal advertisements, which began to appear in newspapers in seventeenth-century England, thus rendering matchmaking a part of mass media. Furthermore, during the eighteenth century, the matrimonial agencies and personal advertisements found in newspapers became a big business in England. In the 1800s, personal advertisements spread to the rest of Europe and became rather popular. With the growth of these advertisements, dating scams and scandals were born. The early 1900s saw a massive increase in and growing popularity of personal advertising in the United States (Dating Site Review, https://www.datingsitesreviews.com/ staticpages/ index.php?page=online-dating-history). As stated in the Dating Site Review (an online site that catalogs the history of dating), these advertisements initially became popular among farmers in rural areas, then after World War I, the lonely returning soldiers began using pen pals as a way to find romantic partners and mates.

In 1959, matchmaking became more technological when, for a class project, two Stanford University students, Jim Harvey and Phil Fialer, developed a system, Marriage Planning Service, using a punch card questionnaire and an IBM mainframe computer (Stanford Magazine, https://stanfordmag.org /contents/the-real-story-about-dating), thus marking the beginning of computerized matchmaking. During the 1960s, two major social and technological developments in the United States and the United Kingdom changed the course of computerized matchmaking and dating. The first change occurred in the UK where personalized advertisements were widely used by lonely people and sex workers as well as by LGBTQIA+ folks who did not want to be identified. As the British police continued to prosecute these LGBTQIA+ individuals who placed ads in the newspapers and other printed mass media until the late 1960s, personal advertisements became part of the youth counterculture. Hence, the nature of these ads and what they stood for in British culture (and subsequently in the United States) began to change (Lee, 2017). The second change marking the commercialization of computerized matchmaking processes occurred in 1965 when a group of Harvard students created Operation Match, which is considered to be the first computerized dating service because the students were charging a $3 service fee (Matthews, 1965).

With the emergence of the Internet in the commercial domain and because of its increasing popularity in 1995, the matchmaking/dating scene and its rules and processes began to change. As the World Wide Web expanded around the world, new platforms began to emerge. Match.com became the first popular dating site. Following its popularity, other sites began to offer similar services. For example, AOL's instant messenger connected people and enabled them to match based on their interests. Because of the popularity of these platforms, a major Hollywood film, *You've Got Mail*, starring Tom Hanks and Meg Ryan, focused on the digitalization of romance and matchmaking. Moreover, Craigslist began offering chatrooms and forums as well as classified ads for those who were seeking romantic partners, which was similar to newspaper ads in some ways (Lee, 2017). People were mentioning their interests, maybe posting their photos and their locations. During the 2000s, several online dating sites emerged, turning dating and matchmaking into a very profitable industry. Needless to say, members of the Millennial generation widely contributed to the popularity of this industry.

By 2010, all sorts of new dating and hookup sites had been developed and entered into our digital culture. These sites and the resultant quick media applications fragmented the population and created special interest sites based on one's sexuality, religious affiliation, geographic location, and other demographic and identity markers. Because the developers of these applications saw their members as customers, they carefully studied their users' interests and behaviors to create very specialized applications in order to satisfy the market interest. According to data from Businessofapps.com, in 2020, the total revenue from online dating applications was $3.08 billion. According to Statista.com, the total revenue of the film industry in the United States and Canada was $2.2 billion, with $12 billion worldwide that same year. Finally, to compare, the data provided by several online sources (such as CISION PR Newswire) shows that Internet porn revenue in 2020 was roughly $2 billion. Hence, the dating industry has become very profitable with the global expansion of the Internet, but more importantly, it has grown with the widespread availability of smartphones and tablets that feature multiple quick media applications.

The new and emerging dating sites have transformed the way individuals meet and form relationships. According to a 2019 Pew Research Center study, three in ten US adults have used or are still using a dating site or app. While 48% of 18- to 29-year-olds (mainly the members of the Millennial generation and Gen Z) say that they have used these applications, only 38% of 30- to 49-year-olds (Millennials and Gen X) admit to using these services and applications. The data also shows that 55% of LGBTQIA+ individuals, regardless of their age breakdown, use these sites and applications (Vogels, 2020). Considering that meeting other LGBTQIA+ people might not be easy in certain geographic locations, rural areas, or even in cities, these percentages are not surprising. I believe that these sites and applications are socialization vehicles for queer individuals and for meeting others in closer proximity and beyond.

Online dating also creates new challenges and frustrations. According to Vogels' (2020) research, "Americans who have used a dating site or app in the past year say their recent experience left them feeling more frustrated (45%) than hopeful (28%)." It is likely that this frustration results from a lack of potential matches with people in closer geographic locations, or it could be the result of matches that do not produce meaningful relationships. In addition to frustration, online harassment and other unwanted online behaviors were reported as some of the challenges of using dating sites and applications to find relationship partners (Vogels, 2020). In the remaining sections of this chapter, I will turn my attention to Tinder as a case study.

TINDER

Tinder is a US-based geosocial networking and online dating application that was launched in 2012. The application is available in several languages and is available globally. Tinder is available for free and through a membership that provides additional capabilities for its paying members. In 2020, Tinder's parent company Match Group earned $2.4 billion, with Tinder accounting for $1.4 billion of the parent company's yearly revenue. To compare, Grindr, a gay dating and hookup application, brought in $620 million in revenue (Goldfine, 2021). It is clear that the quick media and dating application Tinder became a cultural force, thereby gaining larger visibility within our digital culture.

Because of its popularity, scholars in media and cultural studies, communication studies, sociology, and other humanities and social science disciplines began to examine the different aspects of Tinder. Sumter et al. (2017) analyzed the motivations of "emerging adults" for using Tinder. Ranzini and Rosenbaum (2020) were interested in racial dynamics, and they studied the users' attitudes toward interracial dating on the application through survey research. Byron et al. (2021) focused on young LGBTQIA+ people and their friendships on dating applications, including Tinder. Niehuis et al. (2020) examined the communication of sexually explicit content on dating applications, including Tinder. While most of this research used quantitative research methods, in this chapter, I instead narrate my personal experiences on this particular application to further examine the culture of dating sites and applications

TINDER, COMMUNITY, AND COMPANIONSHIP

I have been an active member of several social networks and dating sites (mainly LGBTQIA+) for about two decades now. As I mentioned earlier, my arrival in the United States facilitated the digitalization of my everyday life. As a young queer international student, I turned to queer social network sites, such as Gay.com, Manhunt.com, and others, to make sense of my own sexuality and to connect with others. I spent most of my formative years as a scholar and a transnational body in a small, Midwest college town. Because digital domains served as a physical home, I searched for belonging within them, and I used these sites as I moved from place to place until I took my current job in a small Ohio town. Over time, with the development of mobile communication and smartphones, these computer-based social network sites began to change, transform, and, in some cases, decline. While some of the existing sites successfully transformed into quick media applications on our smartphones, some new sites also emerged. As their popularity grew, the nature of these sites and applications also changed. They became less community-oriented due to the lack of common and centralized chatrooms and more individualized based on one-to-one communication between users.

Over time, I stopped using some of the social network sites and began using some of the online dating applications. Although I am now in a long-distant relationship, I continue to use these sites purely for communication purposes. In the absence of any visible queer community, these sites and applications have helped me to form communities and connect with others, even though all of these relationships have been and remain purely online. Like so many Millennials, I too have spent limitless hours on my computer and smartphone to conduct my digital everyday life and to communicate with people near and afar.

Story 1

Boredom sank in on a rather chilly Friday evening in November. When you work and live in a small town away from larger towns, you have limited options to entertain yourself. Since my closest friend in my town was away, and no one else had invited me to do anything, I decided to spend the evening on my couch. Lately, I had found my couch rather uncomfortable and less inviting, like so many things around me. While living alone has its perks, clearly, it also has its limitations, such as the lack of options to entertain oneself on a Friday evening. After reading 30 minutes of my mystery novel, I got bored with it. Like so many others, I have been reading my novels online, so instead of putting down a physical book, I switched from one tab to another on my computer. I admit that at any given time, I typically have more than 50 open tabs on my computer. I guess I really live my life through computer and smartphone screens.

Over the years, I stopped getting on queer social network sites since my town did not have a geolocation-based breakout room on many of these platforms. Because of the changing computer and mobile technologies, these sites were also changing, while new ones were appearing as quick media applications. Although I was using some of these sites, my purpose was strictly limited to interacting with the people around me. Since I was in a committed relationship, I was really not looking for anything particular on these sites. On that particular Friday night, I decided to look for another quick media application. I do not know how and when I had heard about Tinder, but somehow, I had. A very quick Google search revealed that Tinder was a geolocation-based online dating application. After much contemplation, I decided to download it.

Downloading a new application often gives me some anxieties because it is yet another platform where I will spend valuable time. As the download icon began to move, my heartbeat was elevated. I have no idea what I expected from the site. Each site is almost like a new world, and new discoveries are waiting to be made. "Downloading is completed." The message indicated that my boredom was about to be challenged.

Instead of paying for a membership, I decided to use the app's free but limited version, which only allowed me to swipe 100 profiles. I needed to be careful not to run out of profiles to look at and cut my newly found entertainment short. Like the other online platforms and quick media applications, Tinder also asks for basic personal information. As I hate constructing profiles, I tried to find the best version of me among my recently taken photos. I decided on one even though I had my doubts about it. Every time I upload a photo, like so many, I often wonder what my "audience"(in this case, the other members) will think of me. Is the camera angle right? Is my face taking up too much of the photo? Does my background reveal any information about me? Was I looking in the wrong direction when I took this photo? I hate taking selfies because I often do not get the angle right. I was really taking this rather seriously and was asking way too many questions throughout the process. My anxieties about uploading my photos onto any social network site or quick media application were real; after all, these photos represent a version of us that becomes available to an audience.

Once I uploaded the photo, I turned my attention to constructing the "About Me" section. I dislike writing these blurbs even more than uploading my photos. What do I want to say about myself in 500 words? To be honest, I feel that 500 words are way too many. As I constructed several short sentences about myself and my likes, I was also asking if I had written too much. Do they really want to know about me? Do they want to know something else? I am sure many who know me would very much disagree with what I was writing.

"Your profile is approved." I became someone on Tinder. I am not sure what I was looking for on that Friday evening in November—maybe a place to escape or maybe simply connectivity. I set my age limits and specified my maximum distance of 50 miles. Distance is perceived differently depending on one's location. Since I live in a small town, and I often drive to bigger cities in Ohio, I don't consider 50 miles a long distance. But for the people who live in cities and are looking for people to meet or hook up with, 50 miles is definitely a long distance and often not acceptable. Especially for those Millennials who grew up with instant gratification, driving 50 miles into the countryside to meet a person is definitely not something that many would do.

With one click, I connected to the world of Tinder. When the first person's profile appeared on my screen, I carefully read their information. I looked at their photos. I felt like I was intruding, trying to get a glimpse of their personal lives. Pause. Then what? Am I supposed to swipe to the right because I liked him or to the left because I didn't? What should I do? After a moment of anxiety, I swiped to the right. We did not match. I swiped right again. Then left and left again. And right and right and one more right. We matched. He was 33 with dark hair and blue eyes.

Me: Hi. How are you?
Five minutes later:
Mr. X: I am fine. What are you up to?
Me: Nothing. Killing time really.
Me: Where are you?
Mr. X: Cleveland. You?
Me: Wooster.
Mr. X: How far is Wooster? Never heard of it.
Me: An hour south of you.
Silence.
Ten minutes later:
Me: Are you still there?

Silence means a dead end on social networks or dating sites. Even though I had past experience with silence, and the distance is usually an issue since my town is considered rural, I was still heartbroken. I felt like the whole Tinder community had just rejected me. I had a bitter welcome, and rejection killed my interest. I put my phone down and returned to my computer screen. Although I was only there to talk to people, not necessarily meet them, hitting a digital brick wall on a Friday evening did not settle well with me. As I sat on my uncomfortable couch, I wondered how a transnational queer individual who lives in the middle of nowhere would be able to meet new people and become part of a community. How do Millennials meet others? I had more questions than answers.

Story 2

It was another snowy Friday night in February. I was at home again. Lately, no one wanted to go anywhere because of the frigid weather. Yet again, I sank into my unwelcoming couch and began watching one of my favorite soap operas. In the middle of the show, I had a sudden urge to return to the world of Tinder after months of absence. After my not-so-warm welcome to the application, I did not want to return to and deal with more silence. I punched in my code to access my phone, then opened my Tinder account.

I began looking at the available profiles. Photo after photo, profile after profile, I was trying to decide to swipe to the left and move on to the next person or swipe to the right and hope that I would match with the person on the screen. After a couple of swipes to the right, I matched with someone. Then again, and again. This time, I began talking to everybody I had been matched with. One was in Akron, one in Mansfield, and another in Cleveland. I returned to the profiles and swiped again and again, hoping that I would match with someone who lived a bit closer.

At one point, I realized that I was mindlessly looking at the profiles and swiping. Just as I matched with two other people, I ran out of swipes.

> *Damn! I wish I were a paying member.*
> *I tried to swipe again, and I hit a brick wall.*
> *No more swipes.*

I began to have anxieties over not being able to swipe. When I was online shopping, I was able to look at as many products as I wanted. Why was Tinder any different? Was I not shopping online? Was I not in the market to create a social community provided by this very application?

Most Millennials grew up as part of the online shopping culture, and for those few who did not, they quickly immigrated to it, as did so many of us.

On the one hand, as we occupy more social media platforms and quick media applications, our lives become more fragmented and somewhat isolated. On the other hand, because of the online shopping culture, our lives are shaped by the idea of looking at image after image until we find something we want to pursue. In so many ways, Tinder is built on this very idea. When one is online looking at profiles and photos, one decides if the person on the screen is worthy of a right swipe, and, if not, they are quickly swiped to the left. We treat the members on Tinder as items in a large consumer catalog; their identities and the combinations of photos and texts are either deserving of a right swipe ("Add to Cart") or a left swipe (keep searching until I find what I want). As members, we become products and consumers at the same time, hoping for successful matches. Therefore, our online presentation is critical, and the important question that we need to ask is how Millennials and others present themselves on social network sites and dating applications. The answers are complicated.

Story 3

Back to my couch. Maybe it is not that bad. It has its moments of comfort, like Tinder. They are both convenient. I set my laptop aside and picked up my iPhone to dive into the Tinder world. I realized that I had messages from five different people. I read those and briefly responded. I told myself that I would come back later to write more. Obviously, I did not want these people to think that I was ignoring them. For the time being, I switched the screen and went back to the "catalog" of individuals. Within seconds I was swiping again. This time I made a point to take more time and study the profiles and photos more carefully.

Adam. Age 34. His hair is thinning. Let's try to not be superficial and ignore that fact. *His second photo definitely went through some cosmetic touches with the available filters. Hmmm . . . Adam, is this a recent photo or a couple of years old? Let's ignore that fact as well.*

Martin. Age 37. He says he is a lawyer. *I like your tie, Martin! OMG, that cat is so adorable. In his bio, he says that he is a cat dad. Cat dads gain positive points from me. He says he owns his house. Oh well, I don't. I wonder what Martin would say about that. Look at his third photo. Who is that tall and handsome man next to you, Martin? How would we know if he's attached or not? His bio doesn't say anything.*

John. Age 27. God, he is young! Am I being ageist? *I like your Abercrombie and Fitch shirt! I wish I could pull off that look. John, is that really your car? Ok, here is another preppy outfit. I wonder what John's occupation is. He says nothing about it. Wow. Photo number five. John definitely goes to the gym. The shirtless photo tells us quite a lot and leaves very little to the imagination.*

Hector. *Age 30. From Cleveland. Distance, always distance. I wonder what Hector would think of the 60 miles of distance between us. Divorced, two kids. Occupation unknown. I like the last photo. Swimming pool photos are always welcomed.*

Jaden. *Age 31. 59 miles away. Ok. Photos of two dogs. Photos of Jaden with a man. They are looking for a third party to hang out with. Interesting. Let's think about this later on.*

Michael. *Age 40. Photos of guns. Ok. No thank you. Let's swipe you to the left.*

While each photo and profile revealed aspects of their identities, because of certain limitations, I was only able to obtain some information about these men. Enough information but not too much will definitely lead to more conversations about our likes and interests. Most of the people I was looking at that night had several photos in their profiles. Some featured objects and some just had a blank, empty screen. A quick survey of these photos revealed that most of the men I looked at were displaying aspects of our material culture, such as cars, some were featured participating in a leisurely activity, such as swimming in a pool or working out at a gym, some were holding an alcoholic beverage, some were shirtless, and some were with their pets. Hardly anyone was featured at home or in a family gathering. Hence, none of them was really marking themselves as "family oriented." This particular preference could also speak for the individualistic orientation of our culture. To note, Millennials have been described as self-centered and individualistic. In some ways, these photos were speaking to that categorization and embodying it in some way.

CONCLUSION

As our culture becomes increasingly more digitalized, social network sites and quick media applications continue to occupy a significant role in our daily lives. Hence, online dating applications, such as Tinder, continue to shape our interpersonal communication, how we meet new people, and how we date or find partners. Millennials and Gen Zers heavily partake in this online culture. As communication and media scholars, we must thus pay close attention to these sites and the audiences' participation in them.

We all come to these online platforms and applications for several reasons. Some of us might be searching for people to date, some are looking for long-term relationships, and others are interested in finding sexual partners for hookups. There are also people like me who are on these sites and applications to connect with others to relieve the boredom and loneliness of small-town living. As we come to these sites for different reasons, we also present ourselves differently. While we reveal selected aspects of our identities, we might also borrow from conventional online presentation styles to self-represent. Some people pose differently (laying on a couch, making particular facial expressions, or looking in particular directions), some aim to look cute, and others reveal more skin by sharing shirtless photos or photos with minimal clothing. In each photo, we collectively borrow from the digital culture around us, and we embody some of its popular aspects.

Although Tinder is touted as an online dating application, it is actually more than that. It is a way of connecting people regardless of their geographic location. It is also a way to communicate. Hence, it is not accidental that the majority of its members are Millennials and Gen Zers. These technologies speak to them and represent many aspects of their culture, including fast dating and hookup culture.

I sank back into my couch on this Monday night during a global pandemic. Out of boredom but also my need to communicate, I started looking at photos and profiles on my small screen. I swiped right then left and left again. I knew I was also being swiped left or right. We all are hoping that we match with someone. After all, applications like Tinder promise an escape and give hope for a relationship. Matches mean possibilities, excitement, and in some cases a road to happiness. They also indicate some kind of acceptance.

REFERENCES

Atay, A. (2015). *Globalization's impact on cultural identity formations: Queer diasporic males in cyberspace.* Lanham, MD: Lexington Books.

Atay, A. (2018). Digital life writing: The failure of a diasporic, queer, blue Tinker Bell. *Interactions: Studies in Communication & Culture, 9*(2), 183–193.

Atay, A. (2019). Examination of transnational geo location-based online dating and hookup applications. In A. Atay & M. U. D'Silva (Eds), *Mediated intercultural communication in a digital age* (pp. 99–110). New York, NY: Routledge.

boyd, d. (2014). *It is complicated: The social lives of networked teens.* New Haven, CT: Yale University Press.

Byron, P., Albury, K., & Pym, T. (2021). Hooking up with friends: LBGTQ+ young people, dating apps, friendship and safety. *Media, Culture, and Society, 43*(3), 497–514. DOI: 10.1177/0163443720972312.

Chayko, M. (2010). *Superconnected: The Internet, digital media, and techno-social life* (3rd ed.). Los Angeles, CA: Sage.

Dimock, M. (2019, January 17). *Defining generations: Where millennials and generation z begins.* Pew Research Center. https://www.pewresearch.org/fact-tank/2019/01/17/where-millennials-end-and-generation-z-begins/.

Goldfine, J. (2021, March 1). *The business of dating aps: How do swipes actually make money.* https://www.businessofbusiness.com/articles/how-dating-apps-make-money-tinder-bumble/.

History of online dating. https://www.datingsitesreviews.com/staticpages/index.php?page=online-dating-history.

Jenkins, H. (2006). *Convergence culture: Where old and new media collide.* New York, NY: New York University Press.

Lee, S. (2017, December 6). *The history of online dating from 1695 to now.* https://www.huffpost.com/entry/timeline-online-dating-fr_b_9228040.

Matthews, T. J. (1965, November 3). *Operation match.* https://www.thecrimson.com/article/1965/11/3/operation-match-pif-you-stop-to/.

Niehuis, S., Reifman, A., Weiser, D. A., Punyanut-Carter, N. M., Flora, J., Arias, V. O., & Oldham, C. R. (2020). Guilty pleasure? Communicating sexually explicit content on dating apps and disillusionment with app usage. *Human Communication Research, 46*(1), 55–85. DOI: 10.1093/hcr/hqz013.

Ranzini, G., & Rosenbaum, J. (2020). It's a match (?): Tinder usage and attitude change toward interracial dating. *Communication Research Reports, 37*(1/2), 44–54. DOI: 10.1080/08824096.2020.1748001.

Rosenstiel, T. (2020, March 11). *Millennials, media, and information.* Pew Research Center. https://www.pewresearch.org/2010/03/11/millennials-media-and-information/.

Sujon, Z. (2021). *The social media age.* London, UK: Sage.

Sumter, S. R., Vandenbosch, L., & Ligtenberg, L. (2017). Love me Tinder: Untangling emerging adults' motivations for using the dating application Tinder. *Telematics & Informatics, 34*(1), 67–78. DOI: 10.1016/j.tele.2016.04.009.

The Real Story About Dating. (2005, September/October). Stanford Magazine. https://stanfordmag.org/contents/the-real-story-about-dating.

Vogels, E. A. (2020, February 6). *10 facts about American and online dating.* Pew Research Center. https://www.pewresearch.org/fact-tank/2020/02/06/10-facts-about-americans-and-online-dating/.

Chapter 3

Everything Is an App (Including Us)
The Media Ecology of Generation Z
Brian Gilchrist

INTRODUCTION

As a combined generational group, Generation Z and Generation Y have come of age in the United States during a time of rapid technological advancement. Generation Z refers to the group of people born between 1995/1997 and 2009/2014 (Bump, 2014). This cohort followed Generation Y, known as Millennials, who were born between 1980/1982 and 1994/1996 (Dimock, 2018). According to popular media depictions, Generation Z is the most technologically adept and most tolerant generation in the United States. In less favorable media coverage, they struggle to negotiate conflict, solve problems, or tolerate people who disagree with them. New media such as smartphones, social media apps have shaped Generation Z's communicative practices. Media outlets often depict the negative results of Generation Z's use of new media, but they have failed to show attentiveness to new media's causes of Generation Z's foibles.

The aim of this interpretive chapter is to provide an analysis of stereotypes associated with Generation Z through media ecology. First, I offer an overview of media ecology, which serves as the guiding theory for the chapter. Second, I submit a brief analysis on some of the common stereotypes associated with Generation Z. Third, I identify the effects of new media on Generation Z as the origins of these stereotypes. I contend that new media has influenced members of Generation Z to elevate smartphone mediation over face-to-face communication.

Media ecology rests on the assumption that human beings have free will and may exercise choice when making decisions. By choosing to communicate with technology over people, Generation Z has unintentionally affirmed individualism, rejected community, and developed smartphone addiction, a threat to their mental health. On college campuses across the United States, Generation Z students will often sit by themselves yet be surrounded by new media. They likely wear earbud to listen to music, type on their laptops, check social media through their smartphones, and text their friends. Although other students share proximity with them, they become isolated through their use of new media. If Generation Z chose to interact with technology over other people, then they might also decide to change their behavior and focus on people instead of their smartphones. This chapter considers how new media has influenced Generation Z's behavior and offers suggestions for how they could use their smartphones as tools rather than continue to allow smartphones to use them as apps.

MEDIA ECOLOGY

This section announces media ecology as the major theoretical framework for this interpretive chapter. Postman (1970) explains media ecology as the study of media environments. For Postman, each form of media such as the written word, the page of this chapter, or the clothing our reader is wearing creates an environment that affects human perception. We dwell in mediated environments that have synergistic effects on us. For example, consider the student sitting in the library while typing on a laptop, texting on a smartphone, reading the PDF file of an article from the library's digital database, and listening to a song through headphones. Each medium from our example competes for the student's attention and influences the student's conscious experience of reality.

Although Postman (1970) receives credit as the first person to publish a definition of media ecology, other scholars have made thoughtful contributions as well. Another definition of media ecology would address an interdisciplinary field of study that focuses on how media affect our lives (Anton, 2012; Gronbeck, 2007; Haynes, 2004; Thaler, 2006). I use the term "interdisciplinary" because media ecology does not represent a division of the communication discipline. Rather, the communication discipline would fit under the umbrella of media ecology. I argue that media ecology considers the relationships among human beings, language, and technology in both real and virtual environments (Gilchrist, 2017, 2018). Anyone who examines how technology affects the world could feel welcome in media ecology. In my definition, I included "virtual environments" because our activities in cyberspace have consequences for us in the real world. Although I do not participate in Instagram, most of my students do, and, sadly, some of them admit that content from that site has caused them negative emotions such as anger, frustration, and even depression.

Marshall McLuhan offers a significant voice in media ecology scholarship. McLuhan reached the height of his notoriety as a media guru in the 1960s, but he began his academic career as an English professor who wrote his dissertation on the *trivium*, the verbal arts of grammar, dialectics, and rhetoric (Coupland, 2009; McLuhan, 2006). As a professor, McLuhan began studying comic books and advertisements, two forms of media that his students enjoyed. He moved on to other forms of media and began constructing an entire system that could investigate media's effects on people. McLuhan (2003) defines media as tools/technology/translators of experience/metaphors /hardware/software/extensions of the human body/extensions of the human consciousness. For McLuhan, media move well beyond the scope of mass media communication technologies to other forms of technology such as our cars, roads, airplanes, and the languages in which we speak, write, and think.

McLuhan (2003) is also responsible for the following aphorism: "the medium is the message." Many people are aware of this phrase, few people know the phrase originates with McLuhan, and even fewer people understand what the phrase means. McLuhan and Fiore (1996) note that "societies have always been shaped more by the nature of the media by which men communicate than by the content of the communication" (p. 8). Here, the "nature of the media" refers to the form of the medium, while "content" describes the message. While most people want to argue about the messages they receive from media, McLuhan is far more interested in studying the effects of media on people.

For example, consider how many times violent video games serve as topics for class discussions. One side of the debate will claim that violent video games desensitize people and cause them to steal cars, rob banks, and commit all sorts of mayhem. The other side will suggest that video games are merely a recreational device that allows people to blow off steam and provides a healthy alternative to drinking alcohol or taking drugs. For McLuhan, neither side of this dialogue is compelling because both groups focus on the content (message) of the violent video games and ignore the effects of the form (medium) itself. Is the problem with playing violent video games the content (message) or the demands of playing the video game (medium)? Regardless of the message, the video game often requires people to remain sedentary for many consecutive hours and immerse themselves in a fantasy world. By choosing to shift their consciousness to cyberspace or the imaginary world of the video game, they do not fulfill real-world responsibilities such as family, work, or school.

Scholarship in media ecology contains various perspectives about technology and robust discussions about freewill, technological determinism, and whether technology functions as inherently positive, negative, or as a neutral good in human existence. In other words, media ecology scholars do not represent a monolith of ideas about technology. The point of media ecology is to consider the effects of technology on our lives. No technology should be labeled as a neutral medium because all inventions and innovations have a purpose and, thus, their inventors' biases shape them. Although the inventors envision their products as technology that could help people meet the demands of life, the inventors almost never foresee the unintended, negative consequences of their inventions. The combination of the Internet and social media platforms such as Facebook, Twitter, and Instagram has given children opportunities to access more information at their fingertips than most human beings throughout the history of humankind and instantly communicate with other people from across the globe, but children have also encountered forms of cyberbullying that have left them devastated, depressed, and lead to suicide.

MEDIA DEPICTIONS OF GENERATION Z

This section identifies some of the stereotypes promoted through media depictions associated with Generation Z. I rely on some examples to consider potential connections between new media and these stereotypes. While Generation Z remains the focus of this chapter, it is helpful to juxtapose their stereotypes with Millennials, the preceding generation. According to many stereotypes in the media, Millennials are the laziest, most entitled, narcissistic, victims of bad parenting who cannot solve problems ("Seeing," 2018). Obviously, any Millennial is more complex than the two-dimensional stereotype that proliferates the media landscape. Yet, these generational characteristics have endured for almost a decade. If, as sociologists argue, we are products of our environment (nature) and how our parents or guardians raised us (nurture), then it could be helpful to consider some of the paradigms that informed both generations.

I use the term "paradigm" when considering norms and conventions that shaped Millennials and Generation Z. By "paradigm," I refer to Kuhn (1996) who explains paradigms as lenses that help us interpret our world. For Kuhn, multiple paradigms exist simultaneously at any given moment in society, which means that people choose to uphold one paradigm while rejecting others. For example, Western society debated for many centuries about whether the earth revolved around the sun or if the sun revolved around the earth. Both beliefs functioned as paradigms, the heliocentric model and the geocentric model, respectively. After enough evidence had been gathered, people could prove that the earth revolve around the sun, which led to the acceptance of the heliocentric model and the rejection of the geocentric model. Kuhn's point here is that scientists are very reluctant to change paradigms unless new data emerges that could justify their decision to support alternative paradigms.

Yet, Kuhn's work on paradigm theory can also apply to cultural assumptions that do not require scientific evidence. Kuhn (1996) notes that some paradigms gain more acceptance than others because more people embrace one paradigm over another when their chosen paradigm holds significant value for them. The culturally dominant paradigm becomes "normal" because most of the people in the culture have selected that paradigm. This paradigm remains normal until some disruption occurs, which challenges the viability of the paradigm and might lead people to seek other paradigms to provide them meaning. Millennials and Generation Z might inhabit the same physical spaces in the United States and share many of the same virtual spaces in terms of social media platforms and other apps, but these generations operate under different paradigms as a result of their life experiences. This means that they have divergent interpretations of the world, a composite of factors such as cultures, family values, historical events, personal experiences, religious traditions, and social status. These factors create shared sets of assumptions that act as lenses through which generations view and understand the world. Since Millennials and Generation Z have not been socialized in the same way and have not shared the same experience of significant events in American History, they form a generation gap based on different sets of assumptions that guide how they live in the world. Some historical examples might offer some helpful context with this point.

The oldest Millennials came of age during the Reagan-Bush years, while the youngest Millennials grew up during the Clinton Era. During this historical moment, the United States emerged as the lone, global superpower after the collapse of the Soviet Union. As children, Millennials were introduced to Apple computers in their schools. For Millennials, white-collar jobs offered greater security and stability than blue-collar jobs, so education and a focus on technology could open more doors for future career opportunities. Although the seeds of technological dependency had been planted during the first decade of the Millennial generation, it would take the subsequent generation for those seeds to bear fruit.

For Generation Z, which Twenge (2017) identifies as iGen, media outlets depict them as more technologically savvy than Millennials, but even lazier, more entitled, less aware of the world around them and more interested in withdrawing into their techno-cocoons to get likes on Instagram than initiating social change through activism (Premack, 2018). Unlike the Millennials, the childhood of Generation Z featured some of the most disruptive paradigm shifts in American culture and politics. Consider that some of their earliest memories included watching the collapse of the Twin Towers in New York City during the September 11th terrorist attacks and the subsequent and ongoing War on Terror, while their formative years featured the 2008 financial meltdown and Russia's cyberwar that disrupted the 2016 presidential election for the purposes of undermining American sovereignty.

Millennials have led many different lives than Generation Z. For Millennials, investments in education, aggregate economic prosperity, and peace at home and abroad functioned as factors contributing to their prospects of successfully participating in the American dream. If Millennials wanted better lives than their parents, then all they had to do was follow the playbook: work hard, play by the rules, live within their means, and take risks if opportunities presented themselves. By "playbook," I mean "paradigm." For Generation Z, the playbook that built modern America since post-World War II provided strategies for success in a world that no longer existed. While many Millennials might have presumed to advance along the path blazed by their parents and grandparents, the intense disruptions in America from 2001 to 2016 transformed that path into an obstacle course. Generation Z saw that obstacle course as their "new" normal, which they rejected in favor of creating new paths themselves.

INTERVIEW OF GENERATION Z MEMBERS

NBC's *Today* aired "What You Z Is What You Get," a compelling feature from 2018 about the lifestyle of Generation Z. The responses from the young people in the interviews coincided with many of the stereotypes about Generation Z. A young woman claims that her generation wants to live on their own terms, which the journalist explains as using social media for career opportunities (Sellers, 2018). The young woman avows that college degrees lack importance based on changes in society. "Living on their own terms" reflects their attentiveness to the disrupted American culture in which they were born and raised. The playbook that helped Baby Boomers, Gen X-ers, and Millennials find meaningful lives no longer responded to the dramatic cultural shifts in America. Where previous generations sought to maintain that paradigm, Generation Z is more inclined to discard that paradigm. The young woman announces that she and others like her seek new ways to guide their lives.

By framing a college degree as unnecessary, Generation Z reveals their own cultural assumptions. Initially, the journalist provides a tacit link between social media and job opportunities but then later contends that Fortune 500 companies hire Generation Z as consultants to help these companies target Generation Z as potential customers (Sellers, 2018). She does not ask them what factors influence their assumptions about college. The rising cost of college and the likelihood of crushing student loan debt are two potential reasons for Generation Z to view college with skepticism. As of 2019, 69% of students from the class of 2018 graduated with a debt of approximately $30,000.00, and 14% of their parents had around $36,000.00 in debt from federal parent PLUS loans (Student Loan Hero, 2019). When including the entire American population, the statistics grow direr because approximately 45 million borrowers owe 1.56 trillion dollars in student loan debt. Generation Z watched their Millennial relatives graduate from college in the shadow of the 2008 economic collapse, which resulted in massive student loan debt and competition for low-paying jobs. Many Millennials also returned home to live with their parents because they could not afford to buy their own houses. Generation Z might interpret college degrees as obstacles to the American dream rather than as required rungs on the ladders of upward social mobility. As Millennials and Generation Z operate from different paradigms through which they form assumptions about the world and how they should best dwell in the world, they follow alternate paths when confronting popular cultural assumptions such as multitasking and adopting the latest forms of new media. Although Millennials certainly participate in multitasking and acquiring new media, Generation Z engages in both behaviors much more readily. In other words, Generation Z operates under a paradigm which presupposes that multitasking is inherently beneficial and that people should constantly replace current media with the newest, most advanced form of media such as smartphones and other devices within ubiquitous consumer culture.

THE MYTH OF MULTITASKING

NBC's *Today* feature about Generation Z also upheld the myth of multitasking, a faulty assumption widely held by members across generations. The journalist suggests that Generation Z multitasks with ease because they focus in a different way (Sellers, 2018). A young man explained the process of multitasking related to social media. He claims that he could communicate with his friends on Snapchat and Instagram, but then also read texts from other friends. When the journalist challenged another young man about other generations complaining about Generation Z's obsessions with smartphones, he replies that they do not know what he is doing on his phone, while another young man brags that he is interacting with hundreds of people (Sellers, 2018). Although we can agree about the proclivities of smartphones for Generation Z, I want to caution them about how they interpret "focus" and "interaction," which relates to my concerns about multitasking. Broadly defined, multitasking refers to people's attempts to perform multiple tasks within the same time frame. Proponents of multitasking, such as Generation Z, support this activity because they link multitasking to productivity.

Generation Z is most susceptible to the multitasking paradigm when compared to other generations in American culture. Yet, scientists have developed data identifying multitasking as a dangerous, untenable activity. Dr. JoAnn Deak claims that our brains cannot perform more than one activity at a time, which results in doubling the amount of time we need to complete tasks during multitasking (Morrison, 2014). Multitasking increases the amount of time needed to complete tasks and decreases the quality of the finished products. Dr. Deak declares that multitasking places children at greater risk because the distractions caused by competing stimuli simultaneously increased pleasure, which would emerge from the production of the chemical dopamine, and decreased in-depth understanding (Morrison, 2014). Children gained more pleasure by performing multiple activities than by concentrating on one activity.

Multitasking remains problematic, especially with how this behavior changes how members of Generation Z understand "focus." Phenomenology offers us a helpful way to better understand the importance of focus. Phenomenology, our conscious experience of reality, involves intentionality, where we place our focus of attention (Lanigan, 1982). Although scientists have exposed the dangers of multitasking, too many people interpret multitasking as beneficial. This widely held assumption echoes the points from the interview with the young people described earlier in this chapter. Rather than directing their intentionality on one task, multitasking invites people to shift from one task to another in rapid succession, which also stimulates dopamine in their brains. They feel greater pleasure as they switch from one activity to the next, but they do not give any activity their complete attention.

Multitasking also challenges how Generation Z comprehends "interaction." The young man from the feature boasts about interacting with hundreds of people through social media (Sellers, 2018). I suggest that Generation Z defines interaction as an activity that does not require the physical presence of another person. They embrace a paradigm that positions interaction as an individual exercise where one person communicates with many other people in different locations simultaneously through social media. They might do this through texting or using social media platforms, but they increasingly "interact" with other people as solitary individuals engaging in disembodied discourse because they do not communicate in the physical presence of their dialogic partners. They are alone with their smartphones, which invite them to multitask by accessing multiple apps. Even though they are likely performing these activities in crowded spaces such as restaurants, classrooms, or cafés, they direct their focus of attention almost entirely on their smartphones, a significant example of new media that invites them to ignore everyone and everything around them. As they shuffle from one app to another, their disembodied dialogic partner functions as just another app through which users swipe to get to the next app. Of course, the same applies to the user because they represent one of the many apps used by their disembodied dialogic partner.

NEW MEDIA EFFECTS ON GENERATION Z

While many media depictions focus on general characteristics about Generation Z and emphasize how much time Generation Z dedicates to new media such as their smartphones, social media, and applications, these journalists rarely discuss new media effects on Generation Z. In other words, media depictions usually criticize Generation Z for what they *do* with new media, but they often fail to consider what new media *does* to them. For the purposes of this chapter, I limit my remarks about new media to smartphone and social media apps.

New media such as advanced smartphones facilitate our communication with other people without any concern about spatial distance or time. Jansson (2013) uses the term "mediatization" to describe the "responsive sociospatial transformation" for our communication practices and to articulate "how other social processes in a broad variety of domains and at different levels become inseparable from and dependent on technological processes and resources of mediation" (p. 281). This mediatization refers to the interplay between how we use advanced communication technology as individuals, and how our society establishes norms for using this technology. This relationship features a combination of bottom-up and top-down cooperation.

The sociospatial transformation explains why members of Generation Z boast about interacting with hundreds of people through their smartphones. Jansson (2013) announces two major consequences about mediatization: smartphones "give people accentuated opportunities" to enhance their relationships with others through "more efficient relational coordination" and "these new media" have greater integration "into daily patterns of human communication" and facilitate further "dependencies such as expectations of information disclosure" (p. 289). Although Baby Boomers, Generation X, and some of the oldest Millennials may not rely on new media to maintain personal relationships, they should not disregard the fact that the members of Generation Z embrace new media as the most effective way to uphold personal relationships. Generation Z accepts almost constant interaction with new media as their "new" normal. Consequently, they are more likely to use their smartphones at dinner or other places where members of other generations would deem as inappropriate.

SMARTPHONES

The smartphone serves as the primary new medium that demands Generation Z's attention. The smartphone represents a new medium that has fundamentally challenged many assumptions of contemporary American society, including public education (Gilchrist, 2016). As new media, the smartphone combines different technologies: cordless phone, television, computer, Internet, and an assortment of social media applications. This convergence of hardware and software results in a multisensory experience for its users. While some readers might blame Generation Z for their seemingly constant interaction with their smartphones, those critics should recognize that smartphones affect them too and have transformed our communication practices.

The smartphone offers many implications for media ecology in terms of cultural effects on human beings. As Zhang (2015) suggests, "To be without a smartphone is to be a cultural outcast of sorts. By and by, the smartphone has become many people's existential gyroscope—the last thing to touch before sleep, the first thing to reach for when waking up" (p. 265). "Normal" people in contemporary American society own smartphones. In the previous decade, possessing a smartphone placed people ahead of the technological curve. Yet, the ubiquity of these devices would categorize people without smartphones as the exceptions to the rule. Since so many people own smartphones, only the users with the newest smartphones can be categorized as "ahead of the technological curve." Once they have purchased the latest model, they eagerly wait for the arrival of the next, new device. Since members of Generation Z have been born into these cultural practices, they likely interpret the corresponding social expectations of seeking the next, new technological device as accepted norms rather than as problematic norms driven by consumer culture.

Smartphones function as new media that also affect users' physical bodies. Zhang (2015) intimates that smartphones have "created a bent-head race among us" where people dwell within individual temporal, virtual bubbles "connected with everybody and nobody" (p. 266). At my previous university, students walking across campus with their heads bent toward their smartphones was a normal occurrence. As Rushkoff (2013) cautions, "Instead of demanding that our technologies conform to ourselves and our own innate rhythms, we strive to become more compatible with our technologies and the new cultural norms their timelessness implies" (p. 95). Students also bump into each other with greater frequency because they are too busy interacting with their smartphones while walking. They have adapted their bodies and behaviors to optimize their smartphones.

Product developers have transformed smartphones into mobile computers with Internet access. Sanvenero (2013) reminds us that "the Internet in the 1990s was primarily used for Web browsing and Internet Service Provider email services. The Internet world today has been infected with a disease called social media" (p. 90). The development of social media platforms has transformed the role of the smartphone and consumer attitudes about the Internet. As Rushkoff (2016) notes, "The information superhighway morphed into an interactive strip mall; digital technology's ability to connect people to products, facilitate payments, and track behaviors led all sorts of new marketing and sales innovations" (p. 26). Facebook began as a social media site where college students could share photos with each other but then expanded into a multifaceted platform where Facebook users receive content such as news, photos, and other materials that fit their profiles.

Sending messages such as ads based on data mining directly to users exemplifies one unintended, negative consequence of smartphones. Kanuri et al. (2018) contend that "Because content customization increases the relevance of social media posts, TCA [targeted content advertising] improves content effectiveness by enhancing consumers' propensity to engage with social media content" (p. 91). The smartphone enables advertisers to identify potential customers based on the consumers' social media habits, Internet usage, and zipcode/location. Suciu (2018) reminds us that "Information that reaches each user through social networks is selected by some algorithms which are not made public" (p. 26). Users understand that their smartphones allow advertisements to travel with them wherever they go, but they are often unaware of the specific practices tied to this process.

Smartphones have fundamentally altered Generation Z's approaches to communication and their assumptions about relationships. Pettegrew and Day (2015) warn that face-to-face communication "may be taking a subordinate role to texting as a preferred form of interaction. Students cite the advantage of little or no apprehension or anxiety with texting" (p. 133). Dialogue during face-to-face communication remains open to a multiplicity of possibilities, meaning that one partner must be prepared to respond at the moment to the other partner's discourse. As the dialogic process unfolds, both partners take a journey together in a living, breathing conversation in which both members are present and accountable for their communicative action.

Texting separates dialogic partners even though time and space might collapse through instantaneous access to information. As Turkle (2011) indicates, "Sociable technology will always disappoint because it promises what it cannot deliver. It promises friendship but can only deliver performances [. . .] A machine taken as a friend demeans what we mean by friendship" (p. 101). The conversation moves along at a pace according to the whim of either partner because the smartphone mediates the discussion. The partners may take as much time as they want in formulating a response, which can include editing their messages as much as they want before sending that message as a text.

The irony of the smartphone rests in our belief that this product would facilitate our everyday lives, yet this new medium has greatly disrupted our existence. Newport (2019) explains that Steve Jobs did not "seek to radically change the rhythm of users' daily lives. He simply wanted to take experiences we already found important and make them better." Unintended, negative consequences are one of the main assumptions about inventions and innovations from the perspective of media ecology. As Newport (2019) continues, "this model changes what we pay attention to in the first place—often in ways designed to benefit the stock price of attention-economy conglomerates, not our satisfaction and well-being." Steve Jobs could not foresee the long-term consequences of the smartphone, especially the shift in how and why people use this device.

Smartphone addiction has emerged as one of the major threats to people's mental health. Bian and Leung (2014) note that younger people have grown "increasingly dependent or addicted to the device, not only for mediated interpersonal communication, which is the initial function provided by mobile phones, but also as a tool for other functions such as relying on the device as an entertainment centre" (p. 160). While Steve Jobs might have intended the iPhone to function like an iPod, contemporary smartphones are used as multimedia entertainment devices and personal computers that demand constant attention from their users. During an interview, Twenge (2017) notes how a young person responds that friends "are all on their technology ignoring each other. I am dissatisfied with my life because a lot of my friends are addicted to their phones—they seem like they do not want to talk to me because they are on their phones" (p. 81). For some young people, smartphone addictions developed from their beliefs that they needed constant interaction with these devices.

SOCIAL MEDIA

Social media represents one of the leading causes of smartphone addiction among young people. Users have easy, instantaneous access to social media platforms that appear on their smartphones as apps. Social media platforms enable users to share their activities and their opinions about any topic with other users. Fear of Missing Out (FoMo) is a growing phenomenon related to users on social media. FoMo refers to a person's anxiety deriving from a compulsion to access other people's updates posted on social media accounts (Bratu, 2018). Users might check social media to see what other people are doing and then grow dissatisfied about their own activities. Bratu (2018) suggests that people "high in FoMo tend to overuse their smartphones to gratify their compulsion to remain connected" (p. 131). From an economics perspective, this concern is called opportunity cost. When people make a decision about a course of action to take or a product to buy, the opportunity cost refers to all of the other alternatives that they did not choose. FoMo differs from opportunity cost because FoMo occurs when users decrease the value of their decision by elevating the seemingly infinite alternatives.

Users posting content across their social media platforms have contributed to the growing phenomenon of FoMo. DeAndrea (2012) examines how students comprehend self-portrayals on Facebook and concludes that the co-creation of social media identities provides useful social evaluation data. Users interpret their own identities based on the choices they make about what content to post. Ibrahim (2015) defines "banal images" as pedestrian, trivial experiences uploaded to social media platforms that "become part of self-representation and are bound to a social media economy in which digital presence entails creating personal content; both in commodifying and sharing it" (p. 46). These banal images represent any activities that users might share such as eating lunch, drinking coffee, or sitting on a chair. The currency the users gain from other users derives from the sheer volume of photos posted. The single photo of a user's Chai Latte might not have much value as a commodity, but the dozens or hundreds of similar photos shared by the user create an accumulation of value.

The selfie represents a specific type of photo that users upload to their social media platforms. Senft and Baym (2015) define a selfie as a "photographic *object* that initiates the transmission of human feeling in the form of a relationship (between photographer and photographed, between image and filtering software, between viewer and viewed, between individuals circulating images, between users and social software architectures, etc.)" (p. 1589). As new media, smartphones may also function as cameras or video recorders that enable users to take photos and record videos of themselves. With online software such as the cloud, smartphones have increased photo storage capacity. Consequently, users may take as many selfies as they want and then quickly upload that content on social media platforms.

Selfies can be categorized according to the type and purpose of the picture. Albury (2015) explains a "sneaky hat" as a form of selfie, in which "subjects pose naked with a baseball cap (or other hat) strategically covering their breasts or genitals" (p. 1738). Albury's study originated with a series of interviews with young people to discuss their opinions about selfies. Three focus groups "called attention to the ways the term *sexting* was misapplied to young people's digital practices" because "naked or seminaked images that might be misread by adults" (p. 1738). These interviews revealed a generational gap about what content would be considered appropriate to post. Although young people might interpret sneaky hats and sexting as humorous, potential employers and older family members might interpret their practices as unfit for public consumption.

The desires users might feel to upload personal content have implications for their psychological states. Jin and Ryu (2018) refer to "digital narcissists" as people "obsessed with their own mirror image they voluntarily exhibit in a wide range of 'social media ponds,' with anonymous or targeted audiences in mind" (p. 555). Users gain pleasure from posting content about themselves because they function as their primary audiences, which echoed the Greek myth of Narcissus who fell in love with his own reflection. Digital narcissists experience loneliness by focusing on themselves rather than seeking relationships with others. Jin and Ryu (2018) caution that "selfie/groupie culture in the Instagram Pond functions as a channel for narcissistic self-enhancement, by enabling modern-day narcissists to deploy the two strategies: 'digital mirroring' and 'digital idealization'" (p. 571). Users try to post the best versions of themselves online and they might even use software to correct or hide flaws in their online pictures. The digital narcissists enjoy looking at themselves online, but the person they see is an avatar, a stranger. Although both Millennials and members of Generation Z can engage in digital narcissism, Generation Z is more inclined to this behavior because they have been socialized at earlier ages and for longer periods of time to participate in this activity.

If digital narcissism is placed on one point of a spectrum, then intense, self-hatred can be located on the other end. Interaction on social media sites can contribute to negative, psychological effects on users. Carlyle et al. (2018) identify suicide as "the tenth leading cause of death in the U.S. and the second leading cause for adults ages 18–24" (p. 12). They also provide a horrifying statistic that a young adult will commit suicide every 1.5 hours. I am not suggesting that smartphones and social media applications alone cause young people to commit suicide. This growing trend in the United States has many factors and an extensive analysis of this phenomenon falls well beyond the scope of this chapter.

Smartphones and social media applications exacerbate public health problems among Generation Z. Young people may use social media to discuss suicide, search for methods to commit suicide, and find support to prevent suicide attempts (Carlyle et al., 2018, p. 13). On a positive note, social media may offer an online support group for troubled young people, but these sites may also facilitate their pursuit of self-harm. While these messages differ, the medium remains the same. These isolated young people are turning to lifeless machines for comfort and advice rather than engaging in the living presence of human beings for face-to-face communication to gain strength from other members of their communities.

CONCLUSION

In this chapter, I suggested that the effects of new media have persuaded Generation Z to subordinate face-to-face communication in interacting with social media applications on their smartphones. Through an analysis using media ecology, I focused on the effects of new media on Generation Z. Some of the unintended, negative consequences of new media effects on Generation Z include elevating individualism over the community and developing smartphone addictions, which has threatened their mental health. As Lukianoff and Haidt (2018) warn, "New-media platforms and outlets allow citizens to retreat into self-confirmatory bubbles, where their worst fears about the evils of the other side can be confirmed and amplified by extremists and cyber trolls intent on sowing discord and division" (p. 5). These troubling characteristics of Generation Z emerged from their decisions about how to use smartphones. They chose to direct their attention to the devices in their hands rather than casting their glances at the person in front of them. I remain hopeful that they can reverse these dire trends. I am not suggesting that they should eliminate their use of smartphones entirely, but they could use their smartphones with greater deliberation and decrease their amount of interaction with these devices. Increasing face-to-face communication would open themselves to a much larger world than the smaller, mediated reality offered by their smartphones.

REFERENCES

Albury, K. (2015). Selfies, sexts, and sneaky hats: Young people's understandings of gendered practices of self-representation. *International Journal of Communication, 9,* 1734–1745.

Anton, C. (2012). McLuhan, formal cause, and the future of technological mediation. *The Review of Communication, 12*(4), 276–289.

Bian, M., & Leung, L. (2014). Smartphone addiction: Linking loneliness, shyness, symptoms and patterns of use to social capital. *Media Asia, 41*(2), 159–176.

Bratu, S. (2018). Fear of missing out, improper behavior, and distressing patterns of use. An empirical investigation. *Linguistic and Philosophical Investigations, 17,* 130–140.

Bump. P. (2014). Here is when each generation begins and ends, according to facts. *The Atlantic.* https://www.theatlantic.com/national/archive/2014/03/here-is-when-each-generation-begins-and-ends-according-to-facts/359589/.

Carlyle, K. E., Guidry, J. P. D., Williams, K., Tabaac, A., & Perrin, P. B. (2018). Suicide conversations on Instagram: Contagion or caring? *Journal of Communication in Healthcare, 11*(1), 12–18.

Coupland, D. (2009). *Marshall McLuhan.* Toronto, Canada: Penguin Canada.

DeAndrea, D. C. (2012). Participatory social media and the evaluation of online behavior. *Human Communication Research, 38*(4), 510–528.

Dimock, M. (2018). *Defining generations: Where Millennials end and Post-Millennials begin.* Pew Research Center. http://www.pewresearch.org/fact-tank/2018/03/01/defining-generations-where-millennials-end-and-post-millennials-begin/.

Gilchrist, B. (2016). The smartphone as permanent substitute teacher. In K. G. Roberts (Ed.), *Communication theory and Millennial culture* (pp. 145–156). New York, NY: Peter Lang.

Gilchrist, B. (2017). Papal media ecology: *Laudato Si'* as a medium of technocratic resistance. *The Journal of Communication and Religion, 40*(1), 56–75.

Gilchrist, B. (2018). McLuhan in the digital marketplace: Media effects of online shopping. *Communications, Media, Design, 3*(1), 26–42.

Gronbeck, B. E. (2007). The media ecology tradition of communication studies: Managing legacies, codifying theoretical-critical practice. *The Review of Communication, 7*(2), 180–185.

Haynes, W. L. (2004). Original Sin or saving grace? Speech in media ecology. *The Review of Communication, 4*(3–4), 227–247.

Ibrahim, Y. (2015). Instagramming life: Banal imaging and the poetics of the everyday. *Journal of Media Practice, 16*(1), 42–54.

Jansson, A. (2013). Mediatization and social space: Reconstructing mediatization for the transmedia age. *Communication Theory, 23*(3), 279–296.

Jin, S. V., & Ryu, E. (2018). "The paradox of Narcissus and Echo in the Instagram pond" in light of the selfie culture from Freudian evolutionary psychology: Self-loving and confident but lonely. *Journal of Broadcasting & Electronic Media, 62*(4), 554–577.

Kanuri, V. K., Chen, Y., & Sridhar, S. (2018). Scheduling content on social media: Theory, evidence, and application. *Journal of Marketing, 82*(6), 89–108.

Kuhn, T. S. (1996). *The structure of scientific revolutions resent shock: When everything happens now* (3rd ed.). Chicago, IL: The University of Chicago Press.

Lanigan, R. L. (1982). Semiotic phenomenology: A theory of human communication praxis. *Journal of Applied Communication Research, 10*(1), 62–73.

Lukianoff, G., & Haidt, J. (2018).*The coddling of the American mind: How good intentions and bad ideas are setting up a generation for failure.* New York, NY: Penguin Press.

McLuhan, M. (2003).*Understanding media: The extensions of man.* T. Gordon (Ed.). Corte Madera, CA: Gingko Press.

McLuhan, M. (2006). *The classical trivium: The place of Thomas Nashe in the learning of his time.* Berkeley, CA: Gingko Press.

McLuhan, M., & Fiore, Q. (1996). *The medium is the massage: An inventory of effects.* Berkeley, CA: Gingko Press.

Morrison, N. (2014). The myth of multitasking and what it means for learning. *Forbes.* https://www.forbes.com/sites/nickmorrison/2014/11/26/the-myth-of-multitasking-and-what-it-means-for-learning/#203007e72169.

Newport, C. (2019, January 25). Steve jobs never wanted us to use our iPhones like this. *The New York Times.* https://www.nytimes.com/2019/01/25/opinion/sunday/steve-jobs-never-wanted-us-to-use-our-iphones-like-this.html.

Pettegrew, L. S., & Day, C. (2015). Smartphones and mediated relationships: The changing face of relational communication. *The Review of Communication, 15*(2), 122–139.

Postman, N. (1970). The reformed English curriculum. In A. C. Eurich (Ed.), *High school 1980: The shape of the future in American secondary education* (pp. 160–168). New York, NY: Pitman.

Premack, R. (2018). Millennials love their brands, Gen Zs are terrified of college debt, and 6 other ways Gen Zs and Millennials are totally different. *Business Insider*. https://www.businessinsider.com/gen-zs-habits-different-from-millennials-2018-6.

Rushkoff, D. (2013). *Present shock: When everything happens now*. New York, NY: Penguin.

Rushkoff, D. (2016). *Throwing rocks at the Google bus: How growth became the enemy of prosperity*. New York, NY: Penguin.

Sanvenero, R. (2013). Social media and our misconceptions of reality. *Information & Communications Technology and Law, 22*(2), 89–108.

Sellers, S. (2018). What you Z is what you get. *Today*. https://www.youtube.com/watch?v=dx7SO6SA0UE.

Senft, T. M., & Baym, N. K. (2015). What does the selfie say? Investigating a global phenomenon. *International Journal of Communication, 9*, 1588–1606.

Student Loan Hero. (2019). *Shocking student loan debt*. https://studentloanhero.com/student-loan-debt-statistics/.

Suciu, I. (2018). Credibility and freedom of choice in social media in relation with traditional media. *Journal of Media Research, 11*(3), 24–34.

Turkle, S. (2011). *Alone together: Why we expect more from technology and less from each other*. New York, NY: Basic Books.

Twenge, J. M. (2017). *iGen: Why today's super-connected kids are growing up less rebellious, more tolerant, less happy—And completely unprepared for adulthood*. New York, NY: Atria Books.

Zhang, P. (2015). The smartphone: A media ecological critique. *ETC: A Review of General Semantics, 72*(3), 265–267.

Chapter 4

Millennials and the Gen Z in the Era of Social Media

Anca Serbanescu

This essay investigates the differences between how users from Gen Z digest social media content on the various popular platforms available, and how Millennials alternatively do the same. The intent is to understand the reasons behind their choice of a particular type of content, usually dictated by the specific social and cultural context, in which these two types of users find themselves. What are their social media habits? What are they looking to get out of these platforms? What key drivers lead them to choose one type of content over another? Thanks to statistical evidence provided by Cone Communications (2017), GlobalWebIndex (2017), Google (2017), and Trendera (2017), it can be better understood how to hit a specific target audience through catchy content and capturing Millennials' attention using the most effective language. Taking this objective into account, a broader understanding will be made about these two generations and their substantial differences, due in part to the digitalization process that saw the digital natives as protagonists in developing a new type of intelligence known as *digital intelligence*.

Every day we produce around 2.5 quintillion bytes of data; a significant amount that is produced each time we search for an answer. This piece of information becomes even more valuable when we realize that more than half of our web searches are now being conducted on a mobile device (Marr, 2018). Knowing this, which is the criteria that new generations choose to select, and how is it possible to direct or attract their attention to certain content? The young generation of mobile prodigies is at the forefront of digital technology, but it does not imply that every new interface will succeed in capturing their attention (Bernard, 2018). This proves how essential it is to study them, their habits, their behaviors, and understand their needs, analyzing and taking advantage of the current trends. The goal of this chapter is to create greater awareness about the attitudes of Gen Z and Millennials generations and to provide useful guidelines that can help with the creation of content for anyone who wants to apply a digital strategy on social media.

WHO ARE MILLENNIALS AND GEN Z AND WHAT ARE THEY LOOKING FOR?

For years, Millennials—also called Gen Y—have been the most studied generation and the largest group size in history—more than 80 million according to US Census Bureau of Statistics (Importer, 2012). One strong characteristic of this generation is their approach to using new media as a practical and functional tool, as well as a way to define themselves figuratively (Geraci & Nagy, 2004). It is necessary to first clarify the background, as there is no precise consensus on the year in which the Millennials period ends and when the Gen Z period begins (Strauss & Howe, 1991). The generational shift between Millennials and Gen Z varies from source to source. Usually, demographers and researchers place Gen Z between the mid-1990s to early 2000s and ending birth years ranging from the late 2000s to early 2010s. Sources ranging from Oxford and Merriam-Webster to the Urban Dictionary describe Millennials as the generation of people born in the 1980s or 1990s. For the purposes of this chapter and to work with a clearer distinction between the two generations, Pew Research Center's classification will be used, which is a source deemed reliable and impartial, active in surveys and demographic research. According to this classification, anyone born between 1981 and 1996 is considered a Millennial, and anyone born from 1997 onward is part of a Gen Z (Dimock, 2018). Although there is no exact date on which the start of the Gen Z takes hold, Dimock's article about the report of Pew Research Center made in 2019 will be taken into consideration within this chapter.

Gen Z—also called "digital natives," a term coined for the first time by Marc Prensky in 2001—is meant to refer to those who fluently speak the language of computers, Internet, phones, and video games. Unlike Millennials, they have had a smartphone since they were born, and they are used to navigating on multiple devices. Gen Z do not necessarily understand how technology works and its implications. Even when they don't know the nature of the problem, they have a proactive approach to problems in order to find solutions. The members of Gen Z are generally comfortable with multitasking, but they have a much shorter attention span (Roman, 2017). They do not use manuals to understand how devices work; they just try to figure it out on their own. The digital natives are children of the fast information society; they draw their knowledge from the Internet, unlike the members of the previous generations who were getting their information from encyclopedias.

They learn from experience, a type of learning called "learning by doing" introduced by Dewey (1938). Dewey developed and trained the concept of problem solving and conceives character as a coherent pattern of recurring actions (Cohen, 2007).

At the same time, experience is not acquired in a linear fashion, but through approximations, according to this logic that is similar to Peirce's "abductive" one (Zingale et al., 2007); it is possible to hypothesize new ideas to explain empirical facts. The need to fill a void is a motivation that drives toward exploration, leading to a less dogmatic and more customized approach to knowledge. Digital reality is part not just of their everyday life, but anyone who has a smartphone is inserted in an "onlife" era. According to the Onlife Manifesto, life is a continuous hybridization between being online and offline (Floridi, 2015). For digital natives, virtuality is a manifestation of reality, equally influential and significant for their social relationships. The concept of socializing (as spending time together) is changing, for example, playing online games can help the younger generation connect with their friends and cooperate, or collaborate for the same goals (McGonigal, 2011). The members of Gen Z are different from previous generations, in that they prefer to cooperate with peers and share with them the different ways of approaching a given problem and the multiple plans of interpretation to solve it (Ferri, 2011). Collaborative learning is second nature to them, and social media has only enhanced the importance of relationships (Roman, 2017). Gen Z may be more dedicated to creativity and cooperation than previous generations (Lyons, 2018). The digital natives have grown up in a complex context that prompted them to get adjusted by taking initiative and thriving in agile environments (Roman, 2017). In a study conducted by Wikia,[1] the world's leading collaborative media company, among its 13–18-year-old users it was found that the members of Gen Z like to share their knowledge and opinions with others. Among those who contribute to websites, 60% like to share their knowledge with others, while 55% like to share their opinion. Only 31% of those who contribute to websites do so in order to feel good about themselves and just 14% to show that they are smarter than others. The top two reasons for their contributions are entertainment/fun and to learn new things (Generation Z: A Look at the Technology and Media Habits of Today's Teens, 2013).

USE OF THE MEDIA: MILLENNIAL VERSUS GEN Z

The Internet plays a very important role in the lives of both Millennials and Gen Z; the former spend an average of 7.39 hours online while the latter spend 7.45 hours. Gen Z spend more on their phones each day than on any other devices combined (Gwi, 2018).[2] Their attachment to technologies is a clear contributor to promoting an anytime-anywhere type of social engagement. The time spent in front of screens has increased with the arrival of smartphones. In a study conducted by the DQ Institute that takes into consideration children from 29 countries[3] aged between 8 and 12, it was observed that the children spend 12 hours more than the global average of 32 hours of screen time per week for entertainment use (DQ Institute, 2018). A growing share of teens now reports using the Internet on a near-constant basis. About 45% of them say they use the Internet "almost constantly," another 44% say they go online several times a day, meaning roughly 9/10 teens go online at least multiple times per day (Anderson & Jiang, 2018). But how do Millennials and Gen Z enjoy online content? How is it possible to communicate effectively with the new generation? 71% of Millennials use the Internet mainly to find an answer to their needs, both at work and during the course of study (Coni, 2015). Contrary to what one might think, they prefer to write positive rather than negative reviews on websites and Facebook pages of companies regarding the interested products (Mangold & Smith, 2012), update their statuses on social media, and see what their friends are doing. According to 2018 GlobalWebIndex statistics (see figure 4.1), conducted on a sample of users aged between 21 and 34, it emerged that the most-used social network is Facebook, with a membership of 88%, followed by YouTube, which is ranked as the second-hand social network with a rate of 83%, and Facebook Messenger with a rate of 77% (Millennials, 2018). Millennials enjoy content from computers, tablets, and smart TVs more than Gen Z. They also use more Facebook and less Snapchat than the digital natives, and if they need to search for information about brands, they prefer to visit the official company websites. On the other hand, Gen Z often like to go on social pages, in fact, they are the only generation that use social media to research products rather than search engines or follow their favorite influencer or celebrity to determine the choice of a specific brand (Young, 2018).

Unlike the Millennials, Gen Z is actually more inclined to use social media to fill up the time and entertain rather than stay in touch with friends (Young, 2018). They prefer fun content over friends, spending an average of about three hours per day on social platforms, time spent longer than members of the older generations (Gwi, 2018). While the two generations score equal figures for the majority of the social media usage motivations tracked by GlobalWebIndex, the differences worth noting are how they fill up their time and how they find content.

The digital natives take possession of online content, as Jenkins (2006) suggests "digital appropriation of content" through mash-ups and remixes. They spend more time than Millennials on streaming music, Instagramming and Snapchatting. Over 60% of the content produced by them are of a

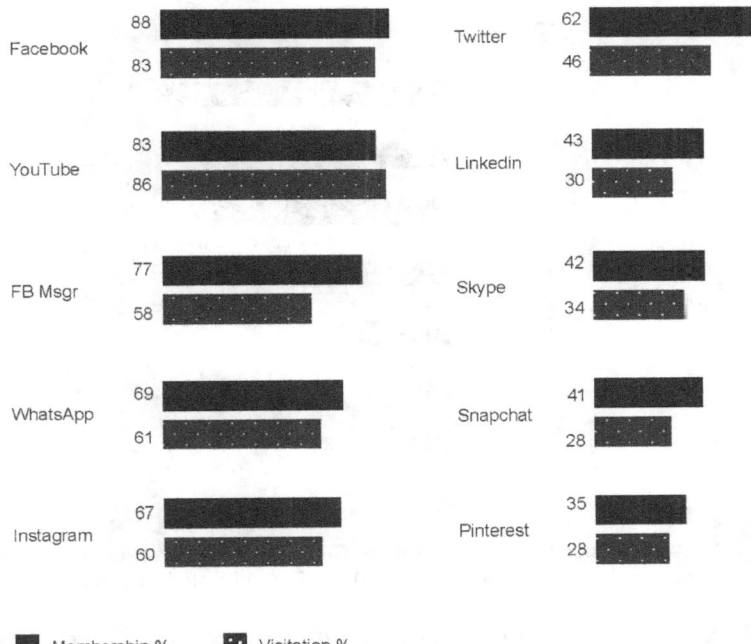

Figure 4.1 Top Social Networks Used by Millennials. Percentage of Internet users aged 21–34 outside China who are members/visitors of the following social platforms. *Source:* Data from GlobalWebIndex audience report 2018. Adapted from GlobalWebIndex Q3 2017. Figure created by authors.

creative nature, very often deriving from other content produced by the cultural industry, or creating new social bonds to negotiate one's identity (Ferri, 2011). Facebook is still a daily habit for most teens for consumption and online stalking, but they rarely post because it is not seen so "cool" anymore (Google, 2017). As it can be seen from figure 4.2, the social network with the largest number of subscribers has been replaced by YouTube, Instagram, and Snapchat. Today, about half (51%) of US teenagers aged 13–17 say they share less content on Facebook, compared to other emerging platforms (Anderson & Jiang, 2018). According to the Pew Research Center, about a third say they visit Snapchat (35%) or YouTube (32%) more often, while 15% say it is the same as Instagram. Only 10% of teenagers say that Facebook is their most-used online platform, and even less mention Twitter, Reddit, or Tumblr as the site they visit most often (Anderson & Jiang, 2018). The members of Gen Z prefer social media platforms that can reflect their desire for privacy and how much they value a curated circle of followers. Instead of focusing on increasing their friend count, for them what matters the most is to develop interpersonal relationships and have quality friends. They manage multiple

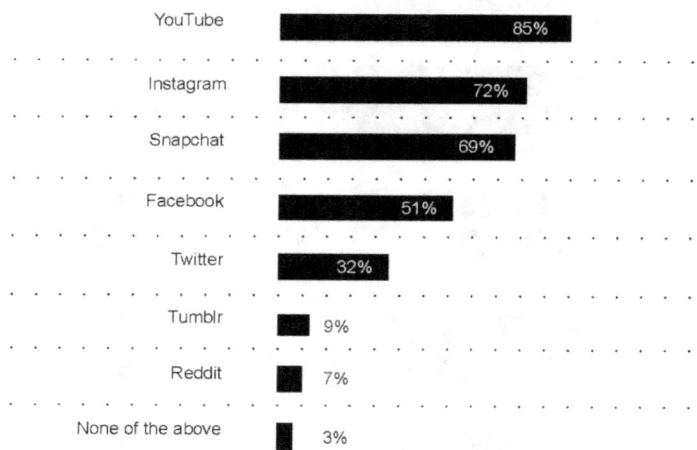

Figure 4.2 Popular Social Networks Used by Gen Z. *Source:* Data from Pew Research Center, "Teens social media and technology 2018." Figure created by authors.

digital identities on social networks, with different levels of privacy, being hyper-aware of what to show and with whom to share it (Basso, 2008).

Instead of posting many public photographs in Facebook albums, digital natives are opting for disappearing posts or stories that can only be accessed by a select group of friends. For example, some of them even have multiple Instagram accounts, one private for friends and other public ones (Beckman, 2018). Stacey Hicks (2018) randomly took 20 profiles of the members of the Gen Z from Instagram and noted that most of these do not share photos and personal information, preferring to use social media to engage with others rather than putting themselves on display. According to statistics published from the Pew Research Center (2018), 31% of teens report that using social media online makes them feel less shy and has a mostly positive impact, compared to 24% that claim they have a negative effect. They, therefore, feel freer to express themselves online and as a result, they can create circles of friends with much greater ease.

The video content is highly relevant for this generation because they can watch an online video tutorial to learn a new skill. In the survey conducted by Trendera (2017), YouTube beat out every other medium as the place where Gen Z watches video content, including Netflix and cable TV. The report also found that YouTube is not only an application that they visit every day but also their number one source for information, surpassing friends, family, and other websites (Trendera, 2017). Gen Zers also have a contradicting relationship with technology, according to MNI Targeted Media Inc. About 50% of them would like to spend more time away from it, while 48% would like to use the phone less frequently and think they spend too much time on social media. Although 90% of them agree that the media helps them stay informed, at the same time they feel overwhelmed and are convinced that spending more time offline can bring them real benefits (Inc., 2018). Teens are not aware of the potential effects social media have on their lives. What are these intergenerational differences due to? Part of the response can be found in the process of digitalization that saw the new generation as a protagonist.

DIGITALIZATION AND A NEW TYPE OF INTELLIGENCE

The contemporary generation will always be more digital than the previous one, and it is possible that this process implies an "epigenetic" modification of the brain of the digital natives (Negroponte, 1995). This statement made by Negroponte may seem a little exaggerated, but it cannot be denied that with the birth of the Internet and new devices, the concentration and approach to information have changed. Why not give the benefit of the doubt that in the near future our brain will change? According to Carr (2011), the plasticity and the malleability of the brain, which is constantly being shaped by experience, can turn us into servants of technology. But the ability for our brain to change neural interconnections does not necessarily mean it has to have a negative connotation. As a matter of fact, the game designer Jane McGonigal (2011) claims that if you train your mind by reaching 10 thousand hours in a specific field before the age of 20, you will become an expert in that field. Today's children and teens possess markable digital intelligence, also called DQ, born in the contemporary information society and present itself as the product of the intersection between co-evolution of some cultural and technological characteristics (Ferri, 2011). Keeping in mind that today's teenagers spend an average of more than seven hours a day on the internet through electronic devices, it can be assumed that they will soon become experts in this field.

What are the advantages that lead you to be a digital expert? Gen Z users are surely multitasking, because they have a wide range of digital tools available at their fingertips, helping them use nonlinear thinking. For example, the way they share music and online experiences takes us back to a collaborative and open-source approach to knowledge. The ability to juggle the fragmentation of information across multiple devices makes it able to have distributed attention, to make connections between multiple topics, and having everything under control. They have developed new skills to handle more interactive, interconnected, visual information, and their natural attitude has adapted to recognize models and react (Basso, 2008). Digital natives through the interfaces of their devices have the opportunity to put in practice the trial and error pedagogy, thus developing problem-solving skills, which is one of the other advantages of being a digital expert. Digital experience is related to digital intelligence. In the same way as IQ and EQ measure general and emotional intelligence, DQ measures a person's ability and command of digital media (Varkey Foundation, 2017).[4] DQ is an intelligence that is stimulated by a type of learning called "learning by doing," for instance, 51% of surveyed students said they learn best by doing, while only 12% said they learn through listening (Kozinsky, 2017). The same students also mentioned they tend to enjoy class discussions and interactive classroom environments over the traditional dissemination teaching method. A first indication can be seen in the percentage of young people currently using computers and connecting to the Internet. A report based on the PISA 2003 database (Wastlau Schlüter, 2005) states that almost 100% of 15-year-old students in European countries have already used a computer, and half of them use it on a daily basis at home and only a few times each week at school. The survey shows that students who have access to a home computer and have already accumulated a few years of experience with them get better grades than those who cannot access computers outside school hours (Pedrò, 2006).

HOW TO ENGAGE THE TWO GENERATIONS

Generation Z will represent 40% of the market's consumers in 2020 (Inc., 2018), so it must be understood how to better target them, and what companies have to do to attract their attention. The members of Generation Z hope to make the world a better place, paying attention to the impact of businesses in the community, verifying if they are environmentally friendly and socially involved. Taking this into account, brands may need to develop more robust programs to help people, communities, and the environment by offering more opportunities for those who work within the company (Forbes Agency Council, 2018). According to a trend report by AwesomenessTV,[5] Gen Z members are also much more involved in organizing and expressing their viewpoints on race relations, gender inequality, LGBTQ rights, and other identity issues (Premack, 2018). For instance, the Nike Women's Instagram account has 7.6 million followers and routinely features photos of strong women of diverse backgrounds and body types and has become an inspiration for the young generation. Kyle Andrew, chief marketing officer of the lifestyle clothing and accessories retailer of American Eagle Outfitters, stated that brand loyalty is not so common among today's teens, because they are less brand-conscious, and they are not spending as much as Millennials (Premack, 2018).

Most members of Gen Z often look for items that match their individual personality and communicate their identity, often trying to create their own mixed style and design from different cultures around the world. Companies should refer to these highlights to meet their needs, which also aim at exclusivity, reciprocity, and social responsibility (Petro, 2018). In fact, 19% of Gen Zers say that it is very important to buy from socially responsible brands (Trendera, 2017). Their purchase decisions are influenced by a socially conscious brand, so companies should start considering how to integrate humanitarian and sustainable elements in their supply chain and how to communicate responsible practice online and in-store, from design to manufacturing and beyond (Petro, 2018). It will be necessary to use a language that is closer to their way of communicating and consuming information. For instance, companies should take advantage of the benefits and potentials of the multichanneled approach, trying to involve them personally through social contests, or live-streaming. In doing so, digital natives can feel like the protagonists of a larger project and be its direct beneficiaries. Therefore, marketing and communication strategies should be stimulating, proposing curious and captivating contents with the possibility of a quick consultation. For example, strategies need to include building a multimedia report with graphics, movement, sound, and narratives. Moving the discourse on touchpoints, it is paramount to ask which channels allow to find and capture their attention. As can be seen in figure 4.3, Gen Zers aged between 8 and 12 don't even consider Instagram as a channel where to spend their time, instead the digital natives aged between 13 and 21 follow brands and post on Instagram. Both age groups use YouTube to have fun, feel inspired, or they just visit it when they get bored, while Facebook still remains the place to contact friends and read about what happen in the world.

Since the awareness on how to reach the Gen Z audience has been addressed, let me move forward with Millennials, who value flexibility, accessibility, and usefulness (Kreyenhagen, 2018). The brands for Millennials should implement communication strategies that can quickly connect with their consumers, making them fall in love immediately with the brand and pursue the official website pages. Since the attention threshold corresponds to the time span of eight seconds, Millennials should be reached within that given time (Todeschini, 2017). Members of Gen Y are more inclined to respond to those announcements with which they can establish an emotional connection and react to short and suggestive videos that attract their attention.

Interactive infographics, quizzes, surveys, and polls are some examples of content that require input from viewers who then provide feedback based on their responses. Quizzes are one of the most widely shared types of interactive content on Facebook and other social media networks, and it is common for these types of content to go viral among Millennials (Hsu, 2018). The

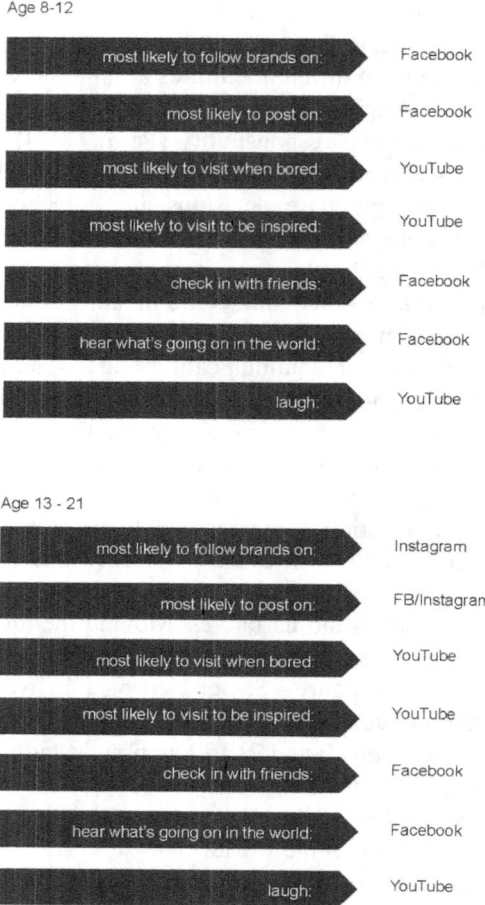

Figure 4.3 Where Gen Z Spends the Most Time. *Source:* Data from "The Trendera files: all about Gen Z, 2017." Figure created by authors.

gamification particularly attracts the attention of Millennials, in fact 46% would like more branded games to play, compared to 23% of Gen Zers, whose interest is much lower (Differenze tra Generazione Z e Millennials, 2018).[6] Half of Millennials prefer to spend their money on experiences that involve material things. Therefore, many brands are turning to experiential marketing in an attempt to connect with their target. This results, for example, in organizing meetups in certain cities or virtual reality experiences (Woo, 2018). They are dedicated to wellness, devoting time and money to exercising and healthy eating. Their active lifestyle influences everything from food and drink to fashion; therefore, the contents of strategic campaigns should be relevant and customized (Millennials coming of age, n.d.).[7] As part of strategic planning, corporations and firms must incorporate research to deepen their understanding of how their brands resonate and connect with their audiences. For this reason, when advertising is taken into consideration, it should be particularly appealing, applicable, friendly, and lively for publication on social media, preferably on multiple platforms (Kreyenhagen, 2018). At this point, the need arises to put in order and clarify the essential differences between the Millennials and the members of Gen Z.

The data collected through desk research were summarized, qualitative data. Intergenerational trends and sentiment were compared and integrated into quantitative data such as statistics on social platforms and used devices. The table also refers to the literature review that investigated the behavior of the two targets with respect to new ways of learning, influenced by the multitude of new devices and the network. The guidelines have emerged as characteristic traits, identifying each generation, but cannot be considered as a scientific result, so much so that they are potentially improvable and upgradeable. The main differences between Millennials and Gen Zers are summarized, subdividing the information that emerged into five categories: behavior, needs, contents, social media, and devices. In the table, the characteristics are divided between the two generations and have been assigned based on the concept of predominance.

This does not mean that a predominant feature in one generation can exclude the other. Generational behavior and differences are partly due to scholastic learning and access to information, in which the mass advent of the Internet has led to the personalization of knowledge. However, at the same time generations are influenced by globalization, allowing access to international trends from all around the world. The members of Gen Z have grown in this climate of instant access to content "anywhere at any time," unlike the Millennials who have discovered it step by step. As for the needs, both generations want to get away from the routine, take time off, and have fun inside of the social media contest. The substantial difference is that Millennials need to feel part of a virtual community and share their thoughts by exposing them on social media in search of feedback from their friends. Members of Gen Y often use social platforms as a showcase to share their daily experiences, while digital natives simply communicate with their peers via instant messaging, maintaining certain degree of privacy and anonymity on the platforms. This does not mean that the Millennials communicate less than the GenZers; they simply love getting noticed by their peers. In fact, the largest number of subscribers to Facebook Messenger and WhatsApp far exceeds that of the generation of digital natives, who prefer to keep a low profile. For both generations, the contents must be aesthetically beautiful, appealing, and engaging. Many ideas are shared by the two generations as political activism, attention to the environment, racial equality, and no gender difference (Collins, 2018). Compared to Millennials, Gen Zers are slightly more likely to favor government involvement over businesses and individuals (Parker et al., 2019). During 2018, the American Gen Zers have taken an active role in political activism on issues like gun control, Black Lives Matter, and MeToo movements. For example, Parkland high-school students started the "March for Our Lives" movement against gun violence (Ginsberg, 2018). Therefore, both generations use different devices; Gen Z prefer the smartphones while Millennials prefer computers, which they also access outside of working hours. Now that a distinction between both generations has been defined based on the collected information, a summary of the data could be the starting point for the brands to create a digital marketing campaign.

In support of research and application of the guidelines, the case example of First Day Feels, a communication campaign for Converse brand, is listed here for discussion. The campaign is targeted toward members of Gen Z and stars Millie Bobby Brown from the Netflix hit, Stranger Things. In this case, Big Spaceship agency was recruited by Converse to strategically promote the new collection of apparel, shoes, and backpacks. Since gifs have become a fundamental form of self-expression for teens (O'Brien, 2017), Converse felt it was important to create a new visual language that teens can use to express themselves. First Day Feels highlights 32 reaction gifs that express the wide range of emotions that come with the first day of school (O'Brien, 2017). The strategy is part of a certain age group and in the relevant context of the first day of school, which sees teenagers as protagonists. The topic of the campaign directly involves the students and is immersed in a social context, thanks to the imagination of the first day of school, which makes them more involved in the moment they are going through. The gif is an emulation of an emotion that triggers the memories of the target; in this case, it is represented by the body movement and facial expressions of the famous celebrity of Stranger Things, an iconic figure for them. The teenagers can make use of the gifs to better express their emotions, not only on the first day of school but at any time, since they are included in the gif database. The right way to attract the digital natives is to build loyalty and provide opportunities for engagement and co-creation (Cheung, 2017). For this reason, they are given an easily accessible tool, with which to have fun and be able to share their feelings among peers in respect of their privacy, without having to publish them on social media. In this situation, Converse created a branded visual language that Gen Z can use on their own terms. The campaign has provided a short one-minute video, uploaded on Converse's YouTube[8] channel in which Brown acts out her emotions from one sequence to another. They have therefore taken into consideration YouTube as the platform most used by teenagers and also because of the shortness of video content. Kyle Andrew, the CMO of American Eagle Outfitters, states the Gen Zers are engaged by brands having their own values (Papandrea, 2017). Ultimately, the message of the campaign is very simple: whatever your sense of back-to-school fashion, Converse offers cool shoes and accessories that will make you look great. Even if the campaign has directly targeted today's teenagers, the emotions expressed by the gifs can be decontextualized from the school desk. In fact, there is always a first time for anything: the beginning of a new job, a new relationship, a new house, and so on. This is how Big Spaceship agency intelligently attracts other indirect targets, such as Millennials, that can enjoy short, engaging, and emotional content.

CONCLUSION

The aim of this intervention is to identify the substantial differences between Millennials and Gen Z in the way in which these generations can benefit from online content and create a base of information that outlines their main characteristics. Trying to answer the primary question at the beginning of this chapter, or what are the media contents and devices preferred by the two generations, I had to deal with the context of digitization and understand their values. Millennials and Gen Z are both involved in the digitization process that stimulates distributed attention and gives the capability to link multiple topics. Gen Z are facilitated in doing this compared to Millennials, because the learning process changed through time between the two generations, considering the arrival of smartphones with Internet access as an instantaneous form of information. Gen Z prefer to learn from video rather than books, trying to put into practice what they have seen. They mainly access contents through smartphones while Millennials prefer computers. Gen Z tend to use social platforms such as Facebook and Instagram to stay informed about what happens in the world rather than socialize with one another. When it comes to cooperating with each other within a specific context such as gaming, Gen z are the first to do so. Millennials put friends first and share their social experiences, while members of Gen Z prefer fun contents and are reluctant to publish personal events on their public profiles. That is the reason why they are more chameleonic than Millennials, having multiple digital identities with different levels of privacy, adaptable to various situations. Despite the fact that members of both generations have grown up in a culture shaped by the economic recession, they have maintained a more positive and hopeful vision of the future. Millennials and Gen Z might want to enjoy aesthetically pleasing and socially involved content, because they believe in a world where diversity is valuable, and in which they can be part of a positive change. Their intention is to improve the world through political activism involvement, attention to the environment, racial equity, and no gender differences. Gen Z use media mostly with the aim to fill up the time to have fun through content reading, while Millennials are engaged in the content that creates an emotional bond. Finally, research within this chapter has revealed guidelines organized in tables that provide concise information, with the possibility of being used as a starting point for further deepening the two generations' behavior.

NOTES

1. The data are available at the following link: http://www.wikia.com/Generation_Z:_A_Look_at_the_Technology_and_Media_Habits_of_Today%E2%80%99s_Teens
2. The data can be downloaded at the following link: https://insight.globalwebindex.net/trends-18
3. The referred countries are Argentina, Australia, China, Dominican Republic, Ecuador, Egypt, India, Indonesia, Italy, Japan, South Korea, Malaysia, Mexico, Nepal, New Zealand, Nigeria, Oman, Peru, Philippines, Qatar, Singapore, South Africa, Spain, Thailand, Turkey, United Kingdom, United States, Uruguay, and Vietnam.
   The data can be downloaded at the following link: https://www.dqinstitute.org/wp-content/uploads/2018/08/2018-DQ-Impact-Report.pdf
4. The information is available at the following link: https://www.educationandskillsforum.org/fr/news-blogs/your-child-s-digital-intelligence-what-is-it-and-how-can-you-increase-it
5. The data are available at the following link: https://awesomenesstvnetwork.files.wordpress.com/2017/05/awesomeness_report_final1.pdf
6. The data are available at the following link: https://coobis.com/it/cooblog/differenze-tra-generazione-z-e-millennials-nel-content-marketing/
7. The data are available at the following link: https://www.goldmansachs.com/insights/archive/millennials/
8. The video is available at the following link: https://www.youtube.com/waxtch?v=Lyxv0z4OcmI

REFERENCES

Anderson, M., & Jiang, J. (2018, May 31). Teens, social media & technology 2018. *Pew Research Center*. http://www.pewinternet.org/2018/05/31/teens-social-media-technology-2018/.

Basso, M. (2008, July 28). 2018: Digital natives grow up and rule the world. *Gartner*. http://www.esearchhawaii.com/cms/uploads/articles/Digital_natives_grow_up.pdf.

Beckman, K. (2018, July 8). Everything you need to know about Gen Z, the newest addition to the workforce. *Ripple Match*. https://ripplematch.com/journal/article/

everything-you-need-to-know-about-gen-z-the-newest-addition-to-the-workforce-38c3b83e/.

Bernard J. (2018, May 25). Emerging interfaces: Millennials and Gen Z on the new tech that will capture their spend. *Forbes.* https://www.forbes.com/sites/forbesagencycouncil/2018/05/25/emerging-interfaces-millennials-and-gen-z-on-the-new-tech-that-will-capture-their-spend/#17b6f14660d1.

Carr, N. (2011). *The shallows: What the internet is doing to our brains.* New York, NY: W.W. Norton & Company.

Cheung, J. (2017). Gen Z brand relationship. Authenticity matters. *IBM.* http://www-935.ibm.com/services/us/gbs/thoughtleadership/genzbrand/.

Cohen, M. D. (2007). Reading Dewey: Reflections on the study of routine. *Organization Studies, 28*(5), 773–786. DOI: 10.1177/0170840606077620.

Collins, M. L. (2018, February 4). Meet generation Z. They're kind of like Millennials, but here's where they're different. *Deseret News.* https://www.deseretnews.com/article/900053886/meet-generation-z-theyre-kind-of-like-millennials-but-heres-where-theyre-different.html.

Coni, R. (2015, October 23). Le caratteristiche del target dei Millennials. *The sixth W.* https://www.tsw.it/journal/archivio/le-caratteristiche-del-target-dei-millennials/.

Differenze tra Generazione Z e Millennials: come focalizzare il content marketing. (2018, August 21). *Coobis.* https://coobis.com/it/cooblog/differenze-tra-generazione-z-e-millennials-nel-content-marketing/.

Dimock, M. (2018, January 17). Defining generations: Where Millennials end and Generation Z begins. *Pew Research Center.* http://www.pewresearch.org/fact-tank/2018/03/01/defining-generations-where-millennials-end-and-post-millennials-begin/.

DQ Institute. (2018). *Outsmart the cyber-pandemic: Empower every child with digital intelligence by 2020.* https://www.dqinstitute.org/wp-content/uploads/2018/08/2018-DQ-Impact-Report.pdf.

Ferri, P. (2011). *Nativi digitali.* Milano: Bruno Mondadori.

Floridi, L. (2015). *The onlife manifesto: Being human in a hyperconnected era* (eBook edition). Springer Open. https://link.springer.com/book/10.1007/978-3-319-04093-6#toc.

Forbes Agency Council. (2018, May 29). Need to reach Gen Z? Here's how to market to a younger demographic. *Forbes.* https://www.forbes.com/sites/forbesagencycouncil/2018/03/29/need-to-reach-gen-z-heres-how-to-market-to-a-younger-demographic/#1d3aaef31fa6.

Frayling, C. (1993). Research in art and design. *Royal College of Art Research Papers, 1*(1). https://researchonline.rca.ac.uk/384/3/frayling_research_in_art_and_design_1993.pdf.

Generation Z: A look at the technology and media habits of today's teens. (2013, March 18). *Fandom.* http://www.wikia.com/Generation_Z:_A_Look_at_the_Technology_and_Media_Habits_of_Today%E2%80%99s_Teens.

Geraci, J. C., & Nagy, J. (2004). Millennials-the new media generation. *Young Consumers, 5*(2), 17–24.

Ginsberg, K. K. (2018, October 19). Generation Z voters could make waves in 2018 mid term elections. *The Conversation.* http://theconversation.com/generation-z-voters-could-make-waves-in-2018-midterm-elections-104735.

Google. (2017). *It's lit: a guide to what teens think is cool.* https://storage.googleapis.com/think/docs/its-lit.pdf.

GWI. (2018). Digital marketing trends report, top trends in marketing strategies. *Global Web Index.* https://www.globalwebindex.com/reports/trends-18.

Hicks, S. (2018, November 14). Why marketers need to stop speaking to Gen Z as if they are Millennials. *Marketing.* https://www.marketingmag.com.au/hubs-c/why-marketers-need-to-stop-speaking-to-gen-z-as-if-they-are-millennials/.

Hsu, J. (2018, June 28). How to reach Millennials with content marketing. *Copypress.* https://www.copypress.com/blog/reach-millennials-content-marketing/.

Importer. (2012, November 12). The Millennial generation research review *U.S. Chamber of Commerce Foundation.* https://www.uschamberfoundation.org/reports/millennial-generation-research-review.

Inc., M. (2018, May 28). MNI targeted media releases data to help marketers win Gen Z-ers. Highlights Gen Z identity, values, behaviors, preferences and more. *GlobeNewswire.* https://globenewswire.com/news-release/2018/05/08/1498624/0/en/MNI-Targeted-Media-Releases-Data-to-Help-Marketers-Win-Gen-Z-ers.html.

Jenkins, H. (2006). *Convergence culture: Where old and new media collide.* New York, NY: New.

Kozinsky, S. (2017, July 24). How generation Z is shaping the change in education. *Forbes.* https://www.forbes.com/sites/sievakozinsky/2017/07/24/how-generation-z-is-shaping-the-change-in-education/#363f29906520.

Kreyenhagen, J. (2018, July 23). How to reach and engage the millennial customer audience. *Forbes.* https://www.forbes.com/sites/forbescommunicationscouncil/2018/07/23/how-to-reach-and-engage-the-millennial-customer-audience/#2a1984a87e2b.

Lyons, L. (2018, October 30). Is your business ready for Gen Z employees? *People Strategy.* https://www.peoplestrategy.com/ready-for-gen-z/.

Mangold, W. G., & Smith, K. T. (2012). Selling to Millennials with online reviews. *Business Horizons, 55*(2), 141–153.

Marr, B. (2018, May 21). How much data do we create every day? The mind-blowing stats everyone should read. *Forbes.* https://www.forbes.com/sites/bernardmarr/2018/05/21/how-much-data-do-we-create-every-day-the-mind-blowing-stats-everyone-should-read/#1b81a23860ba.

Millennials. (2018). Audience report. *Global Web Index.* https://cdn2.hubspot.net/hubfs/304927/Downloads/Millennials-Report-2018.pdf.

Millennials Coming of Age. (n.d.). Goldman Sachs. https://www.goldmansachs.com/insights/archive/millennials/.

Mullenlowe Group. (n.d.). Love at first Taste. *Mullenlowegroupuk.* https://www.mullenlowelondon.com/our-work/love-at-first-taste/.

Negroponte, N. (1995). *Being digital.* Alfred A. Knopf, Inc.

O'Brien, K. (2017, July 27). Converse gifs up Millie Bobby Brown for new back to school campaign. *The Drum.* https://www.thedrum.com/news/ 2017/07/27/converse-gifs-up-millie-bobby-brown-new-back-school-campaign.

Papandrea, D. (2017, September 28). Content marketing to Gen Z. *News Cred*. https://insights.newscred.com/gen-z/.

Parker K., Graf, N., & Igielnik, R. (2019, January 17). Generation Z looks a lot like Millennials on key social and political issues. *Pew Research Center*. http://www.pewsocialtrends.org/2019/01/17/generation-z-looks-a-lot-like-millennials-on-key-social-and-political-issues/.

Pedrò, F. (2006). *The new millennium learners. What do we know about the effectiveness of ICT in education and what we don't* [PowerPoint slides]. http://www.oecd.org/education/ceri/37172511.pdf.

Petro, G. (2018, October 14). Gen Z: New gender norms, fake news, frugality and the rise of retail's next power generation. *Forbes*. https://www.forbes.com/sites/gregpetro/2018/10/14/gen-z-new-gender-norms-fake-news-frugality-and-the-rise-of-retails-next-power-generation/#4a9fd3807382.

Premack, R. (2018, July 12). Millennials love their brands, Gen Zs are terrified of college debt, and 6 other ways Gen Zs and Millennials are totally different. *Business Insider*. https://www.businessinsider.com/gen-zs-habits-different-from-millennials-2018-6?IR=T.

Prensky, M. (2001). Digital natives, digital immigrants Part 1. *On the Horizon, 9*(5), 1–6. DOI: 10.1108/10748120110424816.

Roman, S. (2017). Engaging Gen Z's in the workforce: technology entrepreneurship & culture [Audio Podcast episode]. In *Talent is transforming Podcast*. https://www.top-employers.com/it-IT/analisi-hr/millennials-are-tech-savvy-gen-zs-are-tech-native-shaara-roman/.

Savic, S., & Huang, J. (Eds). (2014). Research through design: What does it mean for a design artefact to be developed in the scientific context? In *Proceedings of the 5th STS Italia conference: A matter of design. Making society through science and technology* (No. CONF, pp. 409–423). STS Italia Publishing.

Strauss, W., & Howe, N. (1991). *Generation Z*. Incomeresult. https://incomeresult.com/generation-z/.

Todeschini, B. (2017, June 21). I brand divisi tra Millennials e Generazione Z. *This Marketers Life*. https://www.thismarketerslife.it/marketing/i-brand-divisi-tra-millennials-e-generazione-z/.

Trendera. (2017). The Trendera files: All about GenZ. *Paramount, 8*(3). https://static1.squarespace.com/static/56a6d045df40f3cc4889f22f/t/59765342db29d6d9c74fe21b/1500926813297/All+About+Gen+Z_CNE.pdf.

Varkey Foundation. (2017, March 18). *Your child's digital intelligence—What is it? And how can you increase it?* Global Education Series. https://www.educationandskillsforum.org/fr/news-blogs/your-child-s-digital-intelligence-what-is-it-and-how-can-you-increase-it.

Woo, A. (2018, June 4). Understanding the research on millennial shopping behaviors. *Forbes*. https://www.forbes.com/sites/forbesagencycouncil/2018/06/04/understanding-the-research-on-millennial-shopping-behaviors/#2f10bfca5f7a.

Zingale, S., Bofantini, M. A., & Bramati, J. (2007). *Sussidiario di semiotica. In dieci lezioni e duecento immagini*. Brescia, BS: ATìEditore.

Section 2

MILLENNIALS AND GENERATION Z IN DIFFERENT CONTEXTS

Chapter 5

Observations in the Classroom

Bridging the Gaps among Media, Technology, and College Students

Mary Z. Ashlock, Yi Jasmine Wang, Lindsay J. Della, Siobhan E. Smith-Jones, and Ralph S. Merkel

INTRODUCTION

In the field of communication, we use perception checking when communicating with others to determine if their perceptions match our own (Alberts et al., 2019, p. 91). We learn that perceptions do not always match reality. As college professors, we see and experience things through different lenses in various ways. Our cultural backgrounds, education, societal forces, and biases affect how we approach our students and the subjects we choose to teach. This chapter attempts to outline teaching experiences among colleagues in the Department of Communication at the University of Louisville with Gen Z and Millennial students. Although these accounts vary, especially due to the generational differences between professors and students, there are some key learning points. Each of the authors of this chapter shares their observations and experiences from a wide range of courses.

First, Strauss and Howe (1991) outlined the generally agreed-upon time frames of each generation. This includes:

- Generation (Gen) Z, iGen, or Centennials: Born in/after 1996;
- Millennials or Generation (Gen) Y: Born between 1977 and 1995;
- Generation (Gen) X: Born between 1965 and 1976;
- Baby Boomers: Born between 1946 and 1964;
- Traditionalists or Silent Generation: Born in/before 1945.

Millennial were first known as "digital natives" and have been described as consummate multitaskers, achievement-oriented, and sheltered. These characteristics also set them apart from the smaller Gen X cohort that followed after the Baby Boomers. Initially referred to as "Generation Y," the more descriptive term "Millennials" slowly took root after being named by Strauss and Howe (1991).

Second, Michael Dimock, president of the Pew Research Center, makes the following key points about Gen Z:

> In this progression, what is unique for Generation Z is that all of the above have been part of their lives from the start. The iPhone launched in 2007, when the oldest Gen Zers were 10. By the time they were in their teens, the primary means by which young Americans connected with the web was through mobile devices, Wi-Fi and high-bandwidth cellular service. Social media, constant connectivity and on-demand entertainment and communication are innovations Millennials adapted to as they came of age. For those born after 1996, these are largely assumed. (Dimock, 2019)

The authors have all had some form of bridging the gap between media and technology with their Millennial generation and Gen Z undergraduate students at their university. Mary Z. Ashlock teaches "Introduction to Communication" (for all nonmajors and majors including those students wanting to pursue a communication major or minor) as well as public speaking, special topic courses, and an upper-level business communication course. Yi Jasmine Wang's courses include "Introduction to Visual Communication," "Adobe Creative Cloud Workshop," and "Documentary Production." Lindsay J. Della teaches "Strategic Communication Campaigns," "Research Methods," and "Health Communication Campaigns." Siobhan E. Smith-Jones' area of teaching includes "Introduction to Mass Communication," "African Americans: American Media," and "Television Criticism." Ralph S. Merkel focuses on teaching "Digital Journalism," "Video Communication I and II," and "Campus Media" (which includes overseeing the publication of the university's student newspaper). The following accounts highlight each instructor's distinctive approaches in connecting with both Millennials and Gen Z students in the classroom. The stories presented below engage students in using new media technologies and platforms, teaching with and through media, and teaching online.

WHO AM I AND HOW DO I COMMUNICATE?

MARY Z. ASHLOCK

I first delved into the topic of Gen Z and Millennials when volunteering to create and teach a special topics class, "Generation Z: Who Am I and How Do I

Communicate?" for sophomores who were undecided majors. Students were to explore an academic topic or theme of personal interest within the topic of Gen Z while developing inquiry skills that would inform their exploration of a major and/or career. At first, I was apprehensive about how this newly created class would add value and be received by the students. Mohr and Mohr (2017) had solid advice for teachers: (1) university instructors need to learn more about their students and their values; (2) instructors should review the major assignments given in their classes to consider ways to increase their value and appeal to students; and (3) instructors may want to adjust the way they talk about their courses and promote them as valuable to students.

During the first week of this class, the class viewed a documentary that outlined the essential characteristics of each generation. When students were instructed to divide into four groups to compare and contrast each generation, I knew they had grasped the theme of the course. I was struck by the students' openness and honesty. For example, they discussed how their generation was much more open-minded than older generations regarding inclusivity and equality for everyone including members of the LGBTQ+ community. They later produced videos and wrote reflection papers showcasing Gen Z's attitudes to music, fashion, sustainability, and authenticity.

My second experience in connecting more closely with my Gen Z and Millennial students came unexpectedly. Students were working together in small groups one morning in my "Introduction to Communication" class (held in a large auditorium with over 200 students). Each group was tasked with applying relational development theories to their own experiences. I randomly called upon various groups to share their experiences and feedback. One group discussed how two students in the class had been posting humorous TikTok videos about dating and relationships with thousands of followers. Within minutes, the two students volunteered to record a TikTok video (up to 60 seconds long) using some of the concepts we had just discussed in class. The students' behaviors align with Xu et al.'s (2019) research regarding how the short video industry is on the rise and plays an important role in the Internet industry. Xu et al. further state the reason for the success of the TikTok application is that the manufacturer uses a variety of effective marketing strategies while meeting the needs of its users. I asked the two students to first practice in front of the class. As a professor, I was making sure the content was acceptable, that is, no profanities before they did the live session. Not to fear, the TikTok video was a success and much laughter and—one hopes—learning ensued. That day we bridged the gaps among media, technology, and a class of college students.

Our university partnered with the Adobe Creative Campus Program in 2020 to provide advanced digital literacy skills throughout our curricula across disciplines. I served as one of the faculty who piloted and implemented Adobe assignments in my "Introduction to Communication" and "Business Communication" courses. For example, students could choose to showcase their written assignments by adding an additional podcast or using other Adobe graphic programs to highlight their key points. Although my colleague, Yi Jasmine Wang, teaches students at a more advanced level (see below), this form of media has allowed students at all levels of technology to enhance their digital media skill sets. Students of the University of Louisville continue to have free access to the Adobe Creative Cloud to learn and use various programs that will give them an edge upon graduating and entering the competitive modern workplace (Adobe Creative Campus, 2021).

HIGH TECH CREATES MEANINGFUL EXPERIENCES

YI JASMINE WANG

I have observed in my "Video Communication" course that students learn faster even using nonintuitive editing software such as Adobe Premiere Pro CC while video-editing software companies are embracing social media and attracting Millennials and Gen Z students. McLuhan and Fiore's (1967) phrase, "the medium is the message," still refers to media and technology today. Federman (2004) explains "that the personal and social consequences of any medium—that is, of any extension of ourselves—result from the new scale that is introduced into our affairs by each extension of ourselves, or by any new technology" (p. 1).

Students are learning how to use video-editing software much faster compared with the classes a few years ago. Then and now, students are introduced to similar concepts, tools, and interfaces of different types of editing, working with visual editing apps on their computers and smartphones with actions as simple as adding a filter to putting a photo on their phones. Yet today, software companies are making their user interface design more intuitive and are incorporating social media export settings.

Students in my "Introduction to Visual Communication" course love the opportunities to learn new technologies but lack necessary data analytical skills such as critical thinking and data visualization. In my "Introduction to Visual Communication" class, I teach Tableau, a platform for data visualization, and I have used Google Cardboard for the discussion of VR storytelling. A few of the students' comments are listed below:

"Strengths: Interesting, relevant, thought-provoking, useful, not overly demanding

Weaknesses: Layout of weekly assignments can be a little confusing because there is a lot of material."

"The material will become an ever-increasing part of our daily lives and specifically will be more important content for communication majors as time advances the more common use of this type of technology. Additionally, I found the content interesting and exciting."

"One of the most beneficial classes I have ever taken, it will translate into something I can use in my professional life immediately."

"Strengths: Introduced the intriguing and more recent concept of data visualization. Enabled students to think critically and understand the schematics of data."

In general, I found our students were weak in data analytical skills as mentioned earlier. Brock Read (2009) stated,

> From information technology researchers, we learn that these digital natives sometimes *overestimate* their tech skills. They may be savvier about how to upload YouTubes and "like" their friends' Facebook posts than they are about performing tasks on industry standard work tools, like PowerPoint, Word, and Excel. (p. 4)

I'M IN YOUR ONLINE CLASS, TOO

LINDSAY J. DELLA

I have been teaching online courses since I began my tenure at the University of Louisville in 2007. When I first started teaching online, most of the interaction was text-based and asynchronous. I also noticed that I either taught "online students" or "traditional students" and the two groups didn't overlap much, except perhaps in the summer when traditional students were away from campus but wanted to complete a course or two. Now I notice that my students in the classroom routinely approach me after class with comments such as, "I'm in your online class, too, and I have a question about X." Thus, I've noticed that my Gen Z students fit less into the category of "online students" as they were once traditionally defined, at least at the University of Louisville (or maybe just in my own mind). Instead, they're just opportunistic students (and I mean that in a positive way) taking advantage of the flexibility that online courses provide them in meeting degree requirements and scheduling other classes and internships (Perreault et al., 2002).

Although some people might argue that this transformation is grounded in the increased availability of technology and online course options, I think it represents a different level of online learning familiarity than Millennials may have had, perhaps because elementary schools have been introducing technology into classroom learning so early (Hew & Brush, 2007). A quick anecdote: I taught my first hybrid/digital graduate-level quantitative methods a year before the COVID-19 pandemic. I was nervous that the lack of in-person face time might result in fewer questions and poorer overall outcomes. In reality, the number of questions was probably on par with a classroom-based course. I was able to record the sessions so students could go back and review a topic if needed, and we communicated synchronously once a week when everyone logged in from home. Students still "came to class" and "participated" in this virtual meeting. It is clear that I was the only one worried about doing everything via technology (Ashrafzadeh & Sayadian, 2015). I routinely asked the students if they liked the virtual format, and everyone seemed pleased with it. Whereas "technology problems" used to be blamed on me and invoked as an excuse for failing to complete course work on time in my earlier online courses, any tech-based problems are now quickly reported, and the students seem willing to collaborate to resolve technological issues without—or at least with a lot fewer—complaints.

MEDIA CULTURE, LITERACY, AND FANDOM

SIOBHAN E. SMITH-JONES

I teach courses that explore media culture, including media literacy and fandom, and I have incorporated various activities in my courses that require students to use a range of media technologies. For example, in my fandoms (subculture of fans who share a common interest in hobbies, fashions, or genres) and adaptations courses, students are required to apply the class concepts found in the daily readings by finding a representative media text. This practice of adapting is central to the storytelling imagination through a range of media such as film, video games, and music. Hutcheon (2012) believes that the practice of adapting is central to the storytelling imagination.

Often, my students provide URLs to movies, television, or video game trailers, advertisements, and critiques/reviews. However, students have even brought in comic books and board games. One of the most fun and interactive activities involved popsicle sticks with happy/sad faces glued to them; classmates were encouraged to respond to the lecture/reading with their responses. Several of us kept our popsicle sticks and used them in subsequent lectures, or to tease each other. In my African Americans and the American Media course, students are required to bring an African American targeted magazine to class (Rooks, 2004). For most of my white students, this is the first time they have ever touched an *Ebony*, *Jet*, or *Essence* magazine, for example. COVID-19 has required me to adjust my courses, and my students and I have been able to achieve camaraderie with Zoom (including both live and prerecorded lectures) and daily discussion boards.

CHRONICLING THE MODERN STUDENT ACTIVIST: DIGITAL NATIVES SUSTAIN ENGAGEMENT WITH BIG ISSUES

RALPH S. MERKEL

On the first day in my "Digital Journalism" class, every student is deputized as a reporter in the newsroom/classroom: they learn that news "is what we say it is." Because all of their work goes online, they also learn the important precept developed for the course, "Nobody searches for nothing."

In a nutshell, I teach an exhilarating and fluid class that operates like a professional newsroom with each student charged with finding true stories, telling them well, and sending them out to the world for audience. "Search engine optimization" means they learn to tag and categorize their work so more people can find it. Today's journalists need a wide range of knowledge and technical skills and need to be digital-savvy (Kawamoto, 2003).

The class provides students with ways of learning professional techniques of modern reporting. The students learn to operate high-end professional equipment and post-produce five video stories at modern network standards.

Because Millennials and Gen Zs are abandoning legacy news outlets in alarming numbers as reported by the marketing firm, Y Pulse (2020), the class takes a student-centric approach to what the students/reporters cover and how they cover it. Because the students choose their topics, they are invested in the storytelling; these are stories they care about (Hackett, 1984).

The first class spends considerable time finding out what interests the students—what they are passionate about. Unlike traditional reporting that maintains the above-the-fray view from nowhere—objectivity—the reporters are encouraged to develop a voice that can help them create a future audience of readers/viewers.

They create beats they will want to write and report about. No editor forces them to cover an assignment on a topic they despise. Any news editor will tell you the best stories are told by interested narrators. "Digital Journalism" seeks to make each student just that.

Over the course of several years, this course has evolved to its current form where students use professional equipment to tell stories as varied as "What's the best place to eat," to "Why are activists picketing across campus?" to "How can I live a more sustainable lifestyle?"

Equipment Is Top-Notch

The class started by using Sony HDV and DVCAM video cameras and migrated to Nikon DSLRs. The University of Louisville is one of only six schools in the country lucky enough to have a Nikon School Locker program (2021) for video production. The students use the $2,000 cameras to shoot high-definition stories. They are fortunate to have more than 25 DSLRs in their equipment arsenal. Through the course of the semester, they become more skilled not only in storytelling but also in the professional use of these high-end cameras (Ascher & Pincus, 2007). They edit their stories using Adobe Premiere (a professional software program). The newsroom for the class has 15 Apple Macs where students produce their stories.

The production of those stories follows a wide variety of formats—they can be just like a television news story with a voice-over and a stand-up reporter, a mixture of sound bites and text to set them up, or just snippets of interviews strung together to tell the story.

Students, perhaps because they are shy or unsure of their presentation skills, often do not want to insert themselves directly into the stories, which is fine. "Digital Journalism" prizes well-told stories over numerous reporter stand-ups that may feed the reporter's vanity more than the narrative of the story.

The introduction to the equipment and its proper use is fast and furious. Within the first 30 minutes of class, students are out shooting personal introductions to their audience. Piecing together these short introductions serves as their first lesson in editing as they follow along on their desktop computers as they are shown the basics of Final Cut software.

Their first video is due within three weeks. Three more videos follow roughly every three weeks. Their final capstone project—a multimedia package including a highly produced video, a slideshow of at least a dozen images, and a 750-word story—is due on the last day of class.

One of the more important aspects of "Digital Journalism" is the feedback students receive not only from the professor but also from the world at large as their personal blogs gain traction and their readership grows. This interactive component of the class gives them the opportunity to engage with a non-University audience.

Foremost though is developing more compelling ways to tell true stories.

The Year of Protests

The year 2020 was a year of racial reckoning in Louisville, Kentucky, sparked by the police-involved shooting death of Breonna Taylor. In May, mass protests broke out in the city that rocked Louisville Metro Police

Department and political leadership. The students' beat focused on the downtown protests. Students interviewed then-Police Chief Yvette Gentry who addressed key questions regarding Louisville Metro Police Department's use of force protocols. Students soon after reported on changes to these protocols including mandatory body-worn-camera use and new limits on use of force. Then in August, students experienced the city of Louisville's historic wrongful death lawsuit settlement awarding Ms. Taylor's family 14 million dollars (Cards Eye View, 2020).

By all accounts, this experience proved to be the exhilarating and fluid "Digital Journalism" class as described in my introduction. Steensen and Westlund (2021) mention how the scholarly field of Digital Journalism studies is built on questions that disrupt much of what previously was taken for granted concerning media, journalism, and public spheres. My students had the opportunity to experience history both within the classroom and on the streets.

CONCLUSION

Bridging the gaps among media, technology, and college students may occur in many ways. Morreale and Staley (2016) point out that instructors need to be aware of the "elephant in the college classroom—the ubiquitous presence of technology and its impact on their lives" (p. 370). This chapter attempted to outline individual teaching experiences with Gen Z and Millennial students among five Department of Communication colleagues at the same university. Although these accounts differ, there are some key take-a-ways for instructors at other colleges and universities:

1. Professors can incorporate new technologies at any level within their classrooms.
2. Gen Z and Millennial students are now learning new technologies at the same time as their professors.
3. Gen Z and Millennial students may not be strong in data analytical skills. Professors need to continue guiding students through critical thinking skills no matter what the technology.
4. Gen Z and Millennial students have many more opportunities to use media and technology for full learning experiences outside of the classroom.
5. Professors can create meaningful, creative experiences through media culture and literacy.

Like most people, professors can become excited about all the new "bells and whistles" surrounding technology. Don't use technology just to say you added something. We recommend carefully considering what would work best within your course? Why do you want to incorporate this new media or technology? What are you planning on using? How will you relate this to your course learning objectives? When will you implement this into your course? In other words, "Pedagogy first, then the medium." We can bridge the gaps between media, technology, and college students. The results are well worth the effort.

REFERENCES

Adobe Creative Campus. (2021, January 15). https://landing.adobe.com/dam/uploads/2018/na/edited_creative_campus.pdf?promoid=D8F91RKC&mv=other.

Adobe Premiere Rush for Android hands-on: Best mobile editing software? (2021, February 1). https://9to5google.com/2019/05/22/adobe-premiere-rush-for-android-review/.

Alberts, J. K., Nakayama, T. K., & Martin, J. N. (2019). *Human communication in society*. Hoboken, NJ: Pearson.

Ascher, S., & Pincus, E. (2007). *The filmmaker's handbook: A comprehensive guide for the digital age*. Manhattan, NY: Penguin.

Ashrafzadeh, A., & Sayadian, S. (2015). University instructors' concerns and perceptions of technology integration. *Computers in Human Behavior, 49*, 62–73.

Cards Eye View. (2020, November 26). *LMPD rebuilding trust under new chief*. https://cardseyeview.wordpress.com/2020/11/26/lmpd-rebuilding-trust-under-new-chief/.

Dimock, M. (2019). Defining generations: Where Millennials end and Generation Z begins. *Pew Research Center, 17*(1), 1–7.

Federman, M. (2004). What is the meaning of the medium is the message. *Preuzetosa*. http://individual. utoronto. ca/markfederman/MeaningTheMediumistheMessage.pdf. Uticajinternetanatradicionalnemedije.

Hackett, R. A. (1984). Decline of a paradigm? Bias and objectivity in news media studies. *Critical Studies in Media Communication, 1*(3), 229–259.

Hew, K. F., & Brush, T. (2007). Integrating technology into K-12 teaching and learning: Current knowledge gaps and recommendations for future research. *Educational Technology Research & Development, 55*(3), 223–252.

Hutcheon, L. (2012). *A theory of adaptation*. New York, NY: Routledge.

Kawamoto, K. (Ed.). (2003). *Digital journalism: Emerging media and the changing horizons of journalism*. Lanham, MD: Rowman & Littlefield.

McLuhan, M., & Fiore, Q. (1967). The medium is the message. *New York, 123*, 126–128.

Mohr, K. A., & Mohr, E. S. (2017). Understanding Generation Z students to promote a contemporary learning environment. *Journal on Empowering Teaching Excellence, 1*(1), 9.

Morreale, S. P., & Staley, C. M. (2016). Millennials, teaching and learning, and the elephant in the college classroom. *Communication Education, 65*(3), 370–373. https://doi-org.echo.louisville.edu/10.1080/03634523.2016.1177842.

Nikon School Online. (2021, February 15). https://online.nikonschool.com/.

Perreault, H., Waldman, L., Alexander, M., & Zhao, J. (2002). Overcoming barriers to successful delivery of distance-learning courses. *Journal of Education for Business, 77*(6), 313–318.

Read, B. (2009, July 20). Students may not be as software savvy as they think, study says. *Chronicle of Higher Education.* http://chronicle.com.echo.louisville.edu/blogs/wiredcampus/students-may-not-be-as-software-savvy-as-they-think-study-says/7276.

Rooks, N. M. (2004). *Ladies' pages: African American women's magazines and the culture that made them.* New Brunswick, NJ: Rutgers University Press.

Social-media export settings in adobe premiere pro: The ultimate guide. (2021, February 1). https://blog.pond5.com/12628-social-media-export-settings-in-adobe-premiere-pro-the-ultimate-guide/.

Steensen, S., & Westlund, O. (2021). *What is digital journalism studies?* New York, NY: Taylor & Francis.

Strauss, W., & Howe, N. (1991).*Generations: The history of America's future, 1584 to 2069.* New York, NY: William Morrow.

Xu, L., Yan, X., & Zhang, Z. (2019). Research on the causes of the "TikTok" app becoming popular and the existing problems. *Journal of Advanced Management Science, 7*(2).

Y Pulse. (2020, July 20). *Gen Z and Millennials have very different news sources.* https://www.ypulse.com/article/2020/07/20/gen-z-millennials-have-very-different-news-sources/.

Chapter 6

Welcoming Gen Z to the Workforce

Leveraging Digital Literacy for Recruitment and Retention

Stephanie Smith and Michael Strawser

INTRODUCTION

Generation Z is entering the workforce, and much like Millennials, this generation is rich in digital wisdom. In fact, they may be the most digitally wise cohort in American history. However, wisdom in one area can often point to inexperience in another. This may explain why Generation Z is often described as "socially awkward" (Adamy, 2018) and in need of greater training about soft/people skills (Morris, 2018). This chapter examines the entry of Generation Z into the American workforce. Recruitment, retention, and communication strategies for organizations seeking to engage with Millennials and Generation Z are discussed through the theoretical framework of digital literacy. Digital literacy builds on existing literacies to argue that a digitally literate person should be able to adapt to new technologies quickly and efficiently (Ng, 2012). Additionally, those who are extremely digitally literate have:

> The awareness, attitude, and ability to appropriately use digital tools and facilities to identify, access, manage, integrate, evaluate, analyze and synthesize digital resources, construct new knowledge, create media expressions, and communicate with others, in the context of specific life situations, in order to enable constructive social action. (Martin, 2006, p. 19)

Using digital literacy as a foundation will help explain and present the existing media representations of Millennials and Generation Z to make inferences about both cohorts' workplace communication strategies.

Organizations must shift into thinking of their workplace as a brand that needs to be developed and nurtured to secure top talent among Generation Z, and strategies to do so are provided. For example, understanding that Generation Z is persuaded more by visual rather than verbal information, organizations can use social media platforms such as Instagram to help recruit talent and tell the story of the organization visually. But, organizations are simultaneously trying to recruit and retain a Millennial workforce, too, so this chapter compares the two cohorts and discusses ways to adjust recruitment strategies to fulfill the needs of both groups. Furthermore, leveraging the existing facts and representations in the media about Millennials and Generation Z provides a robust discussion of workplace retention tactics, explained through digital literacy. Finally, this chapter discusses how organizations can create a mutually beneficial communication environment for Millennials and Generation Z.

UNDERSTANDING GENERATION Z

Generation Z includes the 70 million people born in the United States between 1995 and 2010 (Seemiller & Grace, 2019; Strauss & Howe, 2000). "They are smart, digitally infused, driven, and ready to bring about change in the world" (Seemiller & Grace, 2019, p. 28). This cohort is named Generation Z because it is the generation following Generation Y (otherwise known as Millennials) which follows the generation before them, that is, Generation X. Gen Z has also been referred to as iGen, Digital Natives, the Homeland Generation, Post-Millennials, Plurals, and Founders, to name a few. However, the nomenclature that seems to have resonated the most is Generation Z. Much like the cohorts that came before, Gen Z has many unique and defining qualities that will permanently change society and the groups that follow. For example, some Gen Zers were in kindergarten when 9/11 occurred, which has had a major imprint on their worldviews (Seemiller & Grace, 2019). As previously mentioned in this chapter, this cohort is digital natives, meaning, they have never known a life without technology.

Prensky (2001) first coined the term "digital natives," which has since become a controversial misnomer and replaced with "digital wisdom." Digital wisdom indicates the degree to which a person is fluent in technology, and Gen Zers, much like Millennials, are considered to be rich in digital wisdom or adept at a digital skillset. This is not to argue that members of other generations cannot and have not acquired the same knowledge, but Millennials and Gen Zers possess greater digital wisdom because they were born and raised in digital, media-saturated worlds (Meyer, 2016). Prensky (2009) further argues that people with digital wisdom think and process information fundamentally differently than digital immigrants, or those who were not brought up in a digital world.

In a survey of more than 150,000 Gen Zers, the top strengths included honesty, kindness, fairness, humor, and judgment (VIA, 2018a). This open-minded generation enjoys actively searching for information to help them make informed decisions, view situations from multiple perspectives, and problem solve in unconventional ways (VIA, 2018b). While there is diversity in the strengths of this generation, Gen Z is also the most racially diverse generation in history (Vespa et al., 2018) and has some of the highest rates of non-heterosexual relationships and gender fluidity identification (Tseng, 2016). This is changing the language used in daily conversations and the landscape of many industries including beauty, clothing, and retail (Thomas, 2016; Tseng, 2016).

Due to their digital savviness, Gen Z has mastered presenting their identity in a digital world, and more than 75% of Gen Z members report being comfortable negotiating multiple identities online (Suzuki, 2016). Gen Z can manage their digital preferences through customizing their privacy settings, creating curated online identities across multiple platforms, and only sharing what they want, when they want (Stillman & Stillman, 2017). In addition to their reliance on social media, Gen Z values happiness, relationships, financial security, and their careers the most (Steele Flippin, 2017). Although this may not be a stark departure from the values of previous generations, understanding Gen Z values is essential for communication in professional and interpersonal contexts. Gen Z is also highly motivated by their passions and desire to make a difference (Seemiller & Grace, 2019). While Millennials get tagged as the "participation trophy" generation, Gen Zers prefer to earn their achievements by collecting accolades and reportable skills on resumes and transcripts (Seemiller & Grace, 2019).

To understand how Gen Z will be different than previous generations in the workplace, a brief examination of the unique educational experiences of this group is warranted. In today's educational landscape, there are significantly greater options than ever before, including magnet schools, specialized programs, online education, and charter schools, all of which have seen surges in enrollment from members of Gen Z (National Center for Educational Statistics, 2017). The percentage of students being homeschooled has also doubled among Gen Zers, to nearly 1.8 million (U.S. Department of Education, 2012). Throughout their educational experience, many did not use a traditional pencil and paper for learning, but instead, used tablets, laptops, and smartphones, as well as online platforms and instructional videos (Kiefer, 2013). The digitization of education has become so profound among members of Generation Z that they are now learning how to code instead of how to write in cursive (Wagstaff, 2013). Due to their strong desires for financial security, Gen Z is also influencing the college experience with many students living at home to avoid unnecessary debt, trying to graduate early, and delaying their start of college until they are sure of a major so as not to waste time (Barnes & Noble College, 2015; Fry, 2015). The top majors among Gen Z are business, STEM, computer science, and medicine, all of which are attributed to high-paying jobs (Ologie, 2016).

Perhaps influenced by their YouTube accessibility, Gen Z learns best by watching and then doing (Seemiller & Grace, 2019) because they are very self-conscious about executing tasks correctly, which can have important implications on how Gen Z learns and operates in the workplace. This is also why video-based learning is so popular among Gen Z, especially compared with previous generations. Nearly 60% of Gen Zers use sites like YouTube to obtain new knowledge instead of textbooks and all other forms of media (Bradley, 2019). Gen Zers also like to learn in environments that blur the boundaries between working, socializing, learning, shopping, and discovering, due in large part to their reliance on and accessibility to technology (Figenholtz & Broderick, 2017). Although they like to be in close physical proximity to others, they prefer quiet spaces where they can use their headphones and earbuds to avoid distractions (Seemiller & Grace, 2016).

So, when it comes to understanding what Gen Zers want from their careers, knowing their educational experiences helps. Many Gen Zers report wanting to create things in their careers and believe that they can leverage technology to build things that are new and exciting to older generations (Adobe Educate, 2016). Currently, the trending fields for Gen Z also focus on technology and include business, engineering, and computer and information sciences, according to job recruiters (National Association of Colleges and Employers, 2016). These jobs are also known for being recession-proof, alluding back to the fact that Gen Z values financial security (Strauss, 2016). However, because Gen Z is rich in digital wisdom, this cohort is well aware of the risk of automation for taking jobs that are currently executed by people, which is another reason they are more selective about which industries to work within.

Previous research indicates that when it comes to job searching, the entry-level job seekers are foregoing traditional routes in favor of using technology-based methods like LinkedIn and online networking (Smith, 2017). While job searching, they are hoping to obtain a job that they will enjoy doing every day and find fulfilling, despite their strong desire for good pay (Seemiller & Grace, 2016). In fact, some research indicates that making a difference in society is paramount to Gen Zers, so they want the work they are doing to matter. They also want to feel as though their work is contributing to social change and work for companies that are making positive impacts on society (Stillman & Stillman, 2017). Much like their Millennial predecessors, members of Gen Z also seek advancement and personal growth opportunities from their employers, hybrid work options, and expect diversity and inclusion in the workplace (Seemiller & Grace, 2019). However, Gen Z has distinct differences from their Millennial predecessors when it comes to how they learn, where they learn, their diversity, and their goals. Using the frameworks of media and digital literacy can help organizations better understand how to welcome Generation Z into the workplace and how to retain the unique talents of this generational cohort.

MEDIA AND DIGITAL LITERACY

Media literacy is commonly defined as "the ability to access, analyze, evaluate, and create messages across a variety of contexts" (Livingstone, 2004, p. 3). The addition of Internet and digital communications require users to have a set of skills beyond those required of traditional definitions of media literacy (Eshet-Aklaki & Amichai-Hamburger, 2004). This has led to the development of other skill-based literacies, including digital literacy. As such, digital literacy is defined as "an ability to read and understand hypertextual and multimedia texts" (Bawden, 2001, p. 24). Martin (2006) provides a more elaborate definition:

> Digital literacy is the awareness, attitude, and ability of individuals to appropriately use digital tools and facilities to identify, access, manage, integrate, evaluate, analyze and synthesize digital resources, construct new knowledge, create media expressions, and communicate with others, in the context of specific life situations, in order to enable constructive social action; and to reflect upon this process. (p. 19; Koltay, 2011, p. 216)

According to Ng (2012), digital literacy builds on existing literacies and thus a digital literate person should be able to adapt to new technologies quickly and efficiently.

Digital literacy expands on media literacy by going beyond just examining text-based messages to include sounds and images (Bawden, 2001). Eshet-Alkali and Amichai-Hamburger (2004) suggest digital literacy should include five digital skills: photo-visual skills, reproduction skills, branching skills, information skills, and socio-emotional skills. Scholars have purported media and digital literacy as necessary tools for participating in civic life. According to Kellner and Share (2005), media literacy education empowers individuals to better understand and intelligently use media. Hobbs (2011) suggests that media and digital literacy allow "audiences, especially younger audiences, to seek out information on relevant issues, to evaluate the quality of information available, and to engage in dialogue with others to form coalitions" (p.

421–422). In a meta-analysis of research on media literacy interventions, Jeong et al. (2012) found that these interventions were generally considered to be effective in achieving outcomes.

MEDIA AND DIGITAL LITERACY EDUCATION

According to Kellner and Share (2005), literacy is inextricably linked with education, and it is through literacy that people learn to communicate effectively within a system. Ashley (2015) found that 83% of instructors teaching introductory mass communication classes include media literacy as a component of the course. Schmidt (2013) reported that on average, secondary education faculty teaches media literacy competencies in their courses, although the extent to which this is achieved varies widely. Furthermore, Schmidt (2015) found that students benefitted from media-focused lessons, even if that focus is a marginal aspect of the class. Traditionally, the concept of media literacy was focused primarily on developing interventions and education programs related to traditional media, but as technology evolves so should the application of media literacy interventions. Likewise, Kellner and Share (2005) make the argument that literacy must be extended to include new and digital media.

In the context of organizational communication, an understanding of digital and media literacy can be used to help recruit and retain Generation Z, using similar methods to recruiting and retaining a Millennial workforce because of their digital wisdom. Organizations should rely on technology, as well as other traditional methods, for communication with internal and external audiences.

RECRUITMENT AND RETENTION OF A GEN Z WORKFORCE

Internships

Although Gen Z has unique characteristics like every generational cohort, they are similar in many ways to Millennials. One proven way to engage a Millennial workforce that could be similar for Gen Z is through high-quality internships. Internships are one way for employers to mitigate financial losses by cultivating talent pipelines and helping to ensure a good fit between an organization's culture and values and the prospective employee (Coffey & Strawser, 2018). Knowing that Gen Z values experience and learning, internships are a valuable way to learn training, skills, and communication necessary for success in organizational settings. In essence, internships are another form of experiential learning, which has already been demonstrated as a valuable touchpoint among members of Gen Z. Additionally, understanding the unique values Gen Z expects from their work experiences, internships are one way for Gen Zers to test the fit against their personal expectations without the expense of commitment for the employer.

While Millennials are often described as "job hoppers," it is currently unknown whether or not Gen Zers will follow their lead and similarly leave jobs after short periods of time. Given the financial motivations of Gen Z, it is plausible that they will continually look for new jobs that offer more money, making the understanding of recruitment critical for organizations. Internships can also reduce anxiety and uncertainty among entry-level employees, which can have better effects on employee engagement and retention (Coffey & Strawser, 2018). Finally, internships have important implications for anticipatory socialization. Anticipatory socialization is the process that explains how information that people receive intentionally and unintentionally from their environment affects their career expectations (Jablin, 2001). Just as research indicates that personality traits present in common careers, like accounting and business, influence anticipatory socialization, so too does generational belonging (Coffey & Strawser, 2018). Internships provide an opportunity for socialization, as well as a way to establish identity, reduce uncertainty, and narrow the work-expectation reality gap (Coffey & Strawser, 2018).

Job Searching

Understanding how recent college graduates, which is now beginning to include Gen Zers, search and find jobs is also important for recruiting this generation. Job searching is a difficult, communicative task that "requires the use of complex strategies, substantial self-control, and self-regulation skill" (Price & Vinokur, 1995, p. 192). Job-searching behaviors include preparatory efforts and active behaviors. Preparatory efforts, which happen primarily in a virtual context, include finding information about potential employers, securing leads, and preparing application materials, while active behaviors refer to actually applying to jobs and interviewing (Bretz et al., 1984). In today's world, both preparatory and active behaviors are greatly influenced by technology. Job seekers now turn to websites like Facebook and Instagram to learn about companies, understand company culture, and make assessments about a company's beliefs and values, before applying, making the use of technology a preparatory strategy. However, since many job applications are submitted exclusively online and through websites, using technology for securing employment is also an active behavior. Furthermore, employee-generated review websites are becoming more popular among entry and mid-level employees, which emphasizes how digital wisdom and desire to learn are changing the landscape of job searching for both job seekers and organizations.

Additionally, job seekers are now cyber vetting employers using websites like Glassdoor and Indeed, where employees can leave anonymous reviews about salaries, working environment, and management practices. Research indicates that entry-level employees who use multiple communication methods to search for jobs have greater success in their job search and receive more interviews than those who rely on only one method of job searching (Mau & Kopischke, 2001; Smith, 2017), which has important implications for organizations trying to hire Gen Z.

Due to their digital nativity, today's job seekers use multiple channels, rooted in technology, to find information and apply for available jobs. Organizations need to capitalize on this information and share organizational information as well as job opportunities across various platforms and understand that because of technology, the recruitment period does not end simply because a job may not be currently available. Instead, because Gen Z is so plugged in, organizations should have the mindset that potential employees are always watching and gathering information about whether or not they would ever want to work there. Therefore, sharing information is essential for recruiting a Gen Z workforce.

Millennials and members of Gen Z use a few, specific strategies to search for jobs including personal networking, direct online application, and university career services (Smith, 2017). Interpersonal networking as a job-searching strategy entails communicating with personal contacts for the objective of finding a job. Recent college graduates and those entering the workforce rely on their interpersonal contacts such as friends, family members, online networks, and previous supervisors to help them find and secure available opportunities. Notably, however, the Millennial and Gen Z interpretation of interpersonal networking as a job strategy did not include making new connections with previously unknown people for the purpose of finding a job (Smith, 2017). This is important for employers hoping to recruit Millennials and Gen Z employees because it demonstrates the importance of asking current employees to tell their interpersonal networks about available opportunities at the organization.

Another job-searching strategy is applying directly to positions online. Millennials and members of Gen Z use this strategy because it provides autonomy; it is convenient and can be done on their schedule and does not have the potential for immediate rejection, which they get weary about (Smith, 2017). Popular channels for finding and applying to jobs directly online include websites like Indeed, Career Builder, Glassdoor, LinkedIn, and Monster. Many job seekers report using the function of uploading a standard resume and applying with the one-click feature, rather than tailoring their resume to each specific position posted online (Smith, 2017). Direct application online can also include submitting applications directly through employer's websites. This strategy demonstrates that employers need to share available opportunities across multiple channels, including on its website, so that interested people can easily apply.

Finally, Millennials and Gen Z use university career services as a primary job-searching strategy, even after they graduate from their respective institutions (Smith, 2017). This strategy can include attending career fairs sponsored by their college or university, and/or seeking the resume and cover letter help, interviewing guidance, and using proprietary job postings for job searching (Smith, 2017). Some first-time job seekers report using university career services simply because they do not know another place to search, while others like the variety of opportunities coupled with the availability for coaching (Smith, 2017). This means that organizations looking to recruit Millennial and Gen Z employees should participate in career fairs and share their available opportunities on the career services job posting websites.

Communicating Culture

Organizational culture is a highly studied area in recruitment, retention, and engagement of employees and refers to the complex set of values, beliefs, assumptions, and symbols that define the way organizations conduct business (Deal & Kennedy, 1982). Because Millennials have particular expectations about the cultures they wish to work within, this area of research and practice is seeing a resurgence, and the influence of technology is becoming more prominent. Millennials, and likely Gen Z as well, want to work in flexible cultures (Rawlins et al., 2008) where they can maintain their own lifestyles while still completing their work. This is so important that Millennials are willing to give up some of their salary in exchange for more flexible working arrangements (Chew, 2016). In today's organizational landscape, employees also want to work for organizations that share their values and beliefs, with special consideration for social and environmental issues (Watkins & Smith, 2018). Organizational culture is also strongly linked to employees' level of social identity with their organization which has major implications for retention and engagement. Therefore, understanding how to communicate culture to both prospective and current employees, through the use of technology, is important for organizations.

Instagram is one platform that organizations can leverage to share information about culture. Instagram is unique from other social media platforms because of the visual emphasis in sharing photos and video stories, but it is also the largest visual-based social media platform in the world with over 800 million active users (Etherington, 2017). Specifically, Instagram is an ideal outlet to share information about visual culture because culture represents intangible objects that are often best represented visually (Sriarmesh et al., 1996). Organizations can use platforms like Instagram, as well as its own website and other social media sites, to communicate a distinct organizational identity, share organizational values and the practice of those values, and manage relationships with employees through sharing good news and fun stories about achievements (Watkins & Smith, 2018). Organizations can tell their story by sharing pictures of the current office, the history of the organization, and behind-the-scenes looks into the work of the organization. Additionally, taking advantage of the unique features on each platform like creating branded hashtags, posting short, limited-view stories, and going "live," will help position the organization as an industry leader. Finally, featuring employees living out the values of the organization will make it easier for others, especially Gen Z, to see how they could fit in and ignite their desire to want to identify with an organization (Watkins & Smith, 2018).

Integrating Technology

As previously mentioned, Millennials and Gen Z employees seek flexibility, and due to their digital wisdom, they can find flexibility through teleworking arrangements. Teleworking allows employees to perform their jobs at alternate sites including at home or telework centers through the use of digital communication technology (U.S. Office of Personnel Management, 2018). Employees can also telework through virtual teams, which makes the reliance on technology even more vital. Teleworking has benefits for both employees and organizations alike. Notably, teleworking can be cost-effective for both employees and organizations. In fact, Cisco reports saving over $277 million through teleworking initiatives (Cisco, 2009). Teleworking can also provide employees with greater autonomy and higher levels of job and communication satisfaction (Smith et al., 2018). Teleworking arrangements are optimized for recruitment and retention when they are clearly explained and enforced across the organization. Additionally, organizations need to encourage managers and employees to maintain relationships and provide the necessary tools and guidance to do so. For example, allowing time during regularly scheduled meetings to catch up and to chat with each other helps, as does having a structured schedule (Gajendran & Harrison, 2007). Making use of different forms of communication like email, phone, and instant messaging, as well as video chatting, can also help to maintain relationships (Noronha & D'Cruz, 2008; Smith et al., 2018).

Special care should also be paid to encouraging employee advancement and enhancing employee satisfaction among teleworkers (Gilles & Reese, 2018).

Finally, as younger generations continue to acquire greater digital wisdom, the integration of technology in the workplace will continue to evolve. Employees are now easily accessible at all times, regardless of business hours, and they are constantly plugged in to organizational news (Sczur, 2018). Therefore, organizations need to be mindful to not overwhelm employees with technology to the point where they are plugged in but left out of the more traditional forms of communication that make both employees and organizations thrive.

CONCLUSION

As organizations navigate the new digital workforce trajectory, a clear understanding of available techniques can be a distinguishing factor. The competitive corporate landscape is increasingly complex and in order to attract, recruit, and retain young talent, organizations should develop intentional inroads and tap into the digital wisdom of young workers. The concept of digital literacy provides a coherent framework for workplaces to think about and reach their Generation Z and Millennial workers—and then develop communication strategies appropriately. Workplace retention tactics can save industry leaders both time and money and while recruiting Gen Z workers will be similar to the recruitment process of Millennials; it is nonetheless an area that should be approached strategically and with great intentionality. Just as there are similarities between generational cohorts, there are also distinctions. Both need to be optimized for the recruitment and retention of employees. To retain top talent, regardless of age, organizations need to be conscious and strategic about intergenerational communication. The bottom line, as organizations continue to recruit and attempt to retain top talent, technology should be used as a central tool throughout the entire search, selection, hiring, and onboarding process.

REFERENCES

Adamy, J. (2018). Gen Z is coming to your office. Get ready to adapt. *Wall Street Journal.* https://www.wsj.com/graphics/genz-is-coming-to-your-office/.

Adobe Educate. (2016). Gen Z in the classroom: Creating the future. http://www.adobeeducate.com/genz/.

Ashley, S. (2015). Media literacy in action? What are we teaching in introductory college media studies courses? *Journalism & Mass Communication Educator, 7002,* 161–173.

Barnes & Noble College. (2015). *Getting to know Gen Z: Exploring middle and high schoolers' expectations for higher education.* https://next.bncollege.com/wp-content/uploads/2015/10/Gen-Z-Research-Report-Final.pdf.

Bawden, D. (2001). Information and digital literacies: A review of concepts. *Journal of Documentation, 57*(2), 218–259.

Bradley, R. (2019). *Why Gen Z loves YouTube.* https://medium.com/@the_manifest/why-generation-z-loves-youtube-ec64643bd5b2.

Chew, J. (2016). Why Millennials would take a $7,600 pay cut for a new job. *Fortune.* http://fortune.com/2016/04/08/fidelity-mutual-study-career/.

Cisco. (2009). *Cisco study finds telecommuting significantly increases employee productivity, work/life flexibility and job satisfaction: Increased productivity due to telecommuting generates an estimated $277 million in annual savings for company.* http://newsroom.cisco.com/dlls/2009/prod_062609.html.

Coffey, L. P., & Strawser, M. G. (2018). Engaging the Millennial workforce through high-quality internships. In S. Smith (Ed.), *Recruitment, retention, and engagement of a Millennial workforce* (pp. 177–192). Lanham, MD: Lexington Books.

Deal, T., & Kennedy, A. (1982). *Corporate cultures.* Reading, MA: Addison-Wesley.

Etherington, D. (2017, September 27). *Instagram now has 800 million monthly and 500 million daily active users.* https://techcrunch.com/2017/09/25/nstagram-now-has-800-million-monthly-and-500-million-daily-active-users/.

Eshet-Alkali, Y., & Amichai-Hamburger, Y. (2004). Experiments in digital literacy. *Cyberpsychology & Behavior, 7*(4), 421–429.

Figenholtz, J., & Broderick, A. (2017). *Future-proofing higher education: Understanding Generation Z.* www.bdcnetwork.com/blog/future-proofing-higher-education-understanding-generation-z.

Fry, R. (2015). *Record share of young women are living with their parents, relatives.* www.pewresearch.org/fact-tank/2015/11/11/record-share-of-young-women-are-living-with-their-parents-relatives./.

Gajendran, R. S., & Harrison, D. A. (2007). The good, the bad, and the unknown about telecommuting: Meta-analysis of psychological mediators and individual consequences. *Journal of Applied Psychology, 92*(6), 1524–1541.

Gilles, E., & Reese, M. (2018). Striking the right work/life balance: Best practices in teleworking to retain Millennial employees. In S. Smith (Ed.), *Recruitment, retention, and engagement of a Millennial workforce* (pp. 83–102). Lanham, MD: Lexington Books.

Hobbs, R. (2011). The state of media literacy: A response to Potter. *Journal of Broadcasting & Electronic Media, 55*(3), 419–430.

Jablin, F. M. (2001). Organizational entry, assimilation, and disengagement/exit. In F. M. Jablin & L. L. Putnam (Eds), *The new handbook of organizational communication: Advances in theory research, and methods* (pp. 732–818). Thousand Oaks, CA: Sage.

Jeong, S. H., Cho, H., & Hwang, Y. (2012). Media literacy interventions: A meta-analytic review. *Journal of Communication, 62*(3), 454–472.

Kellner, D., & Share, J. (2005). Toward critical media literacy: Core concepts, debates, organizations, and policy. *Discourse: Studies in the Cultural Politics of Education, 26*(3), 369–386.

Kiefer, A. (2013). *The learning environment sweet spot: Elevating the educational paradigm.* www.ki.com/uploadedfiles/Docs/literaturesamples/white-papers/Learning-Sweet-Spot-White-paper.pdf.

Livingstone, S. (2004). Media literacy and the challenge of new information and communication technologies. *The Communication Review, 7*(3), 3–14.

Martin, A. (2006). Literacies for the digital age. In A. Martin & D. Madigan (Eds), *Digital literacies for learning* (pp. 3–25). London, UK: Facet.

Meyer, K. (2016). Millennials as digital natives: Myths and realities. *Nielsen Norman Group.* https://www.nngroup.com/articles/millennials-digital-natives/.

Morris, C. (2018). 61 Million Gen Zers are about to enter the US workforce and radically change it forever. *CNBC.* https://www.cnbc.com/2018/05/01/61-million-gen-zers-about-to-enter-us-workforce-and-change-it.html.

National Association of Colleges and Employers. (2016). *Job outlook 2016: The attributes employers want to see on new college graduates' resumes* https://www.naceweb.org/career-development/trends-and-predictions/job-outlook-2016-attributes-employers-want-to-see-on-new-college-graduates-resumes/.

Ng, W. (2012). Can we teach digital natives digital literacy? *Computers & Education, 59*, 1065–1078.

Ologie. (2016). *The Gen Z report.* Columbus, OH: Ologie.

Prensky, M. (2001). Digital natives, digital immigrants. *On the Horizon, 9*, 1–6.

Prensky, M. (2009). H. Sapiens digital: From digital immigrants and digital natives to digital wisdom. *Innovate Journal of Online Education, 5.*

Rawlins, C., Indvik, J., & Johnson, P. (2008). Understanding the new generation: What the Millennial cohort absolutely positively must have at work. *Journal of Organizational Culture, Communications and Conflict, 12*, 1–8.

Schmidt, H. C. (2013). Media literacy education from kindergarten to college: A comparison of how media literacy is addressed across the educational system. *Journal of Media Literacy Education, 5*(1), 295–309.

Schmidt, J. E. (2015). Helping students understand media: Examining the efficacy interdisciplinary media training at the university level. *Journal of Media Literacy Education, 7*(2), 50–68.

Seemiller, C., & Grace, M. (2016). *Generation Z goes to college.* San Francisco, CA: Jossey-Bass.

Seemiller, C., & Grace, M. (2019). *Generation Z: A century in the making.* New York, NY: Routledge.

Smith, S. A. (2017). Job searching expectations, expectancy violations, and communication strategies of recent college graduates. *Business and Professional Communication Quarterly, 80*, 296–320. DOI: 10.1177/2329490617723116.

Smith, S. A., Patmos, A. K., & Pitts, M. J. (2018). Communication and teleworking: A study of communication channel satisfaction, personality, and job satisfaction for teleworking employees. *International Journal of Business Communication.* DOI: 10.1177/2329488415589101.

Sriramesh, K., Grunig, J. E., & Dozier, D. M. (1996). Observation and measurement of two dimensions of organizational culture and their relationship to public relations. *Journal of Public Relations Research, 8*(4), 229–261.

Steele Flippin, C. (2017). *Generation Z in the workplace.* Candace Steele Flippin.

Stillman, D., & Stillman, J. (2017). *Gen Z @ work: How the next generation is transforming the workplace.* New York, NY: HarperCollins.

Strauss, K. (2016). *10 great jobs for Gen Z in 2016 and beyond.* www.forbes.com/sites/karstenstrauss/2016/06/02/10-great-jobs-for-generation-z-in-2016-and-beyond/#f1d6fed14267.

Strauss, W., & Howe, N. (2000). *Millennials rising: The next great generation.* New York, NY: Vintage.

Suzuki, J. (2016). *Designing for the identity-fluid Gen Z.* https://medium.com/@ziba-design/designing-for-the-identity-fluid-gen-z-b80209e188fa.

Thomas, E. (2016). *Makeup for men: Fad or future?* http://wwd.com/beauty-industry-news/beauty-features/beauty-brands-market-makeup-men-10678934/.

Tseng, Z. (2016). *Teens these days are queer AF, new study says.* https://broadly.vice.com/en_us/article/kb4dvz/teens-these-days-are-queer-af-new-study-says.

U.S. Department of Education. (2012). *Statistics about nonpublic education in the United States.* www2.ed.gov/about/offices/list/oii/nonpublic/statistics.html.

U.S. Office of Personnel Management. (2018). *What is telework?* https://www.telework.gov/about/.

Vespa, J., Armstrong, D., & Medina, L. (2018). *Demographic turning points for the United States: Population projections for 2020 to 2060.* www.census.gov/library/publications/2018/demo/p25-1144.html.

VIA Institute on Character. (2018a). *The VIA survey of character strengths: United States Gen Z.* Data Prepared by the VIA Institute on Character.

VIA Institute on Character. (2018b). *Honesty.* www.viacharacter.org/www/Character-Strengths/Honesty.

Wagstaff, K. (2013). *Forget cursive: Teach kids how to code.* http://theweek.com/articles/456355/forget-cursive-teach-kids-how-to-code.

Watkins, B., & Smith, S. A. (2018). Best practices for communicating workplace culture on social media. In S. Smith (Ed.), *Recruitment, retention, and engagement of a Millennial workforce* (pp. 37–48). Lanham, MD: Lexington Books.

Chapter 7

The Representations of *Generation Millennials* and Z in the Mass Media
A Text Mining Analysis
Kenneth C. C. Yang and Yowei Kang

INTRODUCTION

Millennials are the most reported market segment in the US media (Dimock, 2019; Nielsen, 2018; Williams, 2015). This segment is also the largest consumer segment in the United States (Nielsen, 2017). According to Pew Research Center (n.d.), *Generation Millennials* often refer to those who are currently 23–38 years old, while *Generation Z* refers to those who are 20 years and below (born after 2001) (Miller & Lu, 2018). Because of their potential as profitable market segments, business researchers and practitioners have been placing a lot of emphasis on researching their attitudes, beliefs, and consumer behaviors (Pew Research Center, n.d.; Resonate, 2019). For example, Nielsen (2017) reports that *Generation Millennials* often multitask with their smartphones when watching television commercials, resulting in the lowest engagement with other devices among different age groups. As a result, only 2% of *Generation Millennials* switch channels during commercials, in comparison with 5.5% among *Generation X* (35–54 years old) and 8% of *Baby Boomers* (aged between 55 and older). In a recent market research report by Resonate (2019), *Generation Millennials* stress the importance of "living an exciting life" (ibid); however, within the *Generation Millennial* segment, older and younger Millennials differ in their retailer selection and purchase decision (Resonate, 2019). For example, the TV icon for *Generation Millennials* in the United States is Hannah Horvath, and they listen to singer Lady Gaga (Williams, 2015).

On the other hand, *Generation Z* is the youngest and most racially diverse generation in the United States (Wang, 2018) and is commonly known as

Post-Millennials, *iGeneration*, or *Homelanders* (Dimock, 2019; Wang, 2018). The terms, *Generation Z* or *Gen Z*, are used by demographers to refer to this generation. This cohort has been receiving increased Google search queries since 2014 with the highest weekly search volume, in comparison with that of *Post-Millennials*, *iGeneration*, or *Homelanders* (Dimock, 2019). *Generation Z* consumers often listen to Lorde and their TV icon is Alex Dunphy in "Modern Family" because Alex is thought to represent the conscientious and hardworking image of their generation (Williams, 2015). Other media-related characteristics include their liking of web stars, such as Lele Pons and Vine, and the role of social influencer, Tavi Gevinson, in affecting the style choice among many *Generation Z* consumers (Williams, 2015).

Although most research on this demographic shift has mainly been conducted in economically developed countries, Bloomberg analyzes cross-national secondary data published by the United Nations and concludes the growing importance of *Generation Millennials* and *Z* is a global phenomenon. Although *Generation Millennials* still account for most demographic cohorts in China, Germany, Japan, and the United States with a combined population of 2 billion, *Generation Z* is catching up (Miller & Lu, 2018). *Generation Z* accounts for 32% of the world population of 7.7 billion by 2019, close to that of 31.5% represented by *Generation Millennials* (Miller & Lu, 2018). In 2019, *Generation Z* in India is expected to have grown to 472 million, compared with China's 312 million (Miller & Lu, 2018).

These two demographic cohorts have presented researchers with the opportunity to examine their technology usage behaviors. In terms of their usage behaviors of information-communication technologies (ICTs), *Generation Millennials* prefer Facebook, while *Generation Z* uses Snapchat (Williams, 2015) and Instagram (Boucher, 2019). *Generation Z* also prefers to engage with a brand through Instagram, followed by Snapchat (49%) and Facebook (12%) (Koch, 2019). Comparatively, the first gadget for *Generation Millennial* consumers was the iPod, conversely, that of *Generation Z* is the iPhone (Williams, 2015). *Generation Millennials* also will opt to watch free ads on their mobile devices but is likely to skip ads, if the skipping function is not disabled in their VOD contents (Nielsen, 2017).

The growing interest of *Generation Millennials* and *Z* is often prompted by the hype in the media about how these two demographic cohorts will change the workplace (Boitnott, 2016; Crouch, 2015), ICT adoption behaviors (Lee, 2014; Suominen et al., 2014; TWICE, 2017a), advertising campaigns (Bartlett, 2016; Campaign Monitor, 2019), business practices (Cummings, 2016; Knowledge@Wharton, 2017), economy (Koch, 2019), and the market around the world (Miller & Lu, 2018). The objectives of this chapter attempt to examine how *Generation Millennials* and *Z* are represented in the mainstream print media around the world. This chapter employs a text mining method to analyze media corpus through the identification of repetitive keywords, phrases, and topics extracted from the media.

LITERATURE REVIEW AND THEORETICAL FOUNDATION

The Rise of Tech-Savvy *Generation Millennials* and Z Consumers

Generation Millennials and *Generation Z* consumers are characterized by their early exposure to a variety of ICTs. In a 2010 report by Pew Research Center, technology use (24%) is mentioned as the most important attribute that makes *Generation Millennials* unique, compared with 12% among *Generation X*. *Generation Millennials* grew up when the Internet technologies exploded around the world (Dimock, 2019). Many *Generation Millennial* consumers are loyal to smartphones and enthusiastic about e-commerce (Dolliver, 2019). About 75% of this cohort have a social media profile (Pew Research Center, 2010). This generation also has the most positive attitude toward technology in general (74%) and believes technology can make their life easier, regardless of their genres and formats (Pew Research Center, 2010).

Similarly, technologies such as the iPhone, Wi-Fi, broadband access, smartphone, and social media have been the daily experiences of *Generation Z* (Carey, 2018; Dimock, 2019). In a UK study, 60% of *Generation Z* agrees that technology will make things better (Statista, 2019a). Compared with older demographic cohorts (such as *Baby Boomer* and *Generation X*), the heavy reliance on these ICTs has transformed their behaviors. For example, *Generation Millennials* are more active on social media than older generations (such as Gen X or Baby Boomers) (Nielsen, 2019). The advent of social media has prompted many *Generation Z* users (60%) to leave online reviews that are often valued by their family and friends, according to a survey by Social Media Link (Nickalls, 2019).

The consumption of traditional television for *Generation Millennials* has been decreasing as they watch 27% less television than other demographic cohorts (Nielsen, 2019). Instead, 61% of *Generation Millennial* households subscribe to over-the-top (i.e., OTT) steaming and pay-per-view TV services, which is higher than the national average of 52% (TWICE, 2016). A survey of 2,500 participants also confirms that *Generation Millennials* tend to favor on-demand content and will skip live TV (TWICE, 2017b). *Generation Millennials* have a higher probability to conduct online searches before purchasing cleaning and food products (Nielsen, 2019). This demographic cohort relies heavily on mobile devices (about 47%) to make online purchases, much higher than *Generation X* (41%), *Baby Boomers* (25%), and the *Greatest Generation* (16%) (Nielsen, 2019). *Generation Millennials* are also eager adopters of new voice-assistant technologies, such as Amazon's Alexa, Apple's Siri, and Google Assistant (Dolliver, 2019). About 47% of *Generation Millennials* have adopted voice-assistant technologies via their smartphone (Dolliver, 2019). Furthermore, *Generation Millennials* in China have a higher interest in reality-creating technologies such as augmented reality (33% vs. 32% for *non-Gen Millennials*) and virtual reality (48% vs. 46% for *non-Gen Millennials*) (Statista, 2019b).

Generation Z has been called "digital natives" (eMarketer.com, 2017). It is estimated that about 78.9% of this generation in the United States were using smartphones in 2018 (eMarketer.com, 2017). Older Generation Z digital natives are more likely to have a smartphone when compared with their younger counterparts (eMarketer.com, 2017). In China, the age cohort, corresponding to *Generation Z*, is called *Post-00* to refer to those born after 2000 (Pan, 2018). They demonstrate similar technology usage behaviors like those in other countries (eMarketer.com, 2018). According to eMarketer.com (2018), 64.9% of the Internet users in this survey spend their free time on social platforms, surfing the Internet (62%), watching digital videos (60.7%), playing digital games (53.7%), and followed by online and offline shopping (37.7%). Due to the widespread use of these ICTs, some are concerned about how these technologies could affect the health of *Generation Z* (Carey, 2018). Instead, previous empirical research has reported the positive social and emotional effects of ICT on teens' performance at school, emotional well-being, and social life (Carey, 2018).

The enthusiasm expressed in popular media and trade publications has led to the hyperbole of these two emerging cohorts using headlines such as "How Generation Z Is Changing the Tech World" by *BBC* and *CBS* (Mastroianni, 2016) or "6 Ways Gen Z Will Change the Tech World" by *Entrepreneur* (Patel, 2016). Despite these anecdotal discussions about the importance of *Generation Millennials* and Z, this text mining study aims to provide a quantitative, and unbiased, analysis of how the world's mass media have portrayed these cohorts. We will derive the popular framing theory to theorize the media practices in portraying *Generation Millennials* and Z.

Framing Theory: Our Interpretive Framework

The concept of framing "refers to how an issue is presented in the media, including the various perspectives and conceptions that people communicate with respect to that issue" (Diakopoulos et al., 2013, n.p.). This concept is also known as "media framing" or "news framing" as it is closely related to the practices of news media organizations (D'Angelo & Kuypers, 2010, p.

1). The practices of framing involve the construction of (media/news) frames that function as "organizing principles that are socially shared and persistent over time, that work symbolically to meaningfully structure the social world" (Reese, 2001, p. 11). Framing theory is commonly defined as "the process of selecting, organizing, and editing information for distribution through a medium" (Novak & Hakena, 2014). Past framing research often focuses on "framing effects" to examine the variations of framing an issue or a subject on the public's opinions through experiments (Hullman & Diakopoulos, 2011). Other framing research also relies on content analysis of various newsworthy subjects to understand the war on terror (Reese, 2001) or debates over climate change and poverty (Nisbet, 2010).

In recent years, conventional framing and media representation research are often constrained and criticized by its data processing ability to content analyze a large amount of media data (Lin et al., 2016; Yang & Kang, 2018). Traditionally framing research often relies on the subjective interpretation and judgment of media contents to develop common themes as identified in the media. Increasingly, computational text processing methods, or commonly known as text mining methods, have been integrated into the identification of frames. Both framing and text mining research techniques attempt to extract meaningful, repetitive, and useful insights and patterns from unstructured textual data (He et al., 2013). However, unlike the qualitative framing method that relies on human interpreters and coders, text mining relies on computational techniques to generate patterns from these media discourses through cluster analysis, categorization, link analysis, and text summarization (Zikopoulos et al., 2013). Among these analytical procedures mentioned above, the topic modeling procedure has similar functions to "organize, understand and summarize large collections of textual information" (KDNugget, n.d.).

RESEARCH QUESTIONS

Based on the above discussion, this chapter aims to answer the following questions:

Research Question 1: How are data mining and text mining methods relevant to the study of *Generation Millennials* and *Z*?
Research Question 2: What are the recurrent keywords, phrases, and topics as found in the collected media corpus on *Generation Millennials* and *Z*?
Research Question 3: What will be cross-country variations in terms of the media representations of *Generation Millennials* and *Z*?

RESEARCH METHODS

The Selection of the Text Mining Method

Text mining is increasingly gaining attention among social science scholars (Diakopoulos et al., 2013; Kang & Yang, 2018; Teso et al., 2018). These text mining techniques have allowed researchers to identify repetitive keywords, phrases, topics in the corpus, and to explore relationships among these recurrent concepts in the media data (Teso et al., 2018). Widely used text mining applications, either commercial or open-source, include *Aika, Atlas.ti, Alceste, Dedoose, HyberResearch, IBM SPSS Predictive Analytics, IRaMuteQ, Lexico3, Leipzig Corpus Miner, MAXDictio, MAXQDA, NVivo, QDA Miner, SAS Text Miner, WordStat, WordSmith, T-LAB*, among others (Silver & Lewins, 2018; Wiedemann, 2016). Text mining techniques offer researchers the opportunity to process a large amount of data systematically, without biases, without human errors, and more objectively (Lin et al., 2016). Text mining methodology has recently emerged as a feasible method for communication scholars to study news frames "with the minimum amount of human interference" (Li et al., 2016, n.p.; Kang & Yang, 2018) to prevent subjectivity and data coding errors by human coders.

This chapter employs *QDA Miner* and its two add-on programs (*Wordstat* and *SIMSTAT*) (Silver & Lewins, 2018) to analyze media data in the corpus. *QDA Miner* "offers good coding, data organization, retrieval, and interrogation functions" (Silver & Lewins, 2018, n.p.). Its add-on *WordStat* program offers content analysis functions to identify keywords, phrases, and topics and to generate graphs such as *WordCloud* or *Link Analysis* to visualize results of the text mining analyses (Silver & Lewins, 2018).

Data Collection and the Compilation of Corpus

To answer the proposed research questions, this study uses *QDA Miner* and *WORDStat* to analyze media data collected from the mainstream English-language print media around the world using a list of keywords ("Generation Millennials" and "Generation Z") to search *Lexis/Nexis Academic* database that contains major world newspaper and magazine publications, trade publications, press releases, and legal documents. The searches have generated 970 articles for *Generation Millennials* and 959 articles for *Generation Z* that are composed of the corpus (see table 7.1). The corpus includes media texts from major world newspapers, industry and trade presses, web-based publications, newswires, and trade press releases. We use keyword extraction, topic modeling, link analysis, map, among others to provide empirical data for the above research questions.

Table 7.1 Newspapers in Our Corpus from Nexis/Lexis Academic Database (Subcategory: Major World Newspapers)

Keywords	Newspaper Titles	N	Valid N (removing duplicates using High Similarity Filter)
"Generation M"	Total (without details)	996	970
	Total (newspapers only)	822	731
	Total (industry and trade presses)	111	111
	Total (web-based publications)	93	93
	Total (newswires and trade releases only)	47	39
"Generation Z"	Total (without details)	999	959
	Total (newspaper only)	808	615
	Total (industry and trade press)	131	116
	Total (web-based publication)	55	53
	Total (newswire and trade releases only)	83	68

Data Pre-Processing and Analytical Methods

Any text mining project begins with the pre-processing of raw data (Lin et al., 2016) to ensure the integrity and relevance of the extracted media texts in the corpus. We read each entry in the media corpus and remove articles after extensive discussions to justify the decision. In the end, the media corpus includes 57 articles for *Generation Millennials* and 659 articles for *Generation Z*. In the end, the media corpus has 716 articles that come from 20 countries and media outlets (such as *The New York Times*, *The Times*, *Global Times*, etc.). There are 153 articles from the United States (21.40% of the corpus), 143 articles from the United Kingdom (20.00%), 125 articles from Australia (17.48), and 58 articles from Canada (63.3%). Countries that have fewer than five articles include South Korea (N = 5), The Philippines (N = 4), Malta (N = 3), Russia (N = 3), Hong Kong (N = 2), Israel (N = 2), and Japan (N = 2).

Findings

To answer our second research question, several text mining techniques are useful to provide empirical data. Text mining research often relies on the

Figure 7.1 Word Cloud Analysis in the Corpus—Keywords. *Source:* Figure created by authors.

extraction of keywords, phrases, or terms to estimate their relative importance by examining the frequency statistics called term frequency (TF) or term frequency inverse document frequency (TF-IDF) (Teso et al., 2018). According to SAS, this text mining technique allows researchers to identify words or phrases that are most prominent and important (Milum, 2018). Word cloud analysis is a widely used text mining technique that represents the frequency of keywords, phrases, and terms in a graphical manner (Srivastava, 2014). Our second research question aims to identify popular recurrent keywords and terms that are used by media outlets around the world to frame *Generation Millennials* and Z. As seen in figure 7.1 below, it is apparent that *Generation Millennials* and Z have often been mentioned with terms such as "Internet," "Information," "Technology," "Digital," "Mobile," "Online," "Social (Media)," and so on. The dominant representations of these two emerging demographics will be recurrent representations of technologies that are demonstrated in the word cloud (see figure 7.1).

Key Phrase Extraction

QDA Miner and *WordStat* offer an easy-to-use tool to extract key phrases in the unstructured texts from our media corpus. However, other popular text mining software, such as *Text Analytics*, also offers a similar capability to enable researchers to identify the main points in the corpus (Microsoft, 2019). This procedure to extract the most salient phrases in the documents is useful for "document categorization, clustering, indexing, searching, and summarization" (DeWilde, 2014). "Social Media" is the most prominent phrase when the world media talk about *Generation Millennials* and Z. The term has appeared 515 times (32.17%) (TF-IDF = 253.3). Another noteworthy key

YOUNG PEOPLE
SOCIAL MEDIA

HIGH SCHOOL BABY BOOMERS
YEAR OLDS GEN ZERS DIGITAL NATIVES
PREVIOUS GENERATIONS MEMBERS OF GENERATION

Figure 7.2 Word Cloud Analysis in the Corpus—Key Phrase Extraction. Note: minimum frequency = 3. *Source:* Figure created by authors.

phrase in our corpus is "digital natives" (N = 119, 13.20%, TF-IDF = 104.3). "Mobile phone" is an important key phrase in our corpus (N = 49, 4.28%, TF-IDF = 67.5), as well as "tech-savvy" (N = 50, 4.20%, TF-IDF = 58.7). The TF-IDF statistics are used in information retrieval and text mining research to measure the importance of a word, a term, or a phrase in the document corpus (Silge & Robinson, 2019). The statistics suggest how these key phrases are used in the media corpus to describe (frame) *Generation Millennials* and Z in the world. The word cloud figures also demonstrate similar results visually (see figure 7.1 and figure 7.2).

Topic Modeling Analysis

In the text mining method, the topic modeling technique helps researchers to organize, search, and understand a large number of data through the discovery of hidden and recurring topical patterns, the annotation of topic-based documents, and the organization and summation of these texts (KDNuggets, n.d.). Commonly used topic modeling techniques include Latent Dirichlet Allocation (LDA) which goes through each document with a mixture of topics to extract common topics across a wide range of documents in the corpus (KDNuggets, n.d.). LDA also assumes that each topic is composed of a mixture of words or phrases (Silge & Robinson, 2019). This technique will allow researchers to treat each document in the corpus as potentially overlapping with others, to mirror how human beings typically use natural language (Silge & Robinson, 2019). Topic modeling techniques such as LDA or Latent Semantic Indexing (LSI) have been used in text mining research to extract and identify main topics in a variety of contexts (see Teso et al., 2018, p. 142 for details). Out of nine topics extracted from over 716 articles in the media corpus, four of them are related to technology that best characterized *Generation Millennials* and *Z* among the print media around the world; these extracted topics are "Facebook" (N = 1197, coherence = .28), "digital natives" (N = 2852, coherence = .27), "mobile phone" (N = 484, coherence = .23), and "shopping habits" (N = 501, coherence =.26). For example, "shopping habits" is extracted from keywords or phrases such as "retailers," "shopping," "store," "shop," "stores," "brands," "consumers," and so on, indicating the strong interest among businesses to better understand the impacts of these two emerging market segments. The topic "digital natives" is extracted from keywords such as "digital," "natives," "born," "media," and so on, while "mobile phones" are from "mobile," "phones," "phone," "Internet," "mobile broadband," "mobile Internet," "mobile devices," "owned mobile phone," and so on.

Cross-Country Comparison

To answer our third research question, we need to examine whether there are cross-country variations in terms of the media representations of *Generation Millennials* and *Z*. To examine if countries vary in their representations of *Generation Millennials* and *Z* in the print mass media outlets around the world, we use the following five figures to demonstrate these differences (see figures 7.3, 7.4, 7.5, 7.6, and 7.7). In figure 7.3, in terms of the key phrase "social media," mass media from Japan, South Africa, and the United States often associate *Generation Millennials* and *Z* with this key phrase, while mass media from Hong Kong, Singapore, and Kenya do not. In figure 7.4, in terms of the key phrase "digital natives," mass media contents from India, Spain, The Philippines, New Zealand, and China often frame *Generation Millennials* and *Z* with "digital natives." In figure 7.5, the key phrase "tech-savvy" mostly appears in the mass media contents of Kenya and South Korea, while in figure 7.6, "social networking" is most commonly used to describe *Generation Millennials* and *Z* among mass media contents from South Korea, South Africa, New Zealand, and China. In figure 7.7, the term "social networks" is often seen in the mass media contents from the United States, Spain, and France when describing *Generation Millennials* and *Z*.

To compare if countries also differ in their framing of topics, we use four figures (figures 7.8, 7.9, 7.10, and 7.11) to report these cross-country variations. In figure 7.8, the extracted topic "shopping habits" is most prominent among mass media contents from Egypt, Thailand, Japan, and India when describing *Generation Millennials* and *Z*, while the topic "Facebook" is most associated with *Generation Millennials* and *Z* in Japan, the United States, and South Korea (figure 7.9). Mass media in Japan, Kenya, and the United

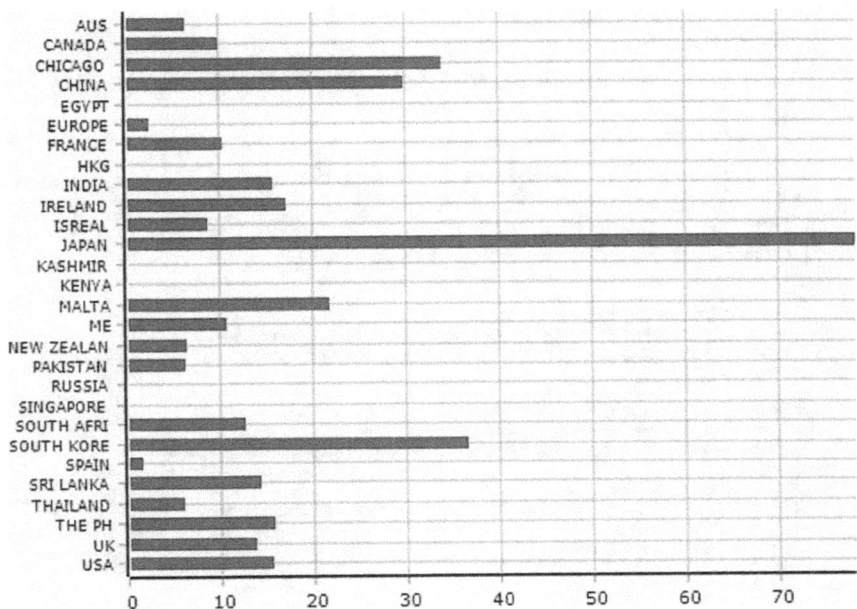

Figure 7.3 Cross-country Variations in Portraying Millennials and Gen Z on the Basis of Extracted Phrases—Social Media. *Source:* Graph created by authors.

States, on the other hand, often discuss *Generation Millennials* and Z by the term "digital natives" (figure 7.10). The topic "mobile phone" is particularly prominent in Kashmir (figure 7.11).

DISCUSSION AND CONCLUSION

It is estimated that *Generation Z* comprises 40% of the total population in North America by 2020 (*India Retail News*, 2017). *Generation Z* also accounts for 630 million world population (Index Mundi, 2019). The combined under 40 generations of X, Y, and younger consumers are now the majority and represent 166 million people in the United States (Schneider, 2020). Older Generation Z consumers (aged between 18 and 23) rely heavily on social media (39%) and online reviews and blogs (26%) when making purchase decisions (Bhargava et al., 2020). Like *Generation Millennials*, social media and digital advertising have become part of their daily lives and important sources of product purchase decisions (Bhargava et al., 2020). Online shopping is popular among *Generation Z* consumers, even though regular visits to traditional brick and mortar malls continue (*India Retail News*, 2017; Bhargava et al., 2020). Due to the COVID-19 pandemic, both *Generation*

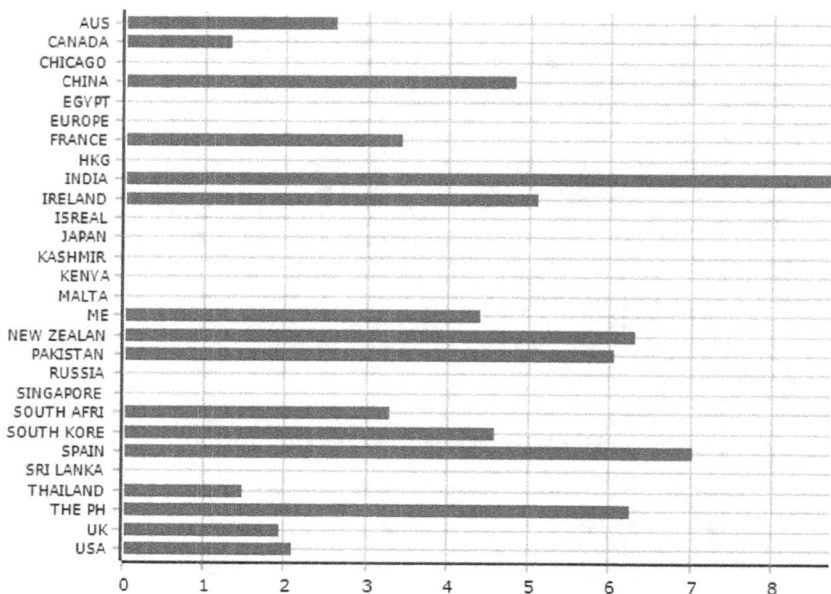

Figure 7.4 Cross-country Variations in Portraying Millennials and Gen Z on the Basis of Extracted Phrases—Digital Natives. *Source:* Graph created by authors.

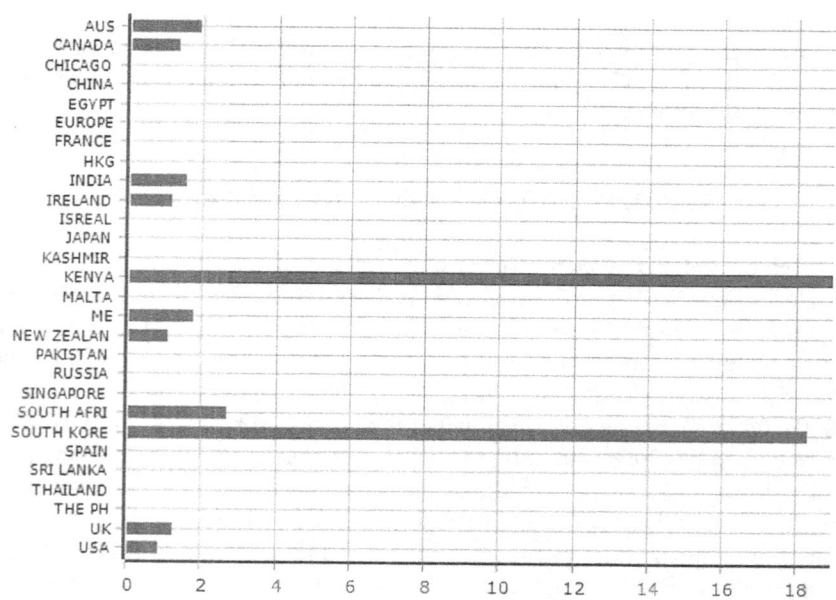

Figure 7.5 Cross-country Variations in Portraying Millennials and Gen Z on the Basis of Extracted Phrases—Tech-Savvy. *Source:* Graph created by authors.

The Representations of Generation Millennials *and* Z   119

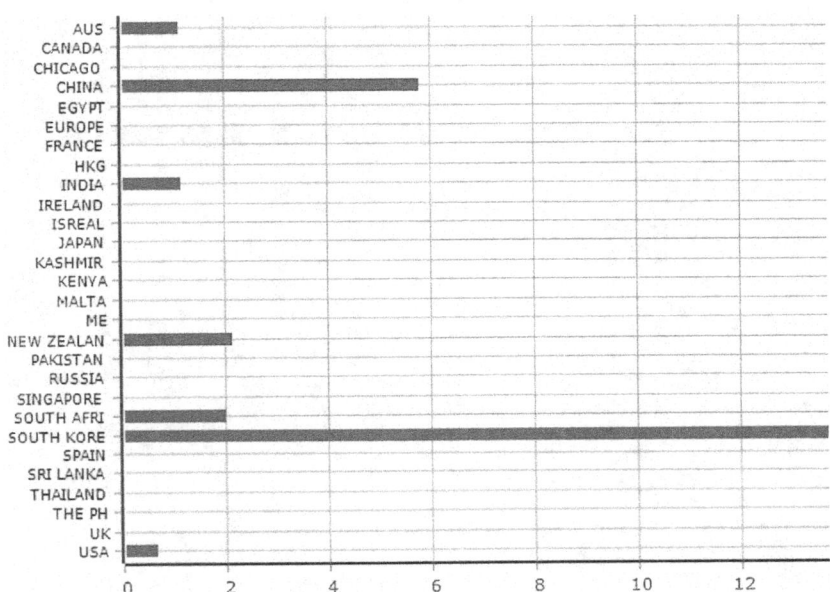

Figure 7.6 Cross-country Variations in Portraying Millennials and Gen Z on the Basis of Extracted Phrases—Social Networking. *Source:* Graph created by authors.

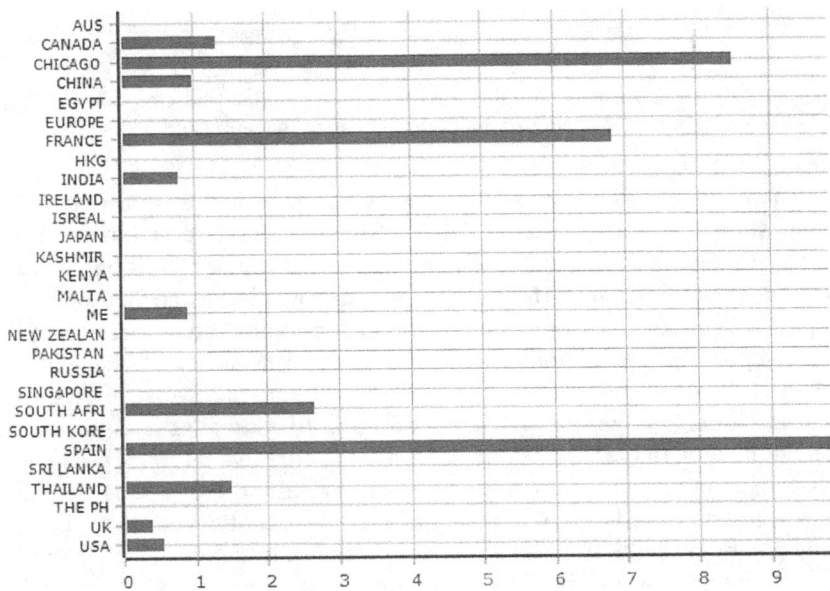

Figure 7.7 Cross-country Variations in Portraying Millennials and Gen Z on the Basis of Extracted Phrases—Social Networks. *Source:* Graph created by authors.

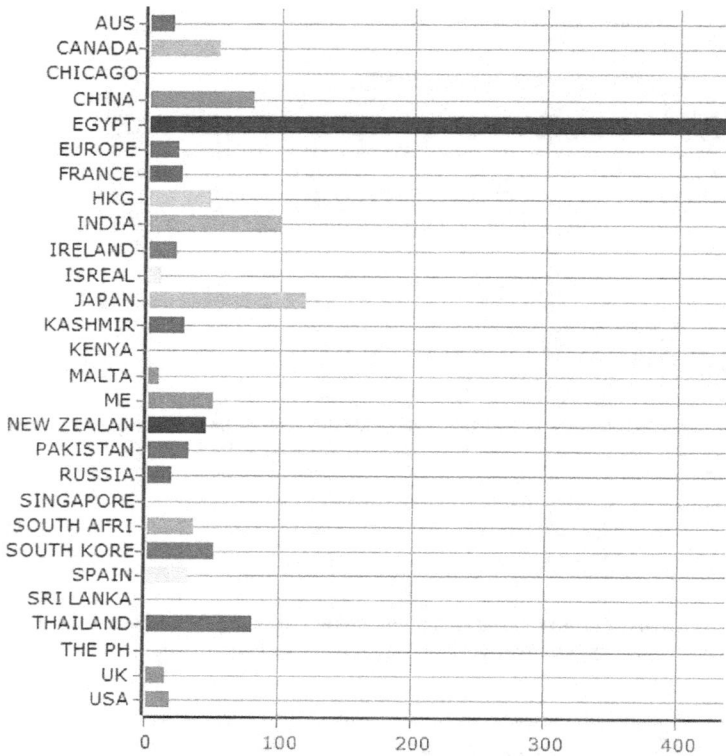

Figure 7.8 Cross-country Variations in Portraying Millennials and Gen Z on the Basis of Extracted Themes—Shopping Habit. *Source:* Graph created by authors.

Millennials and Z consumers have expressed their shift from traditional to online shopping (Bhargava et al., 2020). This trend is observed in the media corpus we have collected and analyzed as many businesses focus on the shopping habits of *Generation Millennials* and Z that will influence their practices. In past consumer behavior and innovation adoption literature, users' generation category, as a predictor variable, has often been assumed to have effects but rarely studied empirically as a stand-alone variable. Most research has used the variable, age, in their data collection to estimate the effect of this demographic variable. For example, Dupagne and Salwen (2005) studied the effect of ethnicity on technology adoption and found that age is a statistically significant predictor of adoption behaviors, regardless of their ethnicity. Even among professional settings, a survey of 292 researchers has confirmed that age negatively predicts users' instant messenger usage (Pearce, 2010). Young researchers tend to use instant messenger technology more than their counterparts (Pearce, 2010). Results from this text mining research of media

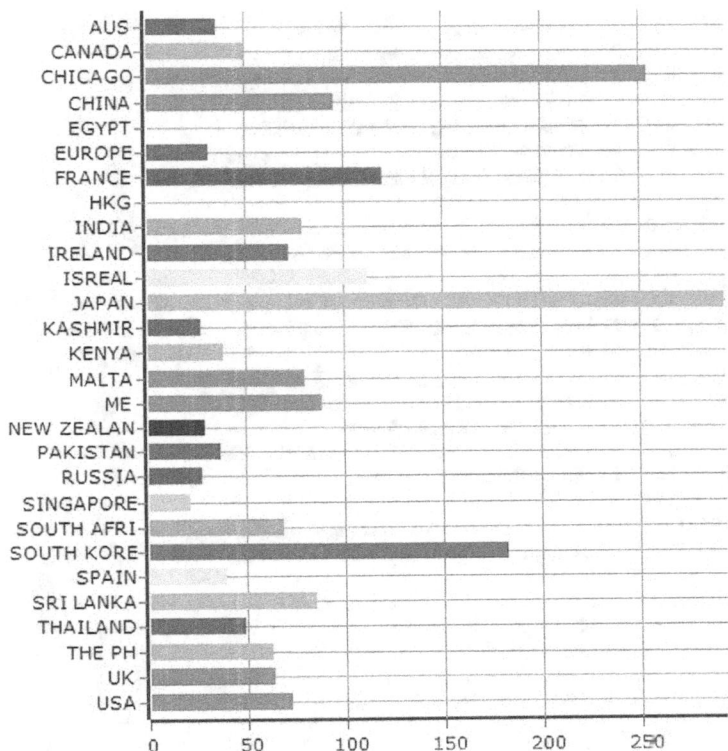

Figure 7.9 Cross-country Variations in Portraying Millennials and Gen Z on the Basis of Extracted Themes—Facebook. *Source:* Graph created by authors.

contents from around the world have confirmed the important role of generation as perceived by these media outlets to characterize these two increasingly important consumer segments.

Both *Generation Millennials* and Z consumers have been framed to "pose major challenges for businesses" (Progressive Media, 2015, n.d.). *The New York Times* in the United States has portrayed *Generation Z* as "the next big thing for market researchers, cultural observers, and trend forecasters" (MediAvataarME.com, 2016). This text mining research has allowed business researchers or practitioners who are interested in *Generation Millennials* and Z to identify keywords, phrases, and topics when describing these two segments. Interestingly, technologies have been closely associated with *Generation Millennials* and Z as demonstrated in the mass media corpus from the world media, suggesting their rise as a global phenomenon. However, cross-country comparative results could help researchers to understand the variations of mass media representations of *Generation Millennials* and Z

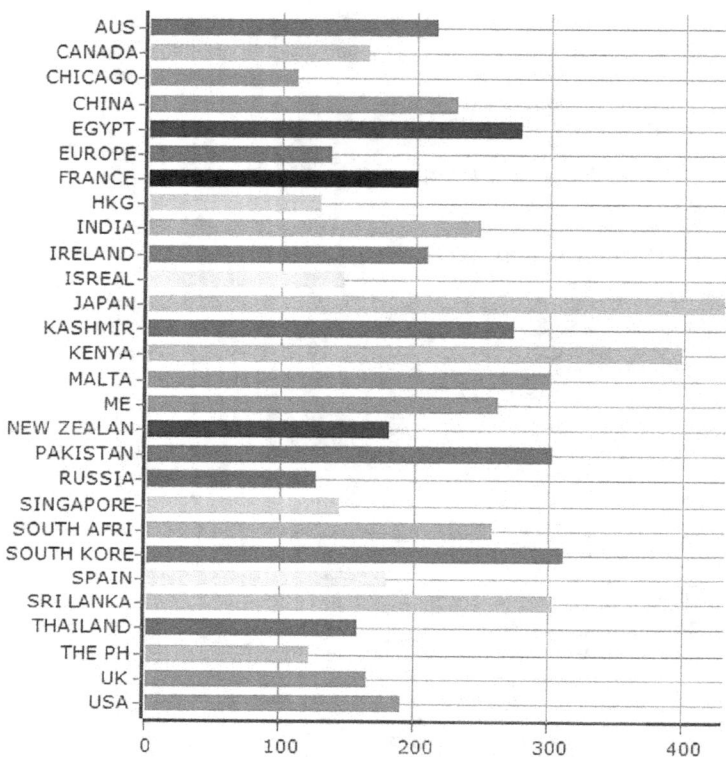

Figure 7.10 Cross-country Variations in Portraying Millennials and Gen Z on the Basis of Extracted Themes—Digital Natives. *Source:* Graph created by authors.

also differ among countries through the visual presentations of word cloud and frequencies. Factors such as a country's politics, technology, economy, and culture are likely to play important roles in affecting the media representations of *Generation Millennials* and *Z*. For example, *Generation Z* in South Africa is also known as "born frees" because they were born after the country became democratic in 1994 (MediAvataarME.com, 2015). Similarly, the advent of social media also collides with when *Generation Z* was born, supporting the importance of these technologies to these tech-savvy consumers as seen in the media corpus.

Limitations

Several limitations need to be taken into consideration when interpreting these research results. Despite the widespread use of text mining techniques,

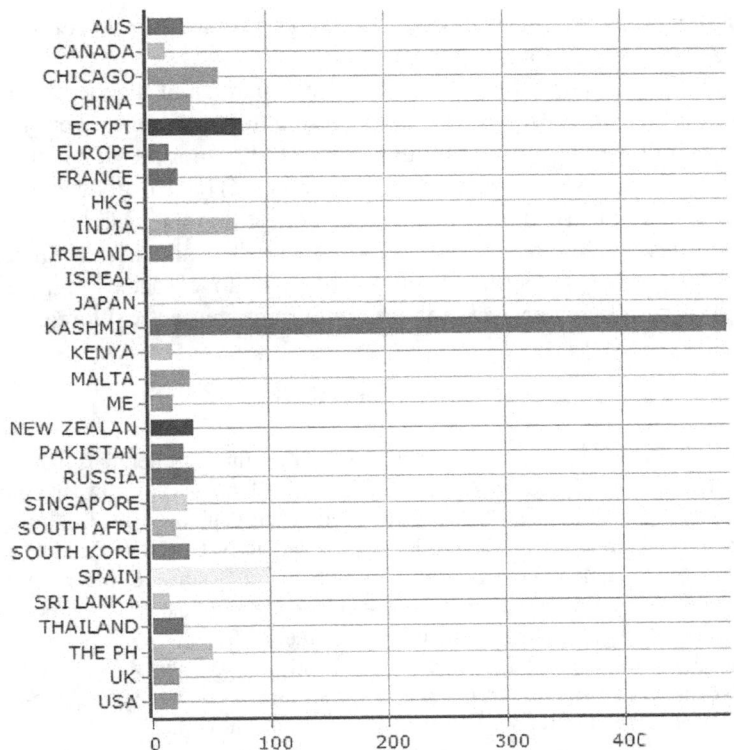

Figure 7.11 Cross-country Variations in Portraying Millennials and Gen Z on the Basis of Extracted Themes—Mobile Phone. *Source:* Graph created by authors.

generation-based communication scholars need to be cautious in interpreting their findings. First, the comprehensiveness of sampled data in the media corpus is often a major concern for any type of text mining research (Yang & Kang, 2019). For example, Tesoa et al. (2018) have cautioned that their research findings may not be generalized to all 28 product categories in the Ciao UK travel site. Second, *Lexis/Nexis* database only collects English-language media; non-English publications are excluded and could limit our understanding of how *Generation Millennials* and Z are represented in these countries where English is not the main language. Third, another limitation is related to the processing of words, keywords, phrases, and dictionaries in identifying recurrent linguistic patterns and trends to generate findings (Tesoa et al., 2018). For example, the reliance on a single word may ignore the diversity of word meanings (i.e., polysemy) (Tesoa et al., 2018). The use of keywords and phrases similarly runs into problems of reducing their importance in different contexts and should be addressed by statistical procedures (Tesoa et al., 2018; Yang & Kang, 2019).

This chapter has presented a descriptive comparison of the media representations of *Generation Millennials* and *Z* around the world. However, the methodology employed in this text mining research does not provide insights into why technologies (such as mobile and social media) have become part of their lives. The current text mining techniques do not allow researchers to examine how these technologies have been used in the daily life of *Generation Millennials* and *Z*. Quantitative survey or qualitative focus group research methods may provide answers to these important, yet less explored, topics.

REFERENCES

Bartlett, B. (2016, February 3). The definitive list of things millennials hate to see in ads. *AdWeek*. Retrieved on April 11, 2019 from https://www.adweek.com/sponsored/2017-words-brands-should-never-ever-say-millennials-169233/#!/.

Bhargava, S., Finneman, B., Schmidt, J., & Spagnuolo, E. (2020, March 20). The young and the restless: Generation Z in America. *McKinsey & Company*. Retrieved on January 27, 2021 from https://www.mckinsey.com/industries/retail/our-insights/the-young-and-the-restless-generation-z-in-america#.

Boitnott, J. (2016, January 27). Generation Z and the workplace: What you need to know. *Inc*. Retrieved on April 19, 2019 from https://www.inc.com/john-boitnott/generation-z-and-the-workplace-what-you-need-to-know-.html.

Boucher, J. (2019). What are Generation Z's social media preferences? *The Center for Generational Kinetics*. Retrieved on January 27, 2021 from https://genhq.com/what-are-generation-zs-social-media-preferences/.

Campaign Monitor. (2019). The ultimate guide to marketing to Gen Z in 2019. *Campaign Monitor*. Retrieved on April 11, 2019 from https://www.campaignmonitor.com/resources/guides/guide-to-gen-z-marketing-2019/?g&utm_medium=display&utm_source=emarketer&utm_campaign=040119.

Carey, G. (2018, October 15). Why marketers don't need to worry about contributing to Gen Z's alleged tech addiction. *AdWeek*. Retrieved on April 11, 2019 from https://www.adweek.com/brand-marketing/why-marketers-dont-need-to-worry-about-contributing-to-gen-zs-alleged-tech-addiction/.

Crouch, B. (2015, May 22). How will Generation Z disrupt the workplace? *Fortune*. Retrieved on April 19, 2019 from http://fortune.com/2015/2005/2022/generation-z-in-the-workplace/.

Cummings, C. (2016, September 18). Infographics: Here's how much engagement brands got from back-to-school social posts. *AdWeek*. Retrieved on April 11, 2019 from https://www.adweek.com/brand-marketing/infographic-heres-how-much-engagement-brands-got-back-school-social-posts-173559/.

D'Angelo, P., & Kuypers, J. A. (2010). Introduction. In P. D'Angelo & J. A. Kuypers (Eds), *Doing news framing analysis: Empirical and theoretical perspectives* (pp. 1–13). New York, NY: Routledge.

DeWilde, B. (2014, September 23). Intro to automatic key phrase extraction. *Burton DeWilde Website*. Retrieved on April 25, 2019 from http://bdewilde.github.io/blog/2014/2009/2023/intro-to-automatic-keyphrase-extraction/.

Diakopoulos, N., Zhang, A., & Salway, A. (2013, October 13–18). *Visual analytics of media frames in online news and blogs*. Paper presented at the IEEE InfoVis Workshop on Text Visualization, Atlanta, Georgia, USA.

Dimock, M. (2019, January 17). Defining generations: Where Millennials end and Generation Z begins. *The Pew Research Center*. Retrieved on April 11, 2019 from https://www.pewresearch.org/fact-tank/2019/2001/2017/where-millennials-end-and-generation-z-begins/.

Dolliver, M. (2019, February 11). US Millennials 2019. *eMarketer.com*. Retrieved on April 20, 2019 from https://www.emarketer.com/content/us-millennials-2019.

Dupagne, M., & Salwen, M. B. (2005). Communication technology adoption and ethnicity. *The Howard Journal of Communications, 16*, 21–32.

eMarketer.com. (2017, September 5). Understanding teens and their smartphone habits. *eMarketer.com*. Retrieved on April 11, 2019 from https://www.emarketer.com/Article/Understanding-Teens-Their-Smartphone-Habits/1016423.

eMarketer.com. (2018, August). How do Post-00* internet users in China spend their free time? *eMarketer.com*. Retrieved on April 22, 2019 from http://totalaccess.emarketer.com/chart.aspx?r=224679.

He, W., Zha, S., & Li, L. (2013). Social media competitive analysis and text mining: A case study in the pizza industry. *International Journal of Information Management, 33*(3), 464–472.

Hullman, J., & Diakopoulos, N. (2011). *Visualization rhetoric: Framing effects in narrative visualization*. Retrieved on April 11, 2019 from http://www.nickdiakopoulos.com/Documents/visRhetoric_final_preprint.pdf.

Index Mundi. (2019, December 7). *World age structure*. Retrieved on January 30, 2020 from https://www.indexmundi.com/world/age_structure.html

India Retail News. (2017, January 23). Retailers must adapt to emerging Generation Z consumers. *India Retail News*. Retrieved on April 25, 2019 from https://www.businesswire.com/news/home/20170123005555/en/Retailers-Adapt-Emerging-Generation-Consumers.

KDNuggets. (n.d.). Text mining 101: Topic modeling. *KDNuggets*. Retrieved on April 25, 2019 from https://www.kdnuggets.com/2016/2007/text-mining-2101-topic-modeling.html.

Knowledge@Wharton. (2017, October 3). *What defines millennials—And how marketers can reach them*. Philadelphia, PA: University of Pennsylvania.

Koch, L. (2019, April 18). Gen Z goes to the 'gram for new products, brand engagement. *eMarketer.com*. Retrieved on April 19, 2019 from https://content-na2011.emarketer.com/gen-z-goes-to-the-gram-for-new-products?ecid=nl1014.

Lee, S. Y. (2014). Examining the factors that influence early adopters' smartphone adoption: The case of college students. *Telematics and Informatics, 31*, 308–318.

Lin, F.-R., Hao, D., & Liao, D. (2016). *Automatic content analysis of media framing by text mining techniques*. Paper presented at the 2016 49th Hawaii International Conference on System Sciences, Hawaii, USA.

Mastroianni, B. (2016, March 10). How Generation Z is changing the tech world. *CBS*. Retrieved on April 20, 2019 from https://www.cbsnews.com/news/social-media-fuels-a-change-in-generations-with-the-rise-of-gen-z/.

MediAvataarME.com. (2015, June 8). Close up and personal with the Generation Zs. *MediAvataarME.com*.

MediAvataarME.com. (2016, July 10). Generation Z: The most complex consumer to challenge marketers? *MediAvataarME.com*.

Microsoft. (2019, April 15). Example: How to extract key phrases using text analytics. *Microsoft*. Retrieved on April 25, 2019 from https://docs.microsoft.com/en-us/azure/cognitive-services/text-analytics/how-tos/text-analytics-how-to-keyword-extraction.

Miller, L. J., & Lu, W. (2018, August 20). Gen Z is set to outnumber millennials within a year. *Bloomberg*. Retrieved on April 19, 2019 from https://www.bloomberg.com/news/articles/2018-2008-2020/gen-z-to-outnumber-millennials-within-a-year-demographic-trends.

Milum, J. (2018). SAS® visual analytics: Text analytics using word clouds (paper 1687-2018). *SAS*. Retrieved on April 25, 2019 from https://www.sas.com/content/dam/SAS/support/en/sas-global-forum-proceedings/2018/1687-2018.pdf.

Nickalls, S. (2019, April 8). Infographic: 27% of Gen Zers say they always write a product review after making a purchase. *AdWeek*. Retrieved on April 11, 2019 from https://www.adweek.com/brand-marketing/infographic-2027-of-gen-zers-say-they-always-write-a-product-review-after-making-a-purchase/.

Nielsen. (2019, January 29). How U.S. Millennials are shaping online FMCG shopping trends. *Nielsen*. Retrieved on April 11, 2019 from https://www.nielsen.com/us/en/insights/news/2019/how-us-millennials-are-shaping-online-fmcg-shopping-trends.html.

Nisbet, M. C. (2010). Knowledge into action: Framing the debates over climate change and poverty. In P. D'Angelo & J. A. Kuypers (Eds), *Doing news framing analysis: Empirical and theoretical perspectives* (pp. 43–83). New York, NY: Routledge.

Novak, A. N., & Hakena, E. A. (2014). Framing theory, social media and. In K. Harvey (Ed.), *Encyclopedia of social media and politics*. Thousand Oaks, CA: Sage. DOI: 10.4135/9781452244723.n9781452244218.

Pan, Y. (2018, May 31). 5 surprising facts on the consumption habits of China's post-00s generation. *Jing Daily*. Retrieved on April 22, 2019 from https://jingdaily.com/post-2000-generation/.

Patel, D. (2016, November 25). 6 ways Gen Z will change the tech world. *Entrepreneur*. Retrieved on April 20, 2019 from https://www.entrepreneur.com/article/285273.

Pearce, N. (2010). A study of technology adoption by researchers. *Information, Communication & Society, 13*(8), 1191–1206. DOI: 1110.1080/13691181003663601.

Pew Research Center. (2010, February). *Millennials: A portrait of generation next*. Washington, DC: Pew Research Center.

Pew Research Center. (n.d.). *Millennials*. Retrieved on April 11, 2019 from https://www.pewresearch.org/topics/millennials/.

Progressive Media. (2015, October 5). Step aside Millennials, Generation Z hungry for business. *Progressive Media*.

Reese, S. D. (2001). Framing public life: A bridging model for media research. In S. D. Reese, O. H. Gandy, & A. E. Grant (Eds), *Framing public life: Perspectives on media and our understanding of the social world* (pp. 7–31). Mahwah, NJ: Erlbaum.

Resonate. (2019). State of the consumer report 2019: Shattering generational perceptions. *Resonate*. Retrieved on April 11, 2019 from https://insights.resonate.com/state-of-the-consumer-2019.

Schneider, M. (2020, August 4). Sorry, boomers and Gen X. Millennials, Gen Z and younger generations are the new majority in the US. *USA Today*. Retrieved on January 27, 2020 from https://www.usatoday.com/story/news/nation/2020/2008/2004/millennials-gen-z-outnumber-boomers-gen-x-brooking-institution-says/3289084001/.

Silge, J., & Robinson, D. (2019, March 23). *Text mining with r: A tidy approach*. Sebastopol, CA: O'Reilly.

Silver, C., & Lewins, A. (2018).Using software in qualitative research: A step-by-step guide. *Sage Publishing*. Retrieved on March 24, 2019 from https://study.sagepub.com/using-software-in-qualitative-research/student-resources/step-by-step-software-guides/qda-miner.

Srivastava, T. (2014, May 7). Build a word cloud using text mining tools of r. *Analytics Vidhya*. Retrieved on April 25, 2019 from https://www.analyticsvidhya.com/blog/2014/2005/build-word-cloud-text-mining-tools/.

Statista. (2019a). To what extent do you agree or disagree with the following statements concerning technology in general? *Statista*, Retrieved on April 11, 2019 from https://www.statista.com/statistics/534554/increased-in-technology-related-to-dcrease-in-exercise-uk/.

Statista. (2019b). Interest in popular emerging technologies among Chinese in 2017, by generation. *Statista*. Retrieved on April 20, 2019 from https://www.statista.com/statistics/805322/china-interest-in-popular-emerging-technologies-by-generation/.

Suominen, A., Hyrynsalmi, S., & Knuutila, T. (2014). Young mobile users: Radical and individual not. *Telematics and Informatics*, *31*, 266–281.

Tesoa, E., Olmedillab, M., Martínez-Torres, M. R., & Toral, S. L. (2018, April). Application of text mining techniques to the analysis of discourse in eWOM communications from a gender perspective. *Technological Forecasting and Social Change*, *129*, 131–142.

TWICE. (2016, June 29). Millennials lead way among cord-cutters. *TWICE*, p. 26.

TWICE. (2017a, September 25). Millennials skipping live TV in favor of on demand. *TWICE*, p. 24.

TWICE. (2017b, September 25). Youthful TV viewers prefer streaming content. *TWICE*, p. 25.

Wang, H. L. (2018, November 15). Generation Z is the most racially and ethnically diverse yet. *NPR*. Retrieved on November 20, 2018 from https://www.npr.org/2018/2011/2015/668106376/generation-z-is-the-most-racially-and-ethnically-diverse-yet.

Wiedemann, G. (2016). *Text mining for qualitative data analysis in the social sciences: A study of democratic discourses in Germany.* Salmon Tower Building, NY: Springer VS.

Williams, A. (2015, September 18). Move over, millennials, here comes Generation Z. *The New York Times.* Retrieved on November 20, 2018 from https://www.nytimes.com/2015/2009/2020/fashion/move-over-millennials-here-comes-generation-z.html.

Williams, K. (2021, January 27). Gen-Z e-commerce influencers. *@Dolescent.* Retrieved on January 27, 2021 from https://adolescentcontent.com/gen-z-e-commerce-influencers/.

Yang, K. C. C., & Kang, Y. W. (2018, October 27–29). *A text mining exploration of mainstream and social media discourses on internet censorship and privacy-invasive information-communication technologies (ICTS) in China: A cultural ecological analysis.* Paper Presented at the New Paradigms Communication Education Stream, The Asian Congress for Media and Communication (ACMC) 2018 International Conference, National Chengchi University, Taipei, Taiwan.

Yang, K. C. C., & Kang, Y. W. (2019, March 11–12). *Using a text mining technique to study gender communication research: A longitudinal and thematic analysis.* Presented at 2019 Women's and Gender Conference, The University of Texas at El Paso, USA.

Zikopoulos, P., Parasuraman, K., Deutsch, T., Giles, J., & Corrigan, D. (2012). *Harness the power of big data: The IBM big data platform.* New York, NY: McGraw Hill Professional.

Section 3

GLOBAL EXAMPLES

Chapter 8

The Role of Technological Change in Facilitating Young People's Experiences with Computer-Mediated Communication (CMC) in the United Kingdom

Lauren Dempsey

The media is rife with speculation about young people. The Millennial generation has been widely discussed in Western media: accused of being shallow, technology-obsessed, and unable to form meaningful relationships (Poindexter, 2012; Rattner, 2015; Turkle, 2011; Williams, 2015). Meanwhile, Generation Z are increasingly portrayed as a new, distinctive type of young person. Journalists argue that they are more thoughtful, open-minded, and earnest as a group (Seemiller & Grace, 2016; Williams, 2015). They, too, are shown to utilize technology for socializing; however, they are doing so in a more considered, private fashion. While technology is positioned as something that unites these two groups, their attitudes and behaviors toward it are argued to vary greatly.

This chapter will consider the existing dichotomies, exploring the differences (and similarities) between these two generations longitudinally to build an understanding of their use of technology in relationship management. I will focus on young people's engagement with computer-mediated communication (CMC) by exploring their relationship with any hardware that facilitates CMC (such as smartphones, laptops, and tablets) and CMC platforms (such as social media, email, and video calling).

This study engages data from the UK's communications regulator Ofcom, utilizing their annually run qualitative study Adults' Media Lives. By engaging with this dataset, I examine young people's experiences with CMC between 2005 and 2018, capturing their journeys as they grow older, develop relationships, and utilize a range of different devices. I am able to explore this multifaceted subject from numerous angles, longitudinally analyzing the experiences of Millennials and Generation Z via first-hand, individual accounts. I examine how technological innovation coincides with a shift in young peoples' behavior and relationship management in a manner that continues to resonate and evolve beyond this research period, as young people utilize technology and CMC throughout the uncertain era caused by the COVID-19 pandemic.

LITERATURE REVIEW

The emergence of the Internet, social media, and mobile technology has led to an influx of studies and critiques on how young people engage with the Internet, such as Prensky's (2001) introduction to "digital natives," boyd's numerous studies on teenagers' varied uses of social networking sites (boyd, 2006, 2007, 2014), and Turkle's (2011) fears for the future of teenagers' social lives. These differ tonally: some scholars argue that this new wave of young people is natural Internet users, capable of surprising previous generations with their aptitude for technology (Papert, 1996; Prensky, 2001; Seiter, 2007; Tapscott, 1998). Others present concerns and fears for new generations, arguing that their supposed "addiction" to technology is damaging their social skills and overall well-being (Lanier, 2010; Turkle, 2011). These concerns are associated with their assumed exposure to technology, leading to a wealth of tech-related identifiers, such as the computer generation (Papert, 1996), digital natives (Prensky, 2001), net generation/N-Geners (Tapscott, 1998), and the Facebook generation (Poindexter, 2012).

Generations have long been described and categorized based on a pivotal moment or period that defines them (such as the Greatest Generation, Baby Boomers, and Millennials). These groupings are often broad, spanning one to two decades and capturing a vast range of individuals under one categorization (Poindexter, 2012). However, it has been argued that due to the range of people within one category—and the multiple significant changes that can take place over two decades—these classifications are at risk of being too broad and nonrepresentative of the nuanced group they describe (Palfrey & Gasser, 2008; Poindexter, 2012). While in this chapter I will identify overarching generations to discuss, I will focus on interrogating the different cultural, social, and technological landscapes each individual came of age, highlighting the importance of moving beyond restrictive categorizations to understand what motivates behavior.

The "Millennial Generation"—a term coined by Howe and Strauss in 2000—refers to those born circa 1983–1995 (although consensus over the exact years each generation begins or ends varies by text (see Brown & Czerniewicz, 2010; Poindexter, 2012)). They are positioned as "unlike any other youth generation in living memory" (Howe & Strauss, 2000, p. 4), and this stance is often linked with the new, complex, and ever-changing technological landscape they grew up in (Poindexter, 2012). This generation is described as the first teenagers to grow up with in-home access to the Internet, the first to experiment with online chat rooms, and the first to step into the world of social media. Their association with the Internet led to it becoming synonymous with their generation and has played a key role in criticism aimed at Millennials in media coverage (Iqbal, 2018; Poindexter, 2012; Rattner, 2015; Williams, 2015). Generation Z follows Millennials, who are classified as those born between 1995 and 2010, again, age ranges vary (Seemiller & Grace, 2016). This generation is often positioned in opposition to Millennials, deemed more private, more thoughtful, and more outward thinking (Iqbal, 2018; Seemiller & Grace, 2016; Williams, 2015).

Despite this splitting of the two generations, scholars have argued the need to explore the grey areas between groups. Poindexter (2012) maintains that just as it is misleading to broadly categorize a wide range of different people under one overarching generation name, it is also problematic to assume that each generation is distinctly different from the last. She argues, "Millennials, like generations that preceded them and generations that will follow, do not exist in a vacuum" (p. 16). Brown and Czerniewicz (2010) state that it is determinist to assume people can be definitively categorized, as it implies that "if a person falls into one category, they cannot exhibit characteristics of the other category" (p. 357). Thus, while grouping in generations is incredibly useful in indicating broad patterns and themes relevant to the time period discussed, they can be restrictive when trying to qualitatively understand individuals. Poindexter (2012) addresses these concerns by categorizing Millennials into two groups: "Wave I" and "Wave II." Dingli and Seychell (2015) rebrand Prensky's (2001) digital natives by arguing that the first-generation digital natives are followed by a second cohort of young people, who they refer to as "2DNs." I will follow these examples by restructuring broader categories into smaller, more fluid groupings, where each group is discussed based on an array of social, technological, and cultural movements.

This chapter closely examines the experiences young people have with technology. It is thus important to note how technological developments over an extended period have facilitated a shift in behavior, usage, and attitudes. However, this chapter rejects a technologically deterministic approach. For example, the belief that technology "does" something to people (Baym, 2010; Quan-Haase, 2015), instead proposing that social processes drive technological development and that it is the user of technology that adapts their usage of devices to suit the needs of themselves or those around them, in response to societal expectations. In her research on the use of technology in relationships, Baym (2010) adopts a "social shaping" approach by positioning her stance as somewhere between technological determinism and social constructivism, and I too shall utilize this stance in this chapter.

METHODOLOGY

Ofcom is the UK communications regulator. Their role is to ensure UK citizens have access to an array of media and the opportunity to develop their media literacy. As part of their role, they conduct regular research into UK citizens' engagement with media. This chapter engages with Ofcom's Adults' Media Lives research, a qualitative study that has run annually since 2005. Participants are visited each year in-home for two hours filmed in-depth interviews, and by interviewing the same participants every year this study is able to develop a cohesive understanding of their experiences with media and how these may alter over time. I observed the raw video footage from the Adults' Media Lives interviews, transcribing each participant's interviews every year between 2005 and 2018. I used NVivo 11 to code the content from these transcripts into themes and then analyzed all content using thematic analysis (Guest et al., 2012), extrapolating key points on the use of CMC in relationships and determining the overarching themes.

Terras and Ramsay (2016) note the importance, but current lack, of longitudinally examining young people's use of technology and the role this plays in shaping their personal relationships. While there have been numerous longitudinal studies conducted on young people's behavior regarding technology (Thomson et al., 2018; Toly et al., 2011), there is a lack of research considering different young people in this manner, over this extensive time period.

In this chapter, I focus on seven of the Adults' Media Lives participants to examine the varied technological experiences of young people. These select participants each fall into the Millennial or Gen Z categories, as described above. In 2018, the oldest was 35, and the youngest was 18. The youngest members of the sample joined the study in 2013/2014, as existing participants grew older and new teenagers were recruited. (See table 8.1 for a full breakdown of their ages and the dates they joined the study.)

Following an analysis of this sample's experiences between 2005 and 2018, I determined that these young people could be loosely grouped into three categories, based on their ages and usage of and attitudes toward CMC. They are classified as "Generation 1," "Generation 1.5," and "Generation 2" and are interconnected. Each generation identified is subject to their own unique experiences with CMC; however, there are similarities across these groups. I will discuss each generation consecutively in the following sections.

Table 8.1 Media Live Sample

Name	Job	Year of Entering Study	Age during Study (year of entering—2018)	Generation (based on lit. review)	Grouping in This Chapter
Daniel	City bank worker	2005	22–35	Millennial	Generation 1
Julia	Junior doctor	2006	17–29	Millennial	Generation 1
Dean	Various: Inc. personal trainer, driver, bar manager	2006	16–28	Millennial	Generation 1
Jenny	Student and makeup artist	2008	16–26	Millennial	Generation 1.5
Robert	University student	2014	18–22	Gen Z	Generation 2
Tim	College/university student	2013	15–20	Gen Z	Generation 2
Chloe	School student	2014	14–18	Gen Z	Generation 2

Note: All names in this chapter are pseudonyms to protect participant identity.

ANALYSIS

Generation 1: Learning Curves

There are three participants incorporated in Generation 1. These include Daniel: a 35-year-old (as of 2018) bank worker based in London; Julia: aged 17 when she entered the study in 2006, who trained to become a doctor and lived across the UK and Australia during the study; and Dean: who entered the study in 2006 at age 16 and took on numerous jobs over time. He also had fluctuating romantic relationships, becoming a father in 2011. Each of these participants expressed different, as well as coinciding, outlooks and behaviors regarding CMC and technology that altered over time. This section examines these experiences, exploring the role of changing technology in how they engaged with CMC.

Academics discussing the subject of media and young people in the late 1990s and early 2000s tended to celebrate this new generation as being enthusiastic, curious, and inherently capable when it came to using computers and CMC (Papert, 1996; Prensky, 2001; Tapscott, 1998). Although these claims have since been widely contended (Buckingham, 2000; Turkle, 2011), some narratives that Millennials are a proficient, technology-fixated generation have prevailed, and Prensky's (2001) coined term digital native is still utilized (Dingli & Seychell, 2015; Palfrey & Gasser, 2008).

Initially, these participants reported behaviors and attitudes associated with the savvy digital natives described: all three began the study enthusiastically utilizing computers and CMC, often claiming that they used computers every day. They were excited by the implications CMC could have for their social lives and eagerly discussed emerging forms of CMC and social media in the mid-2000s, such as Bebo, MSN, and, later, Facebook:

> You started getting emails from people "join me on Bebo" [. . .] and I never bothered, but then people started talking about it at school, so I thought "oh yeah I'll join that," but then got completely hooked, everyone I know is completely hooked it's just—it's addictive. (Julia, age 18, 2006)

Each member of "Generation 1" began the study using desktop computers as their main tool for engaging in CMC. These devices were described as large, static, and slow and are often shared with their family members. Thus, engagement with CMC tended to be limited, where parents were able to enforce rules over actions and time spent online, due to the typically central positioning of the PC (personal computer) in the house. Furthermore, the limits of this technology meant that the use of these platforms tended to take on an "event" nature, where these participants looked forward to using these platforms at designated times in a focused, committed manner for a limited amount of time; the use was a planned occasion. As time and technology progressed, these participants want to utilize CMC in a more private manner, adopting personal devices to do so. Dean bought his own laptop in 2008 so that he could use social media whenever suited him, rather than be restricted to a fixed time shaped by his family's use of the main household computer.

While these participants owned—or at least had access to—mobile phones at the beginning of the study, their access tended to be limited to "basic" mobile phones, lacking the multimedia functionalities and numerous CMC options associated with smartphones. Thus, the manner in which they could use them was restricted, with Daniel noting their limitations: "it doesn't by any means replace my digital camera" (age 22, 2005).

This technological state is also discussed by Dingli and Seychell (2015) who argue that despite early accounts celebrating the new technological landscape that Millennials were supposedly immersed in, Prensky's first generation of digital natives would have actually been "late starters" with technology (p. 1). They argue that "smartphones only penetrated mainstream use towards the end of the first decade [of the 21st century] . . . social media was still in its infancy [and] broadband was still a luxury" (p. 1) for first-generation digital natives. Ofcom's 2006 Media Literacy report enforced this, reporting that only 54% of UK adults had the Internet in their home and only 35% had broadband at the time of research (Ofcom Media Literacy Report, 2006). Dean exemplified this more modest technological exposure, claiming that he lacked the Internet in his house at a young age and therefore did not grow up confident with technology:

> I'm not proper clued up or know a lot about it [. . .] we got the internet not too long ago [. . .] we didn't have the internet when I was [at school . . .] I didn't have a clue, I only learnt about Facebook not too long ago really and things like that, so I haven't really grown up with it properly. (Dean, age 22, 2011)

As such, the narrative that early Millennials supposed traits were generated by growing up with technology at their fingertips appears to be overclaimed.

Furthermore, academics note that mobile technology was still in its infancy as this generation came of age, meaning "the only use which the first DNs had of mobile technology was an expensive teether" (Dingli & Seychell, 2015, p. 2). Generation 1 again reinforced this notion, as Julia encountered numerous issues with mobile phones during her early years in the study, adopting contracts she didn't fully understand (or feel responsible for) and as a result often incurring large fines:

> I got a bit naughty using my data in Australia so I've got to pay for that, I think maybe it's 150? [. . .] so last time I checked it was about 90 plus my 40 for my phone [. . .] It was stupid I know. (Julia, age 24, 2012)

This generation's apparent naivety and lack of understanding when adopting technology illustrate that they were not "naturally" knowledgeable about technology. This inexperience was also evident when they struggled with the sudden access to a wealth of people online. For example, Julia (age 20, 2008) reported that "my friend's boyfriend was cheating on her with another girl and we found out through her wall on Facebook [. . .] everyone can see it." Both Julia and Dean experienced a number of online conflicts, as they and their peers failed to predict the issues that could incur from having networks suddenly converged on one social media platform.

Scholars Rainie and Wellman (2012) and Parks (2017) highlight the problems users may encounter when suddenly finding their different social groups collapsing online. They argue that people naturally categorize and separate different relationships offline, such as workmates, family, and friends, separately in order to avoid overlap and conflict. Thus the sudden collapse of these networks into one place online can cause unexpected social difficulties. This is an issue faced throughout the study period by all participants; however, it is evident that Generation 1 were arguably most susceptible to struggling here, as they were the teenagers making the first steps into social media and had to learn how to navigate an array of platforms through trial-and-error. This approach is far removed from academic portrayals of Millennials inherently knowing how to effortlessly incorporate technology and the Internet into their everyday lives.

These early issues arguably had a lasting effect on these three participants, who went on to have very different experiences with CMC and technology. Julia remained enthusiastic about CMC for the duration of the study, claiming to be "addicted" to her phone and social media. Facebook was of particular interest to her, where "if we're sitting in the library we'll have Facebook open and every sort of 15 minutes you'll click on it to see what's changed" (Julia, age 21, 2009).

Julia took numerous steps in later years to decrease her usage, especially as she continued to have issues with going beyond her contract limitations on her phones and began to worry that she was becoming "antisocial":

> So recently I've started deleting Facebook off my phone when we go out to things [. . .] I just thought "this is really anti-social I spend too much time on it," so it's probably really stupid but I delete Facebook on my phone now when I go out, and it takes less than a minute to download it again when I get home. (Julia, age 26, 2014)

As such, Julia is arguably reflective of the "technology-obsessed" persona associated with Millennials.

By comparison, Dean experienced an almost entirely opposite transition over time. While he was positive about CMC in the mid-2000s, his trial-and-error approach led to him committing a number of his own social faux pas on social media over time, jeopardizing his relationships. This led to him becoming increasingly skeptical about CMC. He lamented a time gone by where the Internet did not factor into everyday life, arguing that it would be simpler to maintain relationships without CMC:

> I wouldn't mind being brought up in [my grandma's] generation where there's not all that technological—like everything's just more simple. Like you meet a [girl] or whatever and you're together and everything is simple, rather than having Facebook and loads of geezers trying to chat her up over the Internet. (Dean, age 24, 2013)

Finally, Daniel appeared to have a much more considered approach to CMC, where he adopted platforms that he deemed useful (notably, WhatsApp) and incorporated CMC into his everyday communication. However, he became increasingly overwhelmed by the sudden influx of options available and rejected numerous CMC platforms, assuming they would take up too much time:

> I mean Facebook I can't remember the last time I logged in, I've got very little interest in it now [. . .] nothing's changed, there's not a great deal I think I get from it [. . .] that there's just nothing on there for me [. . .]. I've thought about on more than one occasion shutting it down, but I can't be bothered. (Daniel, age 29, 2012)

As a result, by 2018 Daniel's Facebook use was "little to nothing" (Daniel, age 35, 2018); he had settled into habitual use of the same devices, and he had stopped attempting to experiment with newer online platforms.

It is evident that despite their close ages and initial experiences with CMC, there were differences between how these three experienced and felt about CMC by the end of the study. This is noteworthy, as it illustrates how age alone is not enough of a determiner of outlook. While they each grew up in a similar technological landscape, their individual differences helped shape very different experiences. However, the core similarity here is their initial enthusiasm dissolving down into routine: they all seemed to choose a "preferred" form of technology and communication to utilize, rather than continuously experimenting with new CMC. Furthermore, there was a sense of resignation in this group, where they felt they had to use CMC and mobile technology in their everyday lives, but sometimes felt "trapped" by it. As such, this generation fits into the Millennial stereotype to a certain extent: they were avid users of CMC, and it was a key part of their everyday lives. However, there was a strong sentiment of frustration and concern, where they still wanted to resist CMC becoming essential for their social lives.

Generation 1.5: The Discoverer

Jenny (aged 16–26) lived with her parents for the duration of the study, undertaking a range of studies and part-time jobs, including working as a makeup artist. She is still—by definition—a Millennial. However, she discussed numerous shifts in behavior that differentiated her from her slightly older counterparts. Despite there only being a three-year age gap between her and Julia, their attitudes, outlooks, and reported behavior varied greatly. I have thus named this group "Generation 1.5" as Jenny sat distinctly between the three aforementioned participants and the three teenagers that followed her but was also a connecting thread between the groups.

Throughout the study Jenny was a high user of multiple CMC platforms across numerous devices. In the time between Julia starting the study as a 17-year-old in 2006 and Jenny starting the study as a 16-year-old in 2008—and in the following years—there were numerous changes in technology and CMC social norms that could arguably lead to some of the profound differences between the two. Between 2007 and 2008 alone, there was a significant increase in household Internet access (62% vs. 73%), and the number of UK Internet users with social media profiles had almost doubled from 22% in 2007 to 38% in 2008 (Ofcom Media Literacy Report, 2009). By 2010, 52% of those aged 16–24 had smartphones, and tablets had been introduced in the UK (Ofcom Media Literacy Report, 2011). As such, Jenny was a teenager in a time where there was a deluge of Internet and CMC facilitating devices and platforms available in the UK.

One key change that occurred during this time was the movement toward the use of CMC on-the-go. As opposed to Generation 1, who began utilizing CMC on fixed desktops in the family home, Jenny entered the study with her own phone and laptop. In her first year of the study, Jenny reported going to her room to use CMC at night, with more freedom to communicate online than Generation 1 initially had. When asked how long she spent on Bebo and MSN after a typical school day, Jenny responded:

> Quite long like. Probably until about—when I get home from school about 4 o'clock, like 4–6 usually, and then I'll have my tea, and then go back on it, until about, well last night it was 11 o'clock I came off. (Jenny, age 16, 2008)

This use rapidly developed during the study, where in the following years she upgraded her mobile phones regularly, adopting the newest device she could and utilizing it throughout the day. Her adoption of technology reflected the period of rapid technological change in which she was growing up: in less than eight years she moved from an avid laptop user, to an avid Blackberry user, and then to an avid iPhone user:

> If I want a new phone I'll probably ask for a Blackberry 'cos I really want one [. . .] It looks quite easy to text 'cos it's got a keyboard, rather than like pushing the buttons like 3 times or something. (Jenny, age 16, 2008)
>
> Now everyone's gone over to the other side and there's only two of us left with Blackberries [. . . iPhones] just seem so much faster and the applications look so much better. (Jenny, age 19, 2011)

The intensity with which she adopted new—and abandoned "old"—technology reflected how she engaged with social media, where she was highly sensitive and responsive to changing trends. In 2008, she noted that "not that many people actually go on Myspace or Facebook: the bigger thing is to go on Bebo, so I'd rather just go on that" (Jenny, age 16, 2008). In 2009, she then reported that "I'm much more on Facebook, like Bebo is kind of like old." By 2011, she had altered her preferred platform again, claiming "it's like when people moved from Bebo to Facebook [. . .] I think that's what's happening with Twitter now, everyone's just getting sick of Facebook" (Jenny, age 19, 2011). In the final years of the study, Instagram was her preferred platform, as "Instagram is probably the one me and my friends use most, and is the most kind of popular one" (Jenny, age 23, 2015).

This was where Jenny again differed from Generation 1. While they tended to find a preferred piece of hardware or platform and commit to it, Jenny constantly explored and trialed new CMC options. She reported approaching each new prospect with excitement and confidence, committing herself to whatever form of CMC she felt was most popular at the time. Her tendency to adapt in this manner was very much driven by her friends and their behavior, and she quickly responded to changes in trends.

Jenny was not young enough to adhere to Dingli and Seychell's definition of 2DNs, who they loosely define as "children born in the wireless age" (2015, p. 10). However, she does display certain characteristics associated with their definition: they argue that for 2DNs "technology is not just a tool but rather an important extension of their life" (p. 3). This description was reflective of Jenny's relationship with her phone, where she often talked about it being integral to her life, and expressed fear over being separated from it:

> Like it's shocking, even when I'm at work I've got [my phone] in my apron, and I'll always be checking it to see if anyone's writing to me or to see if anyone's asked something [. . .] I got my phone back and was like *"oooh thank God,"* like *"we're reunited!"* "We're back together." (Jenny, age 24, 2016)

This is reminiscent of Julia's self-proclaimed "addiction" to her phone; however, their behavior with regard to the device itself varied greatly. First, Julia's attachment to her phone was deeply related to her attachment to Facebook. This was not the case with Jenny, who utilized multiple platforms on her phone for socializing. Second, Julia's "addiction" to her phone came with negative consequences, where she often misunderstood her contract limitations and was penalized as a result. Jenny also claimed to be addicted to her device; however, she didn't encounter the same issues as Julia. Jenny's discussions implied she grew up with more comprehension and awareness about the use of personal devices and CMC. As a teenager, she made an agreement with her parents to pay toward her phone bills, thus taking active responsibility for the costs of using CMC. Furthermore, she repeatedly showed critical consideration of her activities online, protecting her privacy and making the most of possible opportunities. For instance, as she began to build a career she was careful about how she appeared online, reporting that "because I'm applying for summer internships and placements and stuff for next summer [. . .] I've made sure everything I'm on is private" (Jenny, age 24, 2016).

Again, this is a noteworthy difference from Generation 1, who through their trial-and-error approach often discussed encountering numerous unexpected issues online and through CMC specifically, whereas Jenny's reported behavior implied strong literacy skills. She claimed a combination of confidence and curiosity not seen in the first three participants, which arguably propelled her toward high use and experimentation.

Jenny was only a few years younger than Generation 1 and was still a Millennial but showed marked differences in attitude and reported usage. This again illustrates that it is important to assert that people cannot be categorized purely on age because of these discrepancies and that it is essential to take technological changes and cultural shifts in perceptions into account.

Generation 2: The Managers

The final generation I identify in this chapter includes students Chloe (aged 14–18), Tim (aged 15–20), and Robert (aged 18–22). By definition, these three participants were Gen Zers. They were also reflective of Dingli and Seychell's 2DNs, in terms of ages and the types of technology they had access to. Dingli and Seychell (2015) discuss how the introduction of Wi-Fi allowed this generation the freedom to access devices anywhere; touchscreens facilitated easier and more intuitive use; and personal and private devices such as smartphones became standard (see also Bond, 2014). In 2016, Ofcom found that 74% of 16–25-year-olds said their mobile phone would be their most missed device. Adults in the UK were more likely to connect to the Internet via a smartphone than a computer, and 76% of 16–24-year-olds said that they had used public Wi-Fi (Ofcom Adults' Media and Use Attitudes Report, 2017). Thus, for these young people, being always connected to CMC via a portable device was not just a possibility, but a norm.

Despite their attachment to smartphones, Generation 2 still utilized multiple forms of technology, assigning each with a specific role and often claiming to move between two or three devices throughout the day:

> At home I've got like an office with a computer, so if there's a lot of work to do I'll go on there [. . .] I use my iPad more now: I use it for email, Match of the Day [televised football series], I tweet on there, homework on there [. . .] My iPhone is mainly for texting. (Tim, age 16, 2014)

This could reflect a sample that are financially able to purchase three different devices, thus may not be representative of those with more financial constraints. For example, Dean from Generation 1 deemed tablets a luxury he could not afford, and Ofcom found that in 2016 those from DE socioeconomic groups were less likely than ABs to use computers, tablets, and smartphones to go online (Ofcom Adults' Media and Use Attitudes Report, 2017), implying that they may have smaller technology portfolios. However, it is at least evident that this generation had an array of technology to choose from, each able to fulfill a specific need.

Jenny spent her teenage years in the study rapidly shifting between different online platforms, where one form of social media was often replaced with the next (Bebo—Myspace—Facebook). By comparison Tim, Chloe, and Robert claimed to have regularly used numerous platforms at once, managing different people across an array of different sites. Smartphones allowed users to efficiently move between different platforms with minimal effort throughout the day, with Tim saying "[I] constantly use [my phone] all the time, will be just walking somewhere and on Twitter scrolling" (age 18, 2016). Rather than having a "preferred" site, they utilized each platform for a distinctive, specific purpose:

> I think it's quite interesting the distinction between Facebook and Twitter [. . .] I find if I'm speaking to people on Twitter it'll be people I don't usually speak to that much, [. . .] But I mean on Facebook it's very much just my close friends I communicate with [. . .] I don't use Instagram to talk that much, it's more just looking and photos videos. (Robert, age 18, 2014)

They carefully categorized different relationships (such as friends vs. family vs. workmates) via different forms of CMC, adjusting their behavior accordingly. Ofcom found that in 2016 while 95% of UK social media users still had a Facebook profile, the number of users to *only* have an account on Facebook was decreasing, and the amount of other social media used was increasing (Ofcom Adults' Media and Use Attitudes Report, 2017). This is a considerable shift in behavior from Generation 1, who initially utilized computers and laptops to remain on one preferred social media site once or twice a day, for a shorter but more focused time.

In order to navigate these multiple platforms and streamline their communications, Generation 2 discussed "managing" their networks: they carefully considered who they talked to, on what sites, and in what manner. As such, the youngest three participants seemed the most assured with their CMC use. They were confident of the specific roles for each platform and were able to utilize the appropriate literacy skills and knowledge to ensure they behaved in the "correct" way on sites:

> I'd say I'm quite sensible about what I post [. . .] I like the fact that on social media my parents don't know what I'm doing [. . .] I'm friends with my mum on Facebook but I tend to block her on a lot of things I post [laughs] and I don't have family members on anything else. I do like that I have my own privacy and can do what I want on the websites. (Chloe, aged 14, 2014)

This reported awareness of what was and wasn't suitable across certain platforms helped them encounter fewer social faux pas than their older counterparts. They worked hard to make sure only the "appropriate" audience viewed the content they wanted them to:

> I've got a very strong Christian family in Canada [. . .] Facebook will appear on other people's timelines like "Robert commented on this post" [. . .] so you want to be very careful about what you comment on [. . .] so I tend to invite some of my friends into this kind of closed group on Facebook. (Robert, age 20, 2016)

This may explain why this generation is positioned in the media as being more private; they became accustomed to juggling multiple networks at once, ensuring their curated image was protected and other content was hidden. The "correct" use of CMC required work and ever-adapting literacy skills; it was not an inherent skill that came naturally to them. It appears that education is key. While Generation 1 discussed having to adopt a trial-and-error approach with limited help and information from adults around them, Generation 2 claimed to receive education from more knowledgeable parents and teachers on how to utilize computers, technology, and CMC, with Chloe noting in 2016 that there was an emphasis in her school on considering the long-term repercussions of posting content online. Evidently, as time went on those in authority positions had a chance to adapt to the new technological landscape and could provide more cohesive advice to younger generations. This help was arguably pivotal in motivating Generation 2's confidence and ability with CMC.

Given this increased emphasis on education and use, it is unsurprising that this generation also claimed that there was a growing expectation to always utilize CMC, where it became a vital source of social developments within their relationships. As such, they adapted their behavior accordingly, going out of their way to ensure they always had access to CMC even when it was not readily available:

> For me it's important [to access the internet on holiday] 'cos you're not with your friends for a while and want to know what's going on [. . .] I felt like the Greek restaurants were advertising the Wi-Fi like "come to my restaurant, we have Wi-Fi." You could see all the English people in there on their phones. (Chloe, aged 16, 2016)

Although they felt this was typical conduct, Generation 2 did express concerns over this behavior, worrying that young people potentially spent too much time online:

> You kind of wonder a bit like "oh, is it kind of anti-social?" [. . .] it's just a bit depressing sometimes [. . .] I can see it would be very easy for a lot of people—if they're not particularly social and social media is their form of socializing—I can see that it would be very easy to live the kind of life that is dominated by technology. (Robert, age 19, 2015)

Like Generation 1, there was a sense of resignation: Generation 2 were conscious of the dominating role CMC had in their lives, however considered it to be integral to their social lives, something that they would struggle without. While Generation 1 considered CMC to be something they could—to some extent—opt in and out of, Generation 2 felt they did not have this choice. This perception of choice is perhaps the core difference between the generations and is integral to how these groups differ in their attitudes and interactions with CMC.

DISCUSSION

This chapter has explored the experiences of seven different young people across a fourteen-year period, examining their usage of and attitudes toward CMC. This exploration has uncovered two key findings regarding how we segment and discuss generations. First of all, there are numerous notable differences between those within the same generation. For example, although three participants could be classed as Millennials and grew up in similar technological landscapes, it was evident that their personal, cultural, and economic backgrounds all shaped their experiences and led to them reporting varied usage and attitudes toward CMC. This means that it is problematic and limiting to assume everyone from the same generation is the same. Second, there are numerous apparent similarities between the different generations, where regardless of the technological differences they may experience, they have common goals and interests.

It is evident that between 2005 and 2018, devices became increasingly converged and CMC grew more accessible through a range of different platforms. This was supplemented by improved 4G and Wi-Fi connections allowing for easier access to CMC while on-the-go. Alongside—and arguably, because of—these technological changes, there was a reported increase in the social expectation for young people to constantly access CMC. While the teenagers of Generation 1 engaged with CMC as a novel activity, the teenagers in Generation 2 felt that it was imperative for them to use CMC throughout the day, in order to maintain their personal relationships. Despite these variations, each set of young people prioritized socializing and maintaining relationships. The distinction was that they each had different tools and options for doing so. Each set grew up adhering to different social expectations and norms, where the technology they owned facilitated different expectations of use and communication. As each generation was exposed to a very different technological landscape, they learned and adopted new "rules" and codes of behavior. By the end of the study period, all participants, whether they were still teenagers or not, felt a pressure to sustain constant communication via CMC. This further reinforces the notion that it was the shifting technological landscape facilitating a change in social norms regarding relationships, rather than the generations themselves being fundamentally different or insulated.

REFERENCES

Baym, N. K. (2010). *Personal connections in the digital age*. Cambridge, UK: Polity.

Bond, E. (2014). *Childhood, mobile technologies and everyday experiences. Changing technologies = changing childhoods?* London, UK: Palgrave Macmillan.

boyd, d. (2006). Friends, Friendsters, and Top 8: Writing community into being on social network sites. *First Monday, 11*(12).

boyd, d. (Ed.). (2007). *Why youth (heart) social network sites: The role of networked publics in teenage social life*. Cambridge, MA: MIT Press.

boyd, d. (2014). *It's complicated: the social lives of networked teens*. New Haven, CT: Yale University Press.

Brown, C., & Czerniewicz, L. (2010). Debunking the "digital native": Beyond digital apartheid, towards digital democracy. *Journal of Computer Assisted Learning, 26*(5), 357–369.

Buckingham, D. (2000). *After the death of childhood: growing up in the age of electronic media.* Cambridge, UK: Polity Press.

Dingli, A., & Seychell, D. (2015). *The new digital natives: cutting the chord.* Heidelberg, Germany: Springer.

Guest, G., Mac Queen, K. M., & Namey, E. E. (2012). *Applied thematic analysis.* Thousand Oaks, CA: SAGE.

Howe, N., & Strauss, W. (2000). *Millennials rising: The next great generation.* New York, NY: Vintage Books.

Iqbal, N. (2018). Generation Z: "We have more to do than drink and take drugs." *The Guardian.* https://www.theguardian.com/society/2018/jul/21/generation-z-has-different-attitudes-says-a-new-report.

Lanier, J. (2010). *You are not a gadget: A manifesto* (1st ed.). New York, NY: Alfred A. Knopf.

Ofcom. (2006). *Media literacy audit.* The National Archives. https://webarchive.nationalarchives.gov.uk/20090904000659/http://www.ofcom.org.uk/advice/media_literacy/medlitpub/medlitpubrss/medialit_audit/.

Ofcom. (2009). *UK adults' media literacy.* The National Archives. https://webarchive.nationalarchives.gov.uk/20160704101035/http://stakeholders.ofcom.org.uk/market-data-research/other/research-publications/adults/uk_adults_ml/.

Ofcom. (2010). *UK adults' media literacy report.* The National Archives. https://webarchive.nationalarchives.gov.uk/20170112170852/https://www.ofcom.org.uk/cymru/research-and-data/media-literacy-research/adults2/adultmedialitreport.

Ofcom. (2011). *UK adults' media literacy report.* The National Archives. https://webarchive.nationalarchives.gov.uk/20170112170439/https://www.ofcom.org.uk/cymru/research-and-data/media-literacy-research/adults2/adultmedialitreport11.

Ofcom. (2017). *Adults' media use and attitudes: Report 2017.* The National Archives. https://webarchive.nationalarchives.gov.uk/20170714131432/https://www.ofcom.org.uk/research-and-data/media-literacy-research/adults/adults-media-use-and-attitudes.

Palfrey, J., & Gasser, U. (2008). *Born digital: Understanding the first generation of digital natives.* Berkeley, CA: Basic Books.

Papert, S. (1996). *The connected family: Bridging the digital generation gap.* Atlanta, GA: Long Street Press.

Parks, M. (2017). Embracing the challenges and opportunities of mixed-media relationships. *Human Communication Research, 43,* 505–517.

Poindexter, P. M. (2012). *Millennials, news, and social media: Is news engagement a thing of the past?* New York, NY: Peter Lang.

Prensky, M. (2001). Digital natives, digital immigrants. *On the Horizon, 9*(5), 1–6.

Quan-Haase, A. (2015). *Technology and society: Social networks, power, and inequality.* Ontario, Canada: Oxford University Press.

Rainie, H., & Wellman, B. (2012). *Networked: The new social operating system.* Cambridge, MA: MIT Press.

Rattner, S. (2015). We're making life too hard for millennials. *The New York Times.* http://nyti.ms/1HaTVm8.

Seemiller, C., & Grace, M. (2016). *Generation Z goes to college* (1st ed.). Hoboken, NJ: John Wiley & Sons.

Seiter, E. (2007). *The internet playground: children's access, entertainment and mis-education.* New York: Peter Lang Publishing.

Tapscott, D. (1998). *Growing up digital.* New York, NY: McGraw-Hill.

Terras, M., & Ramsay, J. (2016). Family digital literacy practices and children's mobile phone use. *Frontiers in Psychology, 7*(1957), 1–11.

Thomson, R., Berriman, L., & Bragg, S. (2018). *Researching everyday childhoods: Time, technology and documentation in a digital Age.* London, UK: Bloomsbury.

Toly, V. B., Musil, C. M., & Carl, J. C. (2011). A longitudinal study of families with technology-dependent children. *Research in Nursing & Health, 35*(1), 40–54.

Turkle, S. (2011). *Alone together: Why we expect more from technology and less from each other.* New York, NY: Basic Books.

Williams, A. (2015). Move over, millennials, here comes generation Z. *New York Times.* http://nyti.ms/1UZIA01.

Chapter 9

Media and Technology

Generational Differences and Attitude of Nigerian Media Users in Nigeria

Oluwafunmilayo'Bode Alakija
and Anthony Amedu

INTRODUCTION

This article is an exploratory examination of different generations Nigeria has witnessed in media and technology from colonial to the present time. One of the objectives is to situate Nigerians within the debate that has conceptualized various categories of the US generations, according to the age and technology in which each grew up, vis-à-vis the Silent Generation of 1928–1945 (aged 73–90), Baby Boomers of 1946–1964 (aged 54–72), Generation X of 1965–1980 (aged 38–53), Millennial of 1981–1996 (aged 22–37), and Post-Millennial of 1997 to present (aged 0–21 years) (Pew Research, 2019; Serafino, 2018). The Silent Generation in Nigeria we argue would fall within the category of colonial generation, that is, those who were born in the 1914s when Nigeria was birthed as a nation during the colonial administration as a result of the amalgamation of Southern and Northern protectorates.

Our respondents are demographically diverse with regard to generation, profession, ethnic origin, age, and gender that are resident in Lagos and Abeokuta metropolis. This range includes those who were born from 1930 to 1964 (Nigeria's Baby Boomers), followed by 1965–1986 generation (Generation X), the Millennial, those born between 1987 and 1999, and lastly, the Post-Millennial, 2000 to date. The former two categories, The Nigerian Boomers and Generation X, are the ones with political power while the latter, Millennial and Post-Millennial, are contesting that the former should recognize the social and political shifts in the Nigerian system and grant them inclusion, as this chapter shows. In the incidences leading to the last 2019 election, many have clamored for youth recognition. The two presidential candidates were in their mid-70s, Muhammadu Buhari, the elected president, was born on December 17, 1942, and his runner-up Atiku Abubakar on November 25, 1946 (*Premium Times Newspaper*, April 16, 2019), respectively.

From the inception of the first newspaper *Iwe Irohin* in 1859, radio transmission "rediffusion" (Radio Distribution Services from England to the Empires) in 1932, first Nigerian television station in 1959, and mobile communication systems cum digital technologies in 2001 to date, the Nigerian media have served both political and educative purposes. First, used to obtain independence from colonial administration with the establishment of newspapers such as the *Nigerian Tribune, West African Pilot, African Messenger, Lagos Weekly Record,* the *Lagos Standard,* and many others. Even the establishment of *IweIrohin* was set up as a missionary and educational tool for the Yoruba and Egba elites in the South-Western part of the country. Controversy between the then leader of the South-Western Region, Chief Obafemi Awolowo with the central government over the Macpherson Constitution in 1953, provided the grounds for the establishment of the first television station in Africa, the Western Nigerian Television (WNTV) in 1959 (Akinwalere, 2013; Umeh, 1989). Thus, began a series of generational lines where media has been a tool for political propaganda and education for those with the power to establish one.

One of the objectives is to situate Nigeria's media developments and attitude of various generations to both traditional media and digital, ICT technology of the 2000s within this wider global context where different shifts have been acknowledged as to how different age groups experience the world. Many societies in the Global North have created space socially, economically, politically, technologically, and space for the new generations' ideal where even employers have been forced to adapt their management strategy to accommodate the new group as well as to incorporate and update new form of technologies. So, we draw on two epochs in the introduction of media into the social, cultural, political, and economic contexts of Nigeria: the dividing lines, that is, the introduction of traditional media (1859, 1932, and 1959), and that of ICT and social media (2000) in explaining the different generations of Nigerians' attitudes to these new phenomenal events in the history of the nation.

We observe that previous studies in this context have studied Nigerian media use on the political economy of the media and cultural imperialism, to explain the role of media in Nigeria and the resultant erosion of perceived traditional cultures as a result of exposure to the contents of purported media products/texts that are "western" in outlook, with minimal scholarly interrogation of different generations of users of media as technology to argue that, in contrast to international mass media imperialism. This chapter looks at generations with the view of provoking inquiry in generational continuity and discontinuity as well as paying attention to the complexities of cultures beyond the cultural erosion thesis. This chapter, through interviews with a cross-section of three generations, shows how both the older and younger generations who are recipients and users of media technologies in contemporary Nigeria have become a part of globalization and electronic mediation (Alakija, 2016). The latter is, however, savvier and more competent in navigating the terrain of technology usage and media consumption than the former. However, irrespective of this difference in skills and ability to appropriate the media, both generations believe in the power of media technology and its influence on the society's younger generations' exposure to digital technologies through the Internet and its various affordances on the social media platforms are eroding traditional cultures and value systems. Thus, they still subscribe to the powerful media theory and the agenda-setting role of the media, even in a context where scholarship has shown that media provides symbolic space (Madianou, 2014) for the articulation of various media users and industries' contents.

The media as an industry has a significant impact on the social, political, economic, and cultural context of Nigeria. Furthermore, Nigeria in the present dispensation has become a part of the global world where media, one could argue, has become an essential part of everyday life. Thus, in Nigeria, the older generations critique the younger generations who have been exposed to both foreign and local media contents of cultural erosion. Given the visibility of the important role that technology is now playing in the society, both for older generations and younger generations, coupled with the resultant societal developments, we argue that these are crucial distinctions along which generational lines could be drawn. While we have focused on the generations preceding the independence of Nigeria from the colonial administration in 1960, we acknowledged the existence of the pre- and during colonial days. We have however, delineated our discussion in this paper to three major generations, as enumerated above, those who were born in the 1930s and were therefore teenagers when the traditional media were introduced into Nigeria in the 1960s, who are currently between the former, and the 1990s Nigerian youth who, if compared to the US Millennial, have been born into a technological age. They are considered savvy, competent in media use, both traditional and digital with its various affordances on YouTube, blogs, Facebook, Internet, satellite television, and various other platforms.

Although this later generation differs in their competence and global exposure, all categories of respondents are similar in their outlook in the West in terms of its educational standard, and the media can be powerful in molding attitude. Thus, *òlàjú* (exposure) and enlightenment are still measured using these factors as attested to by two of our generations (Ife is 23 years old and her mother, Mrs. Joju, is 55 years old[1]). Some of the 1930s generations, one could argue, were the same generation as of Harris (2006) study of Nigerians in London who were noted as the prominent colonial students of the 1960s. These were the first noticed generation of Nigerians to obtain western education and to return to Nigeria for the task of taking over the reins of governance left with the exit of the British Administration shortly after independence on October 1, 1960. Hence, in addition to media technology, education has been the criteria for Nigeria's generational divide. Media, however, is the major driving line used in this chapter, even though a historical x-ray of the previous generations would show that education, media, and interaction with colonialism have been an offshoot of what the Yoruba tribe in Nigeria see as "*òlàjú*" or "*raré*" (enlightened or inclusion into the elitist social circle) used by Ife and Joju as the "west" continues to set the standard for aspiration among younger and older generations of Nigeria.

The 1930s generation that witnessed colonization as well as the introduction of the first local television stations in 1959, although they were young children, possibly, babies when rediffusion was introduced in 1933, attest to the power of the "magic box" (radio) in the corner of their sitting room around which family and extended members such as neighbors and friends would gather to listen to what was popularly referred to as "*èroasòrò-má-gbèsì*"[2] (a talking gadget to which you cannot respond). Following this generation are those born between the Independence and Post-independence period, which occurred in the 1950s/1960s to early 1980s, shortly after the introduction of the first television in 1959. This generation has matured to become the parents of the 1990s to 2000s generation who are the Millennials. Gaps exist for further investigation of the generation who were born from 2001 to date, in examining if making cultures would replace consuming cultures through the application of media hardware as the generations in this study have been shown to be consumers and users of technologies and media infrastructures from the West.

The difference between consuming culture and using media hardware for social, economic, political, and cultural purposes is based on our notion of the Global North and Global South divide. The media infrastructure and technologies are still produced in the Global North, even though there have been interactions between local and global cultures. Therefore, paradoxically, "Nigeria has a media infrastructure that creates the reality of a nation that is ever connected to a globalized world which, at the same time, emphasizes

Nigerians' marginalization," according to Larkin (2004, p. 308) in his study of the uneven distribution of media outputs such as pirated CDs and DVDs in Kano, an economic center in the Northern part of Nigeria. Nigeria, as a nation and the most populous country in Sub-Saharan Africa, has become a part of the global flow of goods, technologies, and cultural forms, as well as people (Alakija, 2016; Larkin, 2004, 1997) in a contemporary world. Thus, we arguably claim that, as observed by Larkin (2004, p. 292), media in Nigeria has its own parallel structure within globalization in which media goods, as well as technology, circulate and enable the potentials of technologies of reproduction. There is, therefore, a paradigmatic shift in the Nigerian economy and capital where media have become a logic of privatization as well as in everyday life—a transformation effect of media technologies and infrastructures that have a profound impact on Nigeria's everyday life, one which continues to reinvent itself from one generation to another.

Although there has been a change in population in terms of the current population of younger compared to the older generation; and in, media contents, production structure, analysis reception, and consumption have changed since the introduction of *Ìwélròyìn*, rediffusion through distribution to diffusion, television, and ICT in the 1990s, into the nation's social, cultural, political, and economic milieu. The status quo, arguably, is still maintained across generations as all see the media as a tool for social control and a means of inclusion into the wider elite class. Furthermore, the analysis, designing, and reception criticism are still constant (Lakemfa, 2019).

The president of the Federal Republic of Nigeria Muhammadu Buhari (Lakemfa, 2019) recently noted the change in configuration that Nigeria has a very young population who are about 60% of the total national population estimated at 180 million. This 60% is below the age of 30. Earlier, Hall (2002), in his study of Nigerians and the influence of religion on identity construction, has noted the preponderance of young people where 60% are below the age of 31 among his respondents among Nigerians in London (21–40 and 41–50, respectively).

NIGERIA AND ITS MEDIA HISTORY: FROM "MAGIC BOX" TO DIGITALIZATION

Historically and geographically, Nigeria is a diverse society, a creation of the ingenuity of the colonial administration; it is a nation that has 250 different language groups with three as the major along the line of Yoruba education, Igbo commerce, and Hausa governance, although this differentiation is not closed. It is this multicultural, multireligious, and regional context that media was introduced into Nigeria's social, cultural, and economic milieu. Thus, the history of media started in Nigeria in 1859 as a tool for literacy and education that were linked to Christian evangelism with the establishment of "*Ìwé Ìròyìn Fún Àwon Ègbá Àti Yorùbá.*" (A newspaper for the Yoruba tribe, especially, the Ègbá ethnic group.) This publication became the offshoot for others on which the history of journalism in Nigeria is founded, with the publication of other Nigerian newspapers that followed such as *West African Pilot, African Messenger, Lagos Time, Gold Coast Advertiser, Anglo-African* (Akinwalere, 2013), and others that have been mentioned earlier.

Following the print media was the introduction of radio through "rediffusion" (Radio Distribution Services from England to the Empires) in 1932, which later metamorphosed in 1935 to "diffusion" with the establishment of Federal Radio stations and Ibadan Radio station in 1939, culminating in the creation of Nigerian broadcasting service in 1950, subsequently leading to the establishment of radio stations in Kaduna, Enugu, Kano, Ibadan, and Lagos major cities and key areas in geopolitical Nigeria in the British colonial administration. The impact of social shaping by technology and the transformative power of this medium could be perceived with the music composed by a Nigerian popular musician Adeolu Akinsanya according to an 80-year-old retired Civil Servant Interviewee who, in reaction to the medium, sang that *Wóntúngbékinní yen déooo, wáyàburúkúasòrò-má-gbèsìòrò* (a new invention has been developed, an absurd wire that speaks without waiting for a response). This shows an understanding that feedback is needed long before "phone-in programs" were introduced into radio production.

The establishment of the first television station in 1959 served a new purpose beyond its recognized advantage of combining audio with visual. However, this does not equal the power of the medium to accomplish what the political founder conceived as its purpose, established by Chief Obafemi Awolowo, the then regional leader of the Western Region and one of the nationalists that contended from Nigeria's Independence. The television medium was to serve as "a teacher and entertainer, and as a stimulus to us to all to transform Nigeria into modern and prosperous nation" (Umeh, 1989, p. 57). In achieving this objective, the Nigerian broadcasting industry became a political and propagandist medium for various regional governments. The Western Nigerian Broadcasting developed a slogan in 1959 that claimed to be the first in Africa while the Eastern television which, was set up a year later, responded by claiming to be second to none. The North established its own television station in 1962. Although education was the objective, these television stations became an instrument of political and power struggle among the various regional leaders and their owners, culminating in the establishment of the *Voice of Nigeria* in 1990 and various other Federal and State government-owned broadcast media until the passage of Deregulation Decree 38 in 1992, establishing National Broadcasting Commission (NBC) which democratized broadcasting media to include various private ownership.

The late 1990s to date witnessed the introduction of the global system of mobile communication and digital technologies. Digitalization and the establishment of the Internet brought Nigeria into the arena of global media users and scholarship. Today, Internet penetration stands at 73.0%, with over 1540 million Internet users (Internet World Stats, 2021). An analysis in 2011 of the economic impact of wireless broadband in Nigeria found that 70% of users in 2009 visited social networking sites, 65% used emails, and 54% used the Internet for entertainment (Alakija, 2016).

This period marked the birth of a new generation of Nigerian media users, including the introduction of Nigeria into the world of global media infrastructures and technologies—a noticeable feature of globalization. The media that emerged, however, like the Nigerian society itself, many have claimed, is a colonial creation (Crowder, 1973; Onwubiko, 1973), and the importation of "western" structures adapted to local politics and way of life, thereby creating a parallel economy which has become Nigeria's modernity as observed by Larkin (2004) in his study of media piracy, which is part of the organizational architecture of globalization in Kano. This attitude to economy, political, and social systems and structures persists in various generations. It has informed a way of life in which success, social inclusion, and elitism are defined by western education, traveling abroad, media contents and infrastructure, and now social media as tools.

From the inception, it appears that media has been set on fighting against colonial rule and working toward gaining independence from the colonial administration. Thus, nationalist leaders, Chief Obafemi Awolowo, who established the first TV in Africa, Chief Nmadi Azikwe, who established the Eastern region TV and was Prime Minister, Ernest Okoli, Herbert McCaulay, and Anthony Enahoro were all nationalists and media owners. Since they are media owners, they attempted to suppress the freedom of the press, and the government monopolized the media (Umeh, 1989). Today, media ownership in Nigeria cuts across federal, state, and private ownership. This is context when social media was introduced into Nigeria as a new generation of technology that is meant for a new generation. Although social media is beyond the strict government control that is associated with the traditional media because it cuts across time and space, the government of Bauchi State in 2012 fired a civil servant at the State Ministry of Finance and Economic Development, Mr. Abbas Faggo, over a Facebook post on monumental corruption in the state.

While change is inevitable and culture is not static, there is constancy within change that involves the emergence of a new generation, and, according to Winograd and Harris (2009), "every generation defines itself first by making it clear about how and why they are unlike the generation that preceded it. Such moves into a new position of power and influence in that the nation's institutions change to accommodate their beliefs and values" (p. 2). Nigerians have not been able to grasp this and therefore, oftentimes, the status quo is maintained as change has not been fully recognized, even though it abounds in current events and happenings in the society. Usually, as recognized by the American society, such values often are larger than the preceding the new, while that of the United States is more ethnically diverse.

Younger generations in Nigeria still subscribe to the ethnic differences their predecessors have left them, although they are more positive in outlook and have more exposure to the global world than their parents. They recognized the present state of their lives and of the country, and they are aware of the future. They are, however, powerless to do anything except try to meet their own needs like previous generations have done, leaving the future generation to work out their own way through the maze for themselves. Even the importance of scholarly work in acknowledging generational changes and the changing nature of culture in terms of scholarly debates on generational continuity and discontinuity is yet to be understood in the Nigerian academic circle. This is in line with the response of Ife, a 23-year-old young generation lawyer:

> The younger generations are curious enough, the word self-center is too strong, I still believe they are just fighting for what the society is lacking, it is people of the older generation I will refer to as self-center but the word is too strong because the society is lacking the social amenities, we lack things general and from this the young are striving for their living (existence) that is why we have youths going into Yahoo but we have those doing well especially in the entertainment world and fashion designing trying to enjoy life and create opportunities for their children so it is really wrong to say the young are self-center because they are fighting for the future and that of their children because the society does not even provide good place to leave or provide standard of living.

CONCEPTUALIZING NIGERIAN MEDIA HISTORY AND GENERATIONS

The statement from Ife shows that although unrecognized, change has continued to occur in the social and political arena of the national and personal life of Nigerians. Education and media have been prominent influences on the changes in the social, cultural, and political life of Nigerians. Media itself is perceived as all-powerful and authoritarian in setting an agenda and in educating, informing, and entertaining, thus, the reason for political leaders' involvement in its ownership and government control prior to the democratization of social media across space and time. Users also see media as powerful; therefore, the reading of media texts is oftentimes not negotiated, the preferred reading encoded into the message is accepted as reality, not construction, even for the younger generation who are hasty to conclude and accept whatever they received on social media. Arguably, one could surmise that even the social media set the agenda of what they believe and think; the older have critiqued the younger generation of uncritical attitude to media content, while the younger have accused the older generation of the same guilt with regard to their attitude to the traditional media.

With the introduction of colonialism, media, especially television and independence, Nigerian social life changed. Thus, Bisi, a retired female senior civil servant claimed that political life as a result of the availability of education, information, and entertainment changed after the entrance of WNBS (Western Nigeria Broadcasting Station) in the social life of the Yoruba in the Western region where the station was situated. Yet, all the younger generation interviewees are worried about the lack of changes in the political system in the nation and are unanimous with the view that

> it does not make room for the young generation because it is more or less the same people that have been ruling that are still in power, it recycling among the elders and you can't even say the young are not interested. The younger generation are interested even at the universities you see young people in Student Government, the young are not just given the opportunity to lead, for example, if I want to do anything in my community now the first question is who do you know and even when you know somebody they will be asking what can you offer, in Nigeria they will be looking at age saying wait for your turn or time not looking at competence but at age, or trying to settle the young ones with money, then they will tell them to work with the older generation to learn at the end of the day you will see that the older people are the ones influencing the younger generation because they are not setting good example.

This situation, according to the younger generation, only fosters "godfatherism"—a phenomenon in Nigeria which explains a form of political corruption in which an influential, and in this case, older generation assists another to get into political, professional, or any other position of leadership, with the purpose of paying back in cash or in kind. This practice has been set in place since independence by the nationalist leaders and subsequent generations of leadership in Nigeria. In this younger generation's view, "the youths are not given opportunity and are forced to conform to the way the older generations are doing it and just follow them." Thus, the older generations who are in control are denying the new generations the opportunity to thrive:

> The young ones are very curious; we want to know about the happening around us but when they keep pushing us away we have to find other means to survive. Changing your community start from you but when one is not given the opportunity to do so like me I have to focus on my family to know how they will survive because my society is not ready for change or consider me worthy to bring the change to the society. So, let me take care of my family. (Ife, younger generation stresses)

While the older generation of Nigerians, born in the mid-1960s, has critiqued the younger generation's addiction to social media without exercising any critical thinking, the younger generation claims that in terms of politics, they are interested. According to Taiwo, extract of the young generation, 24-year-old solicitor:

> Definitely, majority of us are very concerned about politics and the need for things to get better. Always critiquing the government for their actions or inactions. Our interest goes way deeper into gender-based roles, feminism, patriarchy etc. Thanks to social media, more people get educated daily on this topic.

The above shows how diverse and expansive these younger generations are, and how social media is facilitating the expression of their values and beliefs. Social media

> is an emerging platform for expressing ideas, communication and advertisement. The effect of social media can be streamlined into two cadres—the positive effect and the negative effect. Positive effect. Social media has helped communication easy for the younger generation. Business and professional networking platforms have been created to enhance communication in the business world. It has exposed this generation to a lot of information. We could get any information about anything in the world within the split of seconds. Nigerian youths are forever future leaders until we all come together to change this wrong perception created in our minds by the older generation. Gowon was 32 when he became head of state. Awolowo was a young man who he became the premier of the western region. I wonder why they never saw these guys as our future leaders. I guess it's time we say we are leaders of today not tomorrow because tomorrow is not promised. We only know about today and we will rule our nation today. (Wole, a graduate of business administration)

From the foregoing statement, the younger generation stresses the importance of social media technologies in their everyday professional life and interactions. In their view, social media is enabling the creation of a new generation of Nigerian businesses and networking, even though most of the older generation has actually argued that they spend too much time on social media at the expense of interpersonal relationships and interaction. To the older generation, virtual interaction has replaced face-to-face interaction, where people relate individually and on a personal level, rather than through gadgets, such as smartphones. This incidentally is the global view about the impact of social media and the world of technology on face-to-face interactions, due to the fact that we are living in the digital era (Chen, 2018). Although all the generations interviewed for this article believe in the positive impact of the media and especially social media, the technology-savvy Millennium and Post-Millennium Nigerian professionals have found a voice through social media to critique and to request for their role in society. In this context, the three generations interviewed acknowledged the positive impact of these media, especially social media, on society, yet the younger ones have a high tolerance for lifestyle and ethnic differences and support an activist approach to government, societal, and economic issues. They, unlike their older generations' progeny, recognized change as an empowering force despite its many contrasts and complexities.

GENERATIONAL CONTINUITY AND DISCONTINUITY

While Obama who according to Winograd and Harris (2009) is a later Baby Boomer because he was born "on the cusp of Gen X, recognized and was sensitive to the concerns and political styles of the millennial" (p. 3), the Nigerians' older generations are not as attested to above by the younger generation interviewees. Although the older generations understand the importance of education, they have in turn critiqued the quality of education received by the younger generation as a result of their exposure to and use of technology, which has exposed them to other ways of thinking and lifestyles that are different from their culturally ascribed ones—the ones they attribute to the negative sides of western culture.

Thus, with regard to news and entertainment, the older generation claimed that while their parents' generation encouraged them to watch the news, and in fact sit together to watch the news with their parents in the evening, the current generation have not cultivated such an attitude but instead watch entertainment alone. This is expressed by an older generation, 54-year-old Nigerian pastor, who claims that the younger generation's addiction to video, satellite, YouTube, Facebook, Twitter, and other various affordances has actually replaced their quest to know through news. He claims that as a result, despite the positive impact of communication technologies, there is a lack of focus on the younger generation. The more access they have to information, the poorer their academic performances.

An older generation female, 56-year-old lawyer, Nike, attests to the fact that: "By the present media set up, this particular generation is better than us with regards to media . . . more educated." In the case of this older generation, emphasis was even more on reading as well as watching television. Therefore, a habit was formed that "if I do not read the newspaper ara mi ò nííyá" (I shall feel sick or incomplete). However, most of the new generations after us rely on social media to get their news, which, to the older generation, is junk news. In other words, purporting that social media disseminates useless news, which they are not critically minded enough to examine. To them, the younger generations do not bring a critical outlook into what they receive from social media, because the younger generation reads news about celebrities and entertainment, fashion and trends.

Incidentally, some of the younger generations, born in the 1990s, attest to the timewasting elements of social media, believing the jobless spend more time in media. They, however, admit that more creativity has been advanced as citizen journalism now thrives and audience interaction and creativity enable them to see communication as power, either through their smartphone or laptop. Through major posts, chats, and pictures, personalities and celebrities are created, in addition to watching movies and jokes on their smartphones or laptop. As observed by their older generation counterpart, many admit that they only spend a portion of their time on their devices doing research but rather chat and listen to music more often. However, unlike the previous generation's traditional media, social media and the Internet connect the younger generation to a larger global world through which they interact with others across boundaries. They can watch television on mobile devices and can take them everywhere because of the small size. They can also use them to gain social skills that they can apply to real-life situations.

Social media has succeeded in offering the younger generation a chance to create global connections and online relationships, making global relationships a norm. The younger generation understands that the world is evolving, and further changes are bound to happen in the generation to come, although each generation would have to work it out within their peer-to-peer connectedness. Although it is rare to find a Nigerian youth who sits down to watch national news such as the Nigerian Television Authority (NTA) a federal government network channel, they have, however, recognized the change in age and time, consequently priorities. Thus, there is a dictum among them that those who fail to recognize the shift would lose. According to Ife:

> If you snooze you lose, if you don't move with the world and change, you are going to be the one losing at the end. And you would not enjoy or get anything good out of what is available; therefore, you have to grab it, filter it, do away with where it does not suit you, but use it to the maximum.

She further defends the fact that her counterparts in this younger generation category are aware that social media created its own language among the youth that even the corporate institutions in Nigeria recognize. The corporate world, according to Ife, "use media's commercial value" by employing those youth leaders with the highest following online. Most of the younger generations also access these websites for generational trends and interests. Therefore, pushed out of the mainstream by the older generation, they have created a chain of influences and influencers. Their generations thus use technology for entertainment, for business interactions, and for role models. For instance, Ife says:

> We also pick our role model from the social media people would like to be like social influencers lawyer Olumide for example he has a great number of followers and we see him as role model . . . shows that we can combine social and normal life, even corporate world uses the Internet and social media to attract customers and to recruit staff.

In terms of ownership structures, however, the younger generation still believes that the older generation dominates the media, whether as owners or professionals. For example, a television presenter, Cyril Stober at the Nigerian Television Authority (NTA) network, who has dominated the network for 15 years has recently retired. We would argue that this should create room for the younger generation newscaster to occupy his position; however, they claim that 80% of newscasters are still from the older generation. At a ratio of 80 older newscasters to 20 younger ones, who are only given minor roles to play. However, advancement in media technologies from analog to digital has made possible access to the world's global village (Internet), which has been made to become a small village through social media. These media have incorporated a feedback loop that the older generation found unavailable in radio "*asòrò-má-gbèsì*" as the current medium has both voice interactive open to the expression of opinion and feedback compared to the past. With regard, these younger generations unlike their older ones are already projecting what may or may not happen to the future. Wole is of the opinion that:

> The future generations are going to enjoy more than this generation ever did in terms of communication and getting information. However, the higher the enjoyment the higher their chances of being mediocre if they do not harness the wealth of information at their disposal and channel same to achieve development which includes social, intellectual and political development.

Unlike the older generation, however, these younger generations are considerate and assume their role on how the next generation could utilize further developments that are bound to happen. That is, in Wole, Ife, Frank, and

Taiwo's view, "how we utilize it now; we have to realize that the potential social media have to guide the future generation on how to use same; if we don't, they'll use it wrongfully." We may therefore find ourselves in the same situation as the older see us in the way:

> A few of us use social media. Some of the older generation would see a couple of us as social media/phone addicts with nothing to add to the society, while others might see a couple of us as adding value through social media, educating and mentoring people; and there are those who are hardly on social media.

BETWEEN CONSUMING CULTURE VS. MAKING CULTURE

The media in Nigeria, as discussed above, have acquired a Nigerian infrastructure that has created both its national and political character. Therefore, the media industry in Nigeria has its own parallel structure whereby technologies have been adapted to local, national, and international needs in the form of technologies of reproduction despite the critiques of cultural erosion. With the aid of media technologies and infrastructures, there has been the consummation of culture through the use of media hardware for social, economic, political, and cultural purposes by the various generations discussed in this chapter.

The younger generations through the affordability of social media and all their platforms have agreed to follow trends either mindlessly as the older generation have often criticized them for, or purposefully, in creating a youth economy for themselves in the hope that with their help, the future generation that would follow them shall be guided the way(s) they have utilized it. They have however not failed in pointing out that the older ones have used the media in their own ways too, given the time and epoch, according to Ife:

> I agreed with you we follow trends but the truth about it, these trends are followed by even the older ones just that it is done in different ways to it should not just be on the younger ones because even the older ones introduce the internet which also have negative side, so it is not really correct that the youths are following trend we are following what are already laid down, we are just following it differently but it is still the same thing.

This younger generation recognizes that different generations would have to find their own way in defining themselves, and, irrespective of older generations, antagonism to change must show as they claim that they are different, even though there are similarities. There are bound to be similarities and differences and continuity and discontinuity between generations. It is also the responsibility of the older generation to understand this as President Obama did during his campaign in the United States, giving the opportunity for the Millennium generation to thrive from the vantage of the known, their social media savviness. They were, therefore, able to move up into a new position of power and influence in the society whereby the nation's institutions change to accommodate their beliefs and values (Winograd & Haris, 2009, p. 2).

In this regard, all the younger generation interviewed recognized the change and the cultural mixture which has become part of global interactions and the role of global media and digital technologies as principal agents in this process. This is succinctly expressed by Ife, as follows:

> There are so many things that have been introduced compared to the old; so I believe that the trend then has to do with what was in vogue; but now the trend now have to do with who is who, what do you have to offer and if you have something to offer, show us what you have, and this have been possible by the social media; and then we compare ourselves with the developed world so we are trying to meet up with them.

To the older generation, however, it appears as if the younger ones are mindlessly following trends without critical knowledge of how to set a boundary, yet the status quo cannot continue to be maintained as society continues to evolve and new technologies continue to be more advanced than the previous ones. This changing nature of culture and everyday life necessitate the breaking down of the barrier of fixed cultural mindsets as the Nigerian younger generation are calling their older generation to observe. They acknowledged that they are victims of the current consumer culture perpetuated by media outlets in similar ways the older generations have been in their epoch.

According to Paul, a 24-year-old lawyer, social media is facilitating more virtual contacts than it was in their epoch and

> helps people keep in touch with each other; you're actually never apart. You're always close to each other as if you guys are physically in touch. Well, the down side is that it makes people slaves to their phones, in other words, losing touch with reality and I am guilty of this. Everyone is always on their phones either texting or something. I think the last time our generation had genuine human interaction was when we were little but now, it's all virtual—not real—all electronic, no genuine interaction. Well, because of all these, people don't really know what is happening around them; like for example, people have accidents because they were not paying attention. So, people were not understanding the voice vote, so I sent this out instead, I hope it is still part of what you are looking for.

The fact that culture is consumed through the making and mixture of culture is exemplified in this statement by this young generation lawyer and is shared by most of our younger interviewees that the

> process that is trying to make the world a global village where cultures have to merge, the merging of cultures cannot even stop, the way the old are complaining, that is the way we will complain that, at least we have culture, but our children don't have because the world keep moving. With time, it will be by what is right in a situation, not what culture says, which I think is a good development because culture is good for them, their media perception, so each generation determine what they want. The youths should not be neglected. Where youths show interest, we should not be shot down; there should be no interruption of youths in contributing because at the end of the day, this world is not for one person or for one particular set of people. Generations are coming, and are still to come. So, we should all work hand-in-hand to ensure that different generations are being represented in the society, and even as we are being represented, we should think about the children to come, because if the world is destroyed now, there will not be a world and if there is no world now, there can't be world tomorrow.

Conclusion

Technologies continue to impact the everyday life of Nigerians, from one generation to the next, since its incorporation into the social, political, economic, and cultural life of the nation with the advent of the newspaper. The recognition of the power of the media as a powerful tool with transformative power will continue to have its own dialogue, either in social media or in its traditional forms, with consequent changes in lifestyles and interpersonal relationships.

The need to identify and analyze an entirely new impact of information and communication technologies and their impact on social life rather than the emphasis on the erosion of culture, with a view to continuous maintenance of status quo in the face of change, should be the focus of scholarly inquiries. In sum, this chapter has shown the need for Nigerian scholars and media practitioners to start thinking of developing contextual theories that would guide media practices and generational studies in Nigeria even when we have explored western theories in contextualizing our everyday experiences.

NOTES

1. Pseudonyms have been used for all the interviewees.
2. Associated with a traditional Local Talking Drum that has no feedback loop.

REFERENCES

"Age of Muhammadu Buhari and Atiku Abubakar." *Premium Times Newspaper Online*. Retrieved from www.primiumtimeng.com on April 16, 2019.

Akinwalere, I. (2013). "The history of the Nigerian Television." Retrieved from www.legit.ng.

Alakija, O. B. (2016). *Mediating home in diaspora: Identity construction of first and second generation Nigerian migrants in Peckham, London*. PhD Thesis. London: Department of Communication and Media Studies, University of Leicester.

BRIU Business Day Research and Intelligence Unit and Terragon Insights. (2014). "The state of digital media in Nigeria: Internet penetration." Retrieved from www.africaPractice.com on April 16, 2019.

Chen, J. (2018). "Social media are affecting face to face interaction." Retrieved from www.academia.edu.

Harris, H. (2006). *Yoruba in diaspora: An African church in London*. Gordonsville. Virginia, USA: Palgrave Macmillan.

"Internet users in Nigeria." Retrieved from Internet users in Africa Statistics, 2021. www.internetworldstats.com on June 5, 2021.

Lakemfa, O. (2019). The Nelson Mandela Buhari phenomenon. Vanguard Nigeria, page 7. Retrieved from https://www.vanguardngr.com/2019/03/the-nelson-mandela-buhari/phenomenon/amp/ on March 3, 2019.

Larkin, B. (1997). Indian films and Nigerian lovers: Media and the creation of parallel maternities Africa. *Journal of the International African Institute*, 67(3), 406–440. Retrieved from http://www.jstor.org/stable/1161182.

Larkin, B. (2004). Degraded images, distorted sounds: Nigerian video and infrastructure of piracy. *Public Culture*, 16(2), 289–3145.

Madianou, M. (2014). Smartphones as Polymedia. *Journal of Computer-Mediated Communication*, 19, 667–680.

"Millennials-Pew Research Center." Retrieved from www.pewresearch.org on January 17, 2019.

Serafino, J. (2018). "New guidelines redefine birth years from millennial gen x and post-millennial." Retrieved from www.mentalfloss.com on March 1, 2018.

"The origins of broadcasting in Nigeria." Retrieved from www.legit.ng on March 1, 2018.

Umeh, C. (1989). "The advent and growth of television broadcasting in Nigeria." Retrieved from http://pdfs.semanticscholar.ng on March 4, 2018.

"What is a Millennial?" Retrieved from www. businessdictionary.com on March 2, 2018.

Winograd, M., & Harris, M. D. (2009). *Millennial makeover: MySpace, YouTube and the future of American politics*. Updated with a post-2008 election afterwards. New Brunswick, NJ: Rutgers University Press.

Chapter 10

Digital Children of the Digital Era

A Case Study of Generation Z on Instagram

H. Hale Künüçen and Leyla Akbaş

INTRODUCTION

In a time of ever-intensified digital communication, social media seems to be integrated into the lives of different age groups and generations. When viewed from the perspective of different generations, social media has built environments of virtual reality especially for "Generation Z" which, in popular parlance, includes cohorts born after 1999. Members of Generation Z, also known as the "Internet Generation," have been born into and raised with technology. They tend to exchange information audio-visually online, actively use social media, and frequently share their social lives and self-images on social media platforms—contrary to previous generations.

Instagram a popular social media platform that reaches over a billion users is among the most popular sharing environments for Generation Z. Instead of articulating their feelings such as sadness, happiness, peace, or restlessness in person, this generation shares these feelings on Instagram. They not only share feelings but also find role models on Instagram and emulate them.

This study aimed to identify the impact of these reference groups of role models on members of Generation Z in Turkey. For this purpose, we examined a sample of Instagram accounts of reference groups of role models that Turkish members of Generation Z follow. This qualitative study examines the effects of these role models in the lives of members of Generation Z. It also identifies the communication features of members of Generation Z on Instagram.

FOCUS OF THE STUDY: GENERATION Z

The term generation is used to define cohorts spanning 20–25 years. Generational conflict is a common phenomenon between these cohorts, and the term is used to express behavioral differences between generations and distinguishes them from one another. Based on their differences, generations have been called Traditionalists (the Silent Generation), Baby Boomers, Generation X, Generation Y (Millennials), and Generation Z (see figure 10.1).

The focus of this study is Generation Z, yet it is important to understand the differences of this group from earlier generations. Therefore, we will first briefly discuss the qualities of generations that preceded Generation Z.

The *Traditionalists (Silent Generation)* were born between 1925 and 1945. The Traditionalists experienced the transition from an agricultural to an industrial society (Kuran, 2018, pp. 41–42). One of their most remarkable characteristics is that they play it safe and do not like to take risks (Lehto et al., 2006, p. 239). Another remarkable characteristic of this generation, believed to have introverted and emotional personalities, is that they are obedient to authority. Binark and Karataş (2015) listed the generations starting from Baby Boomers (1946–1964), Generation X (1965–1979), and Generation Y (1980–2001). Akdemir et al. (2013, p. 16) listed the characteristics and values of these three generations (Baby Boomers, Generation X, and Generation Y) as follows:

- *Baby Boomers:* very high sense of loyalty, workaholic, see teamwork as important, moderate, competitive, and distant from technology.
- *Generation X:* shifting sense of loyalty, respect authority, sensitive about society, high work motivation, abstemious, anxious, and little relation with technology.

Silent Generation	Baby Boomers	Generation X	Generation Y	Generation Z
Sessiz Kuşak (1925 - 1945)	Bebek Patlaması Kuşağı (1946 - 1964)	X Kuşağı (1965- 1979)	Y Kuşağı (1980 - 1999)	Z Kuşağı (2000 - 2021)

Figure 10.1 Timeline of Generations from 1925 to 2021 (The Silent Generation to Gen Z). *Source:* Figure created by authors.

- *Generation Y:* little sense of loyalty, have difficulties accepting authority, devoted to their independence, frequently change jobs, individualist, and grew up with technology.

Generation Z is also referred to as the Alpha Generation, the Internet Generation, Digital Children, Indigo or Crystal Children, and Digital Natives (Evran, 2012). Çalışkan (2016) emphasizes that members of this generation earned these descriptions due to their superior mechanical intelligence, high level of technological perception, and skills. In recent years, they have continued to draw the world's attention due to these skills that they possess, which have never been encountered before. Members of Generation Z seek the opportunity to create content instead of being consumers of content. In other words, they want to consume the content that they create (Kuran, 2018, p. 143).

In Turkey, members of Generation Z, who follow and adopt technological developments better than any other generation, begin to use computers at the age of eight, the Internet at the age of nine, and mobile phones at the age of ten (Alikılıç, 2015). Common use of the Internet and mobile phones also resulted in the popularization of social media platforms among the members of this generation. The reason why Generation Z is referred to as quiet is that they react using communication tools rather than using physical gestures and speaking up, as stated in an interview by Dr. Ulaş Çamsarı (2013) in the *Genç Haber Magazine*. This generation loves to express emotions such as happiness, sadness, tranquility, and anxiety on social media platforms. The same interview emphasizes that members of this generation are only active on social media and are lonely and physically inactive.

The members of Generation Z, who were born and grew up in the digital environment, have high levels of interest and skills in information and communication technologies (Kennedy et al., 2008, p. 484). Current education programs in Turkey are believed to be insufficient in meeting the diversifying expectations of Generation Z (Somyürek, 2014, p. 66). The most remarkable characteristics of this generation for which education programs are believed to be insufficient, mainly due to their lifestyles and perspectives, are described differently. In the list below we provide these characteristics:

Karahisar (2013) said that the word that best describes this generation of people born since 2000 is "speed" (p. 79). She characterized this impatient generation that was born into a rapidly expanding consumerist society as people who eat fast, read fast, write fast, and change jobs frequently.

Yavuz (2014) defines the distinctive qualities of Gen Z as follows. They have high self-confidence. They support independence; however, they generally have conservative families. Their intellectual and physiological development is faster. They are not compatible with teamwork. They place importance on education and social status. They prefer to communicate using social media platforms. They have remarkable analytical thinking skills. They have an insatiable desire for knowledge, which makes growing up in the age of technology their biggest advantage. They are introverts and cannot make friends easily. They need technology and luxury. They do not perceive technology and luxury as special needs because they have them. They know exactly what they want. They believe that everything is possible in life.

As a generation, Generation Z is in the identity-building phase due to their age. They were born into a technology-driven culture. They widely use new media technologies, and their social media platforms are YouTube, Instagram, Snapchat, Facebook, and Twitter.

In a study with Adweek and Defy Media, Hadımlı (2017) asserts that Generation Zers communicate with friends on Snapchat while they use Facebook and YouTube to follow news. This study asked approximately 1,500 people between the ages of 13 and 20 what they think about social media platforms and the digital world to learn about the digital habits of members of Generation Z. The study found that Generation Z trusts social media stars more than conventional celebrities. Participants stated that they prefer YouTube for entertainment and also find YouTube useful for practical information such as "how to" or "do it yourself (DIY)" videos. The results of this study showed the importance of social media for Generation Z. To complement this information, Bazilian's (2017) reported usage rates of social media platforms among Generation Z is illustrated in figure 10.2.

Instagram is the second most popular social media platform for Generation Zers. This platform that has been created to communicate and share posts has been getting much attention because it enables its users to capture and share moments by taking pictures and recording videos (Hu et al., 2014, p. 595). Instagram enables its users to share their pictures and videos on affiliated platforms such as Flickr, Tumblr, Facebook, and Twitter. Türkmenoğlu (2014) reported that Instagram stands out from other similar products in terms of cross-platform engagement features and user friendliness. In addition, considering a picture expresses more meaning than thousands of words. Instagram has an important place in people's lives. Instagram as a digital platform for personal and corporate use allows users to express themselves with visuals, which, in turn, allows them to become personal or corporate brands. Artistic posts, posts on favorite places, recipes, DIY ideas, clothing, and makeup suggestions, and posts for only friends gain much attention (Ayvaz, 2015).

Hosting numerous shares and interactions, Instagram is considered to be the second most popular application across the world. Instagram was created by Kevin Systrom (@kevin) and Mike Krieger (@mikeyk) on October 6, 2010.[1] Almost a year and a half later, it reached 100 million active users.

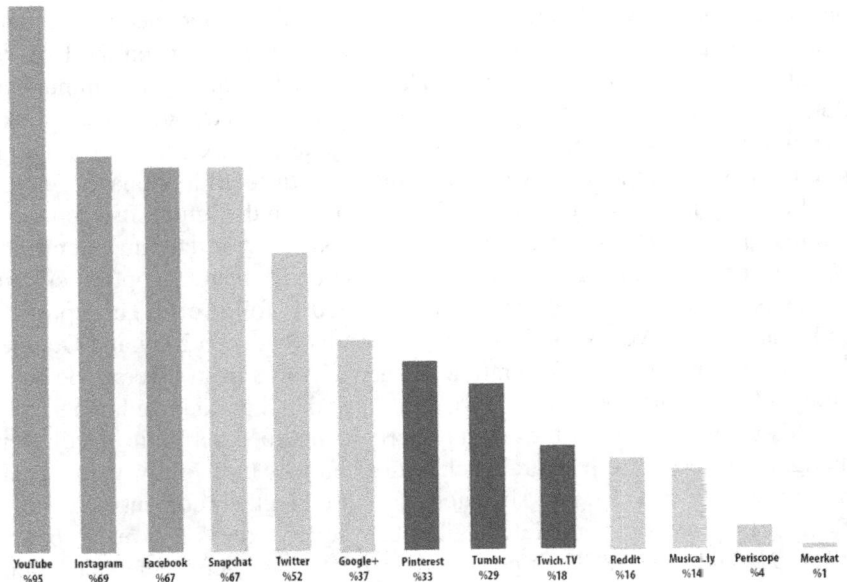

Figure 10.2   Reported Usage Rates of Social Media Platforms among Gen Z. *Source:* Data from Bazilian, 2017. *Figure created by authors.*

Today, it has 400 million daily active users and 600 million monthly active users.[2] Users can edit their pictures and videos on this platform, and they can also put tags and filters on them. They can reach massive numbers of people by putting hashtags (#) on their statuses, and users can communicate with people by messaging.

Apart from our study that highlighted the Internet use by all generations in Turkey, Suat Kolukırık studied Generation Z specifically and asked them "which social media tool they used most?" The answer was Instagram at 72.5% (Karadan, 2017). This result indicates the perceptible effect of Instagram on Generation Z.

STUDY

The aim of this study is to determine the effects of Instagram celebrities as role models for Generation Z. These role models are defined as social media users with very high follower counts that Generation Zers like, closely follow as trendsetters, and try to emulate. We primarily selected users that post frequently and became famous by attracting high numbers of followers with their posts. Subsequently, we tried to observe the effects of their accounts on Generation Z. This descriptive study observes the importance of accounts that were determined to be role models based on its findings on the lives of members of Generation Z. Our study also tried to determine the communication characteristics of this generation's Instagram users through observation. Generation Z was selected for this study to emphasize the effects of Instagram role models on its members who are in their identity-building phase.

This study is a pilot study that will be extended in the future. Its scope was limited to 50 members of Generation Z in Turkey. Six Instagram celebrities, who are popular among members of Generation Z, feature popular culture elements in their posts and have more than 500 K followers.[3] Their profiles and shared posts were examined for six months (between May and October 2017). Fifty members of Generation Z, aged 13 to 18 from diverse sociocultural and economic conditions, were interviewed and participated in a survey for this study. We asked these study participants to describe in detail their thoughts related to the Instagram celebrities and why they follow them. Their responses were grouped into six categories based on their content as follows: "I think they are sympathetic"; "I like their style of dress and makeup, and want to be like them"; "Their posts and the content they create gets my attention, and they are an example for me"; "I like the way they live"; "I want to have their standard of living"; and "They are funny."

Besides these responses, few participants also noted that they either "do not like some of these celebrities; yet, I still follow them" or they "do not follow, but look at their profiles when they show up on the Instagram Explore Page."

We asked an additional question on their own Instagram accounts using *Instagram's Survey Application* based on six months of observation and followers' responses: "What is your attitude toward seeing Instagram celebrities on your Explore Page?" Two responses were offered: "I view their profiles because I get curious" and "I do not pay attention."

The number of members of Generation X and Y who followed the researchers' questionnaire page was 262. Of them, 183 responded, "I do not care." Of the other 79, 42 answered, "I view their profiles because I get curious," and 32 did not see the question, and thus did not respond. Of the 50 members of Generation Z, 42 responded, "I view their profiles because I get curious," and only one chose "I do not care." The other 7 members of Generation Z did not see the questionnaire and did not respond.

CONCLUSION

This pilot study aimed to reveal the defining traits of Generation Z Instagram users in Turkey in terms of how they communicate. Instagram, as a communication medium and tool, is an important social media platform for personal communication like other social media platforms. For the purposes of this study, Instagram also presented a source from which we could observe the behavioral features of Generation Z. There are differences among generations regarding processes and methods of interpreting communication and how much time they spend doing so. Each generation has a way of communicating based on their perceptions and interpretations of the world they live in, which are unavoidably influenced by the available tools of communication in respective eras (radio, print media, TV, social media, etc.). The tools of communication available to Generation Z through social media have broken down the traditional barriers between the two sides of communication, as this generation gained the ability to not only consume but also create content.

This study revealed that members of Generation Z in Turkey have the following traits. They are interested in people with marginal lifestyles (unlike Generation X and Y); they are drawn toward unconventional behavior by social media celebrities that defy commonplace cultural values; they want to create their own content (in a way that resembles the content they prefer to consume); and they show an interest in celebrities' luxurious lifestyles.

In other words, this study revealed that they are close followers of popular culture and digital media through the celebrities who they follow and accept as role models. Moreover, we found that they care more about their lives on social media platforms than their offline social lives. In addition to these findings, Generation Z also considers the Internet and social media as more real than anything else, so they tend to socialize with people who are just like them. This generation frequently develops and socializes new trends and accompanying jargon, which gets mimicked fast and wide. Good examples of this phenomenon are "selfies," "challenges" (e.g., bottle flip), and "Salt Bae" moves.

Generation Zers' communication habits tend to favor visual forms rather than written or oral forms. We argue that this is influenced by or a by-product of Instagram's structural features that are based on communication through images and videos. Moreover, Generation Z, which is known to have stronger motor synchronization than previous generations, appears to prefer socializing on the Internet. As a communication tool, Instagram enables its users to engage in short, fast, and, at the same time, audiovisual sharing, which enables and defines Generation Zers' preferred way of communicating. Finally, it needs to be noted that the scope of our analysis was limited to members of Generation Z in Turkey and their distinctive features in communicating as observed through Instagram. We recommend more comprehensive studies to be carried out on how Generation Z communicates, taking into consideration other social media platforms while examining multiple countries.

NOTES

1. "Instagram" Accessed September 18, 2018, https://www.instagram.com/about/us/
2. "CNN Türk" Accessed September 18, 2018, https://www.cnnturk.com/teknoloji/instagramin-aktif-kullanici-sayisi-aciklandi
3. Six celebrities whose profiles, posts, and followers were examined got some reactions from large groups due to the ongoing legal cases against them, and media coverage has shared information about their lifestyles.
    The names of these celebrities were not included in the pilot study to preserve their personal rights.

REFERENCES

Akdemir, A., Konakay, G., Demirkaya, H., Noyan, A., Demir, B., Ag, C., Pehlivan, C., Ozdemir, E., Akduman, G., Eregez, H., Ozturk, I., Balci, O. (2013). Y Kusaginin Kariyer Algisi, Kariyer Deigisimi ve Liderlik Tarzi Beklentilerinin Arastirilmasi. *Journal of Economics and Management Research*, 11(2), 42.

Aşman, A. Ö. (2015, January 1). *Y'eniveZ'ekikuşağıtanıyın!*. Sözcü. https://www.sozcu.com.tr/egitim/y-ve-z-kusagi-dogru-anlayin.html.

Ayvaz, T. (2015, July 15). *Milenyumkuşağınınen Çokkullandığımobiluygulamalar*. DijitalAjanslar. http://www.dijitalajanslar.com/milenyum-kusagi-mobil-uygulamalar/.

Bazilian, E. (2017, May 21). *Infographic: 50% of Gen Z "can't live without YouTube" and other stats that will make you feel old*. Adweek. https://www.adweek.com/digital/infographic-50-of-gen-z-cant-live-without-youtube-and-other-stats-that-will-make-you-feel-old/.

Binark, M., & Karataş, Ş. (2015, December 5). Dijital kuşaklar dijital kuşaklar nasıl Çalışılmalı?*32. UlusalBilişimKurultayı*. Ankara, Turkey.

Çalışkan, N. (2016, December 12). *X Y ve Z kuşağıÇocuklarınınÖzelliklerineler?* Indigo. https://indigodergisi.com/2016/12/x-y-z-kusagi-ozellikleri/.

Çamsarı, U. Dijitalnesil (Z kuşağı) nedir?—Burukkalplerin Z hikayeleri. Accessed May 10, 2017. http://www.blog.ulascamsari.com/2013/07/dijital-nesil-z-kusagi-nedir/.

Evran, B. (2012, March 8). *Dijitalyerliler (Z kusagi)*. Dijitalyerlilervedijitalyerlil erdeÖğrenme. http://www.zkusagi.blogspot.com.tr.

Hadımlı, G. (2017, May 23). *Z KuşağıYoutubeolmadanyaşayamıyor.MediaCat*. http://www.mediacatonline.com/Z-Kusagi-Youtube-Olmadan-Yasayamiyor/.

Karadan, C. (2017, August 25). *Z kuşağıhayatanasılbakıyor?* CNN Turk. https://www.cnnturk.com/video/yasam/z-kusagi-hayata-nasil-bakiyor.

Karahisar, T. (2013). Dijital nesil, dijital iletişim ve dijitalleşen (!) Türkçe. *Online Academic Journal of Information Technology*, 4(12), 71–83.

Kemp, S. (2017, January 24). *Digital in 2017: Global overview*. We are Social. https://wearesocial.com/digital-in-2017-global-overview.

Kennedy, G., Dalgarno, B., Bennet, S., Judd T., Gray K., & Chang R. (2008) Immigrants and natives: Investigating differences between staff and students' use of technology. *Proceedings of the Annual Ascilite Melbourne* (pp. 484–492).

Kuran, E. (2018). *Telgraftantablete"Türkiye' Nin 5 kuşağınabakış*. DestekYayınları, Turkey.

Odabaş, H. (2017, June 11). *Sosyal bilimlerde araştırma yöntemleri* [Power Point slides]. https://odabashuseyin.files.wordpress.com/2011/04/2.pdf.

Somyürek, S. (2014). ÖğrenmesürecindeZkuşağınındikkatiniÇekme: Artırılmışgerçeklik. *Educational Technology Theory and Practice, 4*(1), 63–80.

Türkmenoğlu, H. (2014). TeknolojiilesanatilişkisivebirdijitalsanatÖrneğiolarakInstagram.*Ulakbilge, 2*(4), 87–100.

Xinran, Y. L., Soo Cheong, S. J., Francis, T. A., & Joseph T. O. (2006). Exploring tourism experience sought: A cohort comparison of baby boomers and the silent generation. *Journal of Vacation Marketing, 14*(3), 237–252.

Yavuz, M. (2014, April 16). *Z kuşağınedir?* HT Hayat. http://hthayat.haberturk.com/anne-ve-cocuk/cocuk/haber/1020781-z-kusagi-nedir.

Yuheng, H., Lydia, M., & Kambhampati, S. (2014). What we Instagram: A first analysis of Instagram photo content and user types. *Proceedings of the 8th International Conference on Weblogs and Social Media ICWSM* (pp. 595–598). Ann Arbor, United States.

Index

Adobe, 82–84, 88, 96
ASOS, 13, 17, 21–24

Baby Boomers, 31, 48, 51, 81–82, 107, 109–10, 132, 149, 159, 168
Bebo, 136, 140–41, 143
blogger, 16
brand hashtaging, 16
branding strategies, 5, 13
brand public, 16, 18–22, 24

campus, 44, 52, 85, 87; campus media, 82
celebrity, 64, 72
classroom, 1, 6, 50, 68, 85–87, 89
coding, 18, 112
computer-mediated-communication (CMC), 7, 131–32, 134, 136–46
consumer, 2, 4, 8, 13, 15–17, 20–23, 39, 49, 52–53, 68, 107–8, 117, 120–21, 152, 169; consumer culture, 29, 163
content analysis, 13, 17, 111–12
content producer, 8
convergence culture, 30, 52
COVID-19, 29–30, 86–87, 117, 132

data mining, 53, 111
data visualization, 84
digital culture, 3, 29–31, 33–34, 41
digital literacy, 7, 83, 93–94, 97–98

digital native, 4, 61–64, 66–69, 71–72, 81, 85, 87, 94, 110, 115–18, 122, 132–33, 136–37, 169

editing, 7, 15, 19, 22–23, 53, 84, 88, 111
education, 1–2, 6, 47–48, 52, 81, 95–98, 144–45, 150, 152–56, 159, 169–70
educator, 4
emoji, 21–22

fandom, 86
Facebook, 6, 14–15, 17, 46, 53, 55, 64–66, 69, 71, 73, 85, 99, 108, 116, 121, 132, 136–39, 141–44
fashion, 5, 15, 17–19, 22–24, 70, 83, 86, 156, 160; fashion brands, 5, 13, 17–18, 20–23; fashion industry, 13, 15
Filter, 15–16, 18–19, 21–22, 39, 55, 84, 113, 160, 171; Geofilter, 5, 20–21
focus group, 13, 17–18, 55, 124
framing (theory), 7, 110–11, 116

generation studies, 2
Global North, 150, 152
Global South, 152
global village, 161, 164
Goffman, Erwin, 15
Google, 36, 61, 84, 108, 110

177

Index

hashtag, 15–16, 19–22, 24, 102, 171

iGen, 47, 94; iGeneration, 108
influencer, 16–22, 24, 64, 108, 161
Instagram, 5, 8, 13–24, 31, 44, 46–47, 49, 56, 64–66, 68, 73, 94, 99, 101–2, 108, 141, 143, 167, 170–74
Instant messenger, 31, 33, 120
iPhone, 3, 31, 39, 54, 82, 108–9, 141, 143
iPod, 54, 108

Jenkins, Henry, 30, 64
job searching, 96, 99–101

laptop, 7, 39, 44, 95, 131, 137, 140–41, 144, 160

McLuhan, Marshall, 45, 84
media corpus, 109, 111, 113–16, 120–23
media data, 112–13
media ecology, 2, 5, 43–46, 52, 54, 57
media literacy, 86, 97–98, 134, 137, 140
millennial culture, 1, 2, 4, 5, 29
multitasking, 49–50, 67

new media, 1–7, 29–30, 32, 43–44, 46, 49–52, 55–57, 62, 82, 90, 170
Nigeria, 7, 149–64

Ofcom, 131, 134, 137, 140, 142–44
online platform, 4, 8, 15, 36, 40, 95, 139, 143
organizational culture, 101

photo, 13–15, 18–23, 31, 33, 36–41, 53, 55, 66, 68, 84, 97, 101, 143
popular culture, 1, 29, 172–73
Postman, Neil, 44

quick media applications, 5, 31–36, 39–40

self, 15, 40–41, 56–57; self-brand/ing, 13, 15, 18–19, 21–23; self-documentation, 14; self-esteem, 15; self-hatred, 56; self-identity, 15; self-image, 15; self-portrayal, 55; self-presentation, 14–15, 21, 55; self-promotion, 5, 23
selfie, 36, 55–56
sexting, 55
shopping, 32, 39, 96, 116, 120; online shopping, 31, 38, 110, 117
smart phone, 3–7, 30, 33, 35–36, 43–44, 49–57, 62–64, 72–73, 84, 95, 107, 109–10, 131, 137, 140, 142–43, 159–60
Snapchat, 5–6, 13–24, 49, 64–65, 108, 170
social network site, 5, 29, 35–36, 39–40
social shaping, 134, 154
story, 14, 18, 20–22, 29–30, 35, 38–39, 66, 82, 87–88, 94, 101–2; storytelling, 84, 86–88
surveillance, 14, 23

technological dependency, 47
television, 31, 52, 82, 86, 109, 150–54, 157, 160, 161; television commercials, 107; television news, 88
teleworking, 102
text mining, 7, 110–15, 120–24
thematic analysis, 18, 134
TikTok video, 83
Tinder, 5, 29, 34–41
Topshop, 13, 17, 21–23
Turkey, 7–8, 167, 169, 171–73
Twitter, 47, 65, 141, 143, 159, 170

UK, 7, 13–14, 32, 109, 123, 131, 134, 136–37, 140, 142–43
university career service, 101

video game, 45, 62, 86

workforce, 2, 6, 93–94, 98, 100, 103

YouTube, 64–66, 69, 72, 85, 96, 151, 159, 170; Youtuber, 16

About the Contributors

Leyla Akbaş is a lecturer in the Department of Finance, Banking, and Insurance, Isparta Applied Sciences University. She has an MS degree from Suleyman Demirel University and her thesis topic is "Environmentally Responsible Consumer Behaviour Effect on Green Product Consumption in the Health Sector: Antalya Area Investigation." She has been a PhD candidate at Burdur Mehmet Akif Ersoy University since 2018. Her research interests are green marketing, generations, social media, subliminal marketing, behavioral sciences, and consumer behavior.

Oluwafunmilayo "Funmi" Alakija is a senior lecturer and the current head of department in the Department of Mass Communication of Moshood Abiola Polytechnic, Abeokuta, Nigeria. She has a bachelor of arts degree in Theatre Arts (University of Benin, Nigeria, 1985), a master of arts degree in Communication and Language Arts (University of Ibadan, 1938), and a PhD in Media and Communication from the University of Leicester, Leicester, UK (2016). She is also interested in ethnography, qualitative research that critically analyzes and explains historical trends and events. Generally, her research interests include migration, diaspora, diasporic media, cultural studies, and globalization. She is a member of the Nigerian Institute of Public Relations, Association of Communication Scholar and Professionals in Nigeria, Women in Technical Education, Association for the study of Worldwide African Diaspora, and the International Association for Media and Communication Research. She has published various articles in journals and speaks English and Portuguese fluently.

Amedu, Anthony is an assistant lecturer in the Department of Mass Communication and Media Technology, Lead City University Ibadan, Oyo

State, Nigeria. He is currently undergoing his PhD in the same university. Anthony is a member of the Association for the study of the Worldwide African Diaspora (ASWAD), USA, Nigeria Institute of Public Relations (NIPR), African Council for Communication Education (ACCE), and Association of Communication Scholars and Professionals of Nigeria (ACSPN). He is an author of over ten publications.

Mary Z. Ashlock is an associate professor in the Department of Communication at the University of Louisville. She earned her BS degree in Education, an MS in College Student Personnel, and a PhD in Communication from Florida State University. Mary has worked in higher education and business for over 30 years. She worked as a senior consultant for 13 years at a training and consulting firm specializing in areas of teamwork, leadership development, and project management. Mary has experience speaking to regional, national, and international associations and enjoys involving her students in these endeavors. During Mary's tenure at the university, she has been named as a Faculty Favorite, Distinguished Teaching Professor, and Faculty Mentor. Mary has published numerous articles, book chapters, and coedited several books. Her current research focuses on Generation Z and Millennials in higher education and organizations.

Ahmet Atay (PhD Southern Illinois University, Carbondale) is an associate professor of Communication at the College of Wooster. His research focuses on diasporic experiences and cultural identity formations; political and social complexities of city life, such as immigrant and queer experiences; the usage of new media technologies in different settings; and the notion of home; representation of gender, sexuality, and ethnicity in media; queer and immigrant experiences in cyberspace, and critical communication pedagogies. He is the author of *Globalization's Impact on Identity Formation: Queer Diasporic Males in Cyberspace* (2015) and the coeditor of several books. His scholarship appeared in a number of journals and edited books.

Lindsay J. Della (PhD, University of Georgia) is an associate professor in the Department of Communication at the University of Louisville. She is also the codirector of the Institute for Intercultural Communication at the University of Louisville. Della is a health communicator with an emphasis on the design of lifestyle-based health improvement campaigns. She teaches research methods, strategic communication campaign planning, and health communication at the undergraduate and graduate levels. She earned her doctorate in Health Promotion and Behavior from the University of Georgia's College of Public Health. Prior to joining the faculty at the University of Louisville, she completed fellowships with the Centers for Disease Control and Prevention (CDC) and the Oak Ridge Institute for Science and Education (ORISE) as postdoctoral training. Della also holds a master's degree in Integrated Marketing Communication from Northwestern University.

Lauren Dempsey has recently completed her PhD at the University of Nottingham, collaborating with the UK communications regulator Ofcom to longitudinally examine the cyclical connection between the use of computer-mediated communication and relationships. She specializes in studying the everyday experiences of technological engagement, examining how the use of multiple platforms, devices, and the Internet may shape digital literacy and social experiences.

Brian Gilchrist (PhD, Department of Communication and Rhetorical Studies at Duquesne University) joined St. Gregory Catholic School as a Middle School Teacher in 2020. He teaches the following classes: Language Arts 7, Language Arts 8, Social Studies 8, and Science 6. His instruction promotes diversity, equity, and inclusion through the lens of Catholic Social Justice. The *trivium* (grammar, dialectics, and rhetoric) influences his research of media ecology, philosophy of communication, and rhetorical theory. His publications include scholarly articles and chapters that address the interplay of human beings, language, technology, and existence by engaging the projects of Marshall McLuhan, Martin Heidegger, and John of Salisbury.

Yowei Kang (PhD) is an assistant professor at Bachelor Degree Program in Oceanic Cultural Creative Design Industries, National Taiwan Ocean University, Taiwan. His research interests focus on new media design, digital game research, visual communication, and experiential rhetoric. Some of his works have been published in the *International Journal of Strategic Communication* and *Journal of Intercultural Communication Studies*. He has received government funding to support his research in location-based advertising and consumer privacy management strategies.

H. Hale Künüçen is a professor and department chair in the department of Radio, Television, and Cinema at the Faculty of Communication, Baskent University. She has an MŞ degree from Anadolu University and two doctorate degrees from Marmara University and Gazi University. Her research interests are visual and effective communication, communication form, media literacy, film studies, history of Turkish cinema, film theories, acting in cinema, and scriptwriting.

Ralph Merkel is a journalist and TV producer who has been teaching at the University of Louisville for nearly 20 years. He created the video production curriculum and also teaches digital journalism classes. Every year he is among those honored as a "favorite professor" by students.

Cristina Miguel, PhD, is a senior lecturer at Leeds Beckett University, UK. She received her PhD in Media and Communications from the University of Leeds, UK. Cristina is a multidisciplinary Internet researcher. Her research interests include digital culture (network intimacy, online communities, and online privacy) and digital economy (sharing economy, the political economy of social media, and influencer marketing). She is the principal investigator of the Erasmus+project COLECO, which examines different aspects of the collaborative/sharing economy, with a special focus on peer-to-peer accommodation.

Sophie Nightingale is a senior PR executive based in Leeds, UK, with an undergraduate degree in Creative Media Technologies and a master's degree in Marketing. Her specific interests include using social media to promote the self and how generations perceive different digital technologies. Sophie's study on the use of social media engagement—Generation Z's engagement with fashion brands on social media—revealed how connections are formed between Generation Z and brands on social media and how the users present themselves following this.

Anca Serbanescu graduated with honors in 2018 in Communication Design at the School of Design of the Politecnico di Milano, with a thesis on territorial promotion through cycling tourism. She is a PhD student in Design, investigating human-AI social relation through interactive narratives and currently works as a teaching assistant at various courses at the School of Design of the Politecnico di Milano.

Stephanie Smith, PhD, APR, is an associate professor of Public Relations in Virginia Tech's School of Communication. She studies the multigenerational workforce and how to recruit, retain, and engage entry-level employees. She also examines the role of technology in workplace communication and employee recruitment.

Siobhan E. Smith-Jones (PhD, University of Missouri) is an associate professor in the Department of Communication at the University of Louisville. She is a graduate of Xavier University of Louisiana and Louisiana State University. Her current research interests include explorations of African American women as interpretive communities. She teaches courses in mass media, race, culture, fandom, and media literacy.

Michael G. Strawser (PhD, Communication, University of Kentucky) is an assistant professor of Communication at the University of Central Florida.

Yi Jasmine Wang (PhD, University of Connecticut) is an assistant professor of communication at the University of Louisville. Her research interests focus on information processing and design, as well as the role of social media in communicating health and risk information.

Kenneth C. C. Yang (PhD) is a professor in the Department of Communication at the University of Texas at El Paso, USA. His research focuses on new media advertising, consumer behavior, and international advertising. Some of his many works have been published in *Cyberpsychology*, *Journal of Strategic Communication*, *International Journal of Consumer Marketing*, *Journal of Intercultural Communication Studies*, *Journal of Marketing Communication*, and *Telematics and Informatics*. He has edited or coedited three books: *Asia.com: Asia Encounters the Internet* (2003), *Multi-Platform Advertising Strategies in the Global Marketplace* (2018), and *Cases on Immersive Virtual Reality Techniques* (2019).

www.ingramcontent.com/pod-product-compliance
Lightning Source LLC
Chambersburg PA
CBHW061716300426
44115CB00014B/2709